FRIDAYS
with my
FOLKS

Also by Amal Awad

The Incidental Muslim
Courting Samira
Coming of Age: Growing Up Muslim in Australia (anthology)
This Is How You Get Better
Beyond Veiled Clichés
Some Girls Do (anthology)

FRIDAYS
with my
FOLKS

Amal Awad

Stories on ageing, illness and life

VINTAGE BOOKS
Australia

A Vintage Australia book
Published by Penguin Random House Australia Pty Ltd
Level 3, 100 Pacific Highway, North Sydney NSW 2060

penguin.com.au

Penguin
Random House
Australia

First published by Vintage Australia in 2019

Addresses for the Penguin Random House group of companies can be
found at global.penguinrandomhouse.com/offices.

A catalogue record for this
book is available from the
NATIONAL
LIBRARY   National Library of Australia
OF AUSTRALIA

ISBN 978 0 14378 979 6

Cover image of car © Depositphotos; image of Amal Awad courtesy of
the author
Cover design by Alex Ross © Penguin Random House Australia Pty Ltd
Typeset in 11.5/16 pt Sabon by Midland Typesetters, Australia
Printed in Australia by Griffin Press, an accredited ISO AS/NZS
14001:2004 Environmental Management System printer

MIX
Paper from
responsible sources
FSC
www.fsc.org   FSC® C009448

CONTENTS

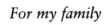

For my family

I have been easy with trees
Too long.
Too familiar with mountains.
Joy has been a habit.
Now
Suddenly
This rain.

−*Rain,* Jack Gilbert

PROLOGUE

I will write the truth gently.

Since I was a girl, I have admired the wedding photo that hangs on my parents' bedroom wall. It has a surreal quality to it. It's not black and white; rather, it's been colourised in a way that makes it look more like a hyper-colour painting. My mother's almond-shaped eyes, lined in black kohl, are the first thing you notice. But then, to the side, is my father, handsome and impossibly young, embracing her, beaming with pride.

My mother looks glamorous, mature for her age and experience, and my father also captivates. Bright eyes, optimism and strength. That's how I have always known him. Somehow invincible, even if he was a remote figure. He wasn't demonstrative when I was growing up; he was matter of fact and deeply immersed in work.

I stare at the wedding photo with fresh eyes now, because in 2013 my father was diagnosed with kidney failure.

I was in my mid-thirties, in the process of immense personal change, when my world was turned upside down. Not just my world – that of my entire family. We quickly

1

saw that life would evolve into a new reality. A schedule for my father filled with appointments rather than retirement luxuries. My brothers and I never without our phones in sight. Every year since has seen a longer visit to the hospital, always unexpected, a shattering of the peaceful revised norm.

It does something to you. As resilient as I am, even I had to concede at one point that my emotions, turbulent and overwhelming, were a caution. But we are not alone. During one hospital visit for my father I found myself reaching out to friends, something I have always struggled with – asking for support, privately asking them to pray for my dad, for the whole family. I asked for positive vibes, healing – love in any form – to be telegraphed towards us.

These were friends who themselves were navigating painful, disrupted realities, so I knew they would understand. Eventually, as we discussed the ins and outs of hospital visits, the time we put aside for our parents, I realised how many of us were experiencing similar issues. We half-jokingly compared schedules. Three appointments next week for Patty and her dad. Marcela has one. Lucky. Acquaintances, colleagues, strangers – they had their stories too, and they shared them easily, relieved to be unloading an experience that had felt isolating – as though they were speaking a language not everyone can understand. We were immediately connected. An ageing parent, someone we love not in perfect health – the war stories were fierce, painful. Maybe sharing them was not only connection but also a way of normalising things. The commonality helped. Friends helped. So did the therapist I finally acknowledged I must see, because life felt full, overwhelmingly so at times, and I realised how important it was to talk about things. To express fear so that it lost power rather than consumed me.

There were dark moments, but I was strangely calm. Tired, probably overdosing on caffeine. But I was present, the daughter I needed to be for my father, and for my mother, Dad's constant companion.

For a time I retreated into my usual interests and stayed busy with work. Strangely, the activity that helped me best decompress was doing puzzles, usually a thousand pieces, which I put together while a TV show played in the background. It's the therapy of them. Knowing that concentrated purpose and persistence pay off; that sliver of relief you feel each time you lock a piece into place. I wondered if there was a metaphor in my puzzles: it will all come together. Persistence that yields the desired results.

Still, I was asking myself, how do we transform ourselves from children to people who care for a parent in a similar fashion as they cared for us?

Although there are many books on ageing, it's only when you are experiencing it for yourself, or with a close family member or friend, that you realise how painful and life-changing it is. Moreover, you come to understand how universal the story is: no matter how our winding paths vary or converge we are all born and one day we will all die; and fears around death and illness tend to be universal.

As a writer and observer, I was naturally driven to record some of the stories my friends, and strangers, were sharing with me, to make sense of what was unfolding in my family's life; and also to pull away the veils of mystery that surround ageing, and cause the anxiety that marbles into fear. There is pain and stigma associated with sickness and our bodies getting older, and they are experienced not just by the elderly. I felt strongly that it was time we all talked more about this and listened to others' stories.

Fridays

I often think back to my father's reaction to his diagnosis of kidney failure. 'I'm going to stay hopeful,' he told me. And his positivity worked – until he had to face the limitations of his body as it deteriorated. He was still driving, but less so. Still active, but things like getting to the mosque on a Friday became more difficult.

I needed to see my parents more often, to take them places that would be harder to get to themselves. In a moment of inspiration I committed every Friday to them. I wanted them to have as much normality to hold on to as possible. I needed to ensure Dad could get to the mosque, and sit in the company of other men in worship as he had always done. I wanted to be beside my mother, accompany her in the process of a changing lifestyle.

My eldest brother, Alex, has claimed Sundays, with his wife Kelly and their children. My older brother Hossam spends a couple of days with Mum and Dad, too, traversing Sydney and finding new and interesting things to do. My younger brother, Anwar, cleverly brought the DVD box set into their lives, purchasing *Columbo* (which Mum and Dad have watched twice).

And then there's me, every Friday, exploring different possibilities, a dutiful, respectful daughter. I wondered at first if the Fridays made a difference. At the very start there was a teething process, resistance from my mother. She felt I was wasting my day (a sentiment I didn't share). My father seemed fine with the arrangement – or at least he didn't object to it. Considering it now, I think he was simply quiet, trying to make sense of things.

Fridays began in this tentative way, like we were all trying out a new pair of shoes that should have been the right size, but felt a little too tight. Over time perhaps they'd stretch out, but for now the discomfort ran deep. Each week I looked for signs that Dad was back. This life-loving man who liked to talk, took pleasure in exploring Sydney, and enjoyed going out with my mother. So much quieter now.

My parents brought me up in a loving but strict household: Dad always working, Mum always around. I spent many years negotiating my identity as a female Arab-Muslim in a conservative family. I was used to asking for permission for everything. I lived according to customs and cultural structures that meant I looked ahead to a future of being able to do whatever I liked – when I got married. So this was all new for me. How would our relationship change? I was no longer a timid daughter afraid of breaking the rules. I was a daughter facing change: being more helpful to her parents. Yet always a daughter.

+

I'll tell you what Fridays with my folks look like. At their best, we spend a day together that is filled with stories and reflections, as we take in Sydney. At their most interesting, I'm part-counsellor, part-observer, as my mother harvests her grief from the first thirty years of her time in Australia. As my father sits still in his quietness. Relief – that's what they're seeking in their outbursts and remembrances. The universe as jury, and it's time for a hearing.

Sometimes my parents just make me laugh. I think Mum likes to get a rise out of Dad. One day as she stares out the car window she tries to provoke him with an accusation. Something or other about men and how they don't like women. I can't tell if Mum means it. I suppose if I said something similar she'd probably agree with me.

Dad offers no response, so I prod him gently. 'Dad, Mum's trying to tell you something.'

Dad's a passenger now, though, so his interest lies in the world around him. Mum pulling at threads; Dad stepping over them and looking in another direction. He finally speaks. 'Look at that building, it's so tall,' pointing to a development site.

Sometimes Fridays take a lot of warming up.

A *lot* of warming up.

But there are moments, piercing, sharp, emotional. It might be a beat of forgetfulness, redolent of times past. Other times it's pathos, the kind you often find threaded through memories. Dad unpacking his life, his travels from his birthplace, a small town in Palestine, through Germany, before finally landing in Australia. My mother, young, hopeful, innocent, a new arrival to a country that was neither hostile nor welcoming to her.

And then moments of reflection, acceptance. The five stages play out in no particular order. Denial. Bargaining. Depression. Anger. Acceptance.

Diabetes runs in my father's family but he's been good at managing it since he was diagnosed in his mid-fifties. Still, one day in the car Dad pierces the silence. 'I never thought this would happen to me,' he said.

1.

STORIES FROM FELLOW TRAVELLERS

One day, in traffic, I notice a bumper sticker:
*'We're all in this **together.***'

Our stories vary and diverge. In our minds, none of us shares the same strands of experience and pain. The similarities are striking, nonetheless, invoking a camaraderie in conversation. When I set out on this journey, my explorations began with people in similar situations to mine. People around midlife, often parents themselves, whose lives were evolving into a new normal – that of caring for parents, in big ways and small.

What I found most remarkable in these conversations was how each person tackled their changing reality. Some valued the refurbished parent–child relationship, born of growing wisdom and compassion. Others expressed frustration and resentment at the revised family dynamics being forced upon them.

'Meet them where they're at'

Patty is about to tell me how spiritual tools help her, when she stops mid-sentence. Beside me, her ailing but sweet dog, RuRu, is hovering, sniffing in my handbag, around my ankles, sending doe-eyed glances my way, though he's half-blind. A few days earlier he fell down some stairs and ruptured a disc.

'Amal, I've just figured out what's going on. Can you put your pen down for one second? And mimic me, but to him,' says Patty like a school teacher, pointing to RuRu, 'and just go, "No more." He thinks you have food.'

I do as Patty asks, feeling guilty.

'And hold his gaze, because he is going to be like, "Yeah, you do . . ."' Ruru slowly backs away. 'Okay, there you go. That's what it is.'

Patty smiles knowingly but I feel for poor RuRu. His hungry energy throws me off. 'He reminds me of a kid,' I tell Patty.

'Yeah. Totally, because he's regressing now. He's got dementia.'

That's what it is. He reminds me of an old man, the kind who has progressed full circle, more child-like in his approach to things – completely dependent on and devoted to Patty. An old man with dementia, an affliction I'm hearing so much about lately that I feel like I've seen it up close.

Patty's already switching gears. 'So, the only difference between the bumps that invariably happen is that I have spiritual tools, so I'm less reactive. I don't get caught up in a vortex of stress that isn't mine to embody.'

Patty is in her forties, has a voice that goes from soft to commanding in a heartbeat, and the healthy, trim body of a yoga instructor. She's a marriage celebrant, healer and counsellor, so she's bursting with practical life advice. Nowadays, she's a helpful daughter, too, who is pliable with her time. She considers herself lucky that she works in professions that allow her a level of autonomy and flexibility – both help when you're the designated Dad driver.

Like mine, Patty's parents are ageing, and her father has health problems. Her mother has had some minor scrapes with poor health – a couple of endoscopies and colonoscopies; she's lost a lot of weight, and is stressed by a rupture in the extended family. But her father is diabetic and 'like most diabetics who have the good sense to self-medicate with alcohol and cigarettes', his vision is impaired.

'It's also caused a little bit of dementia. And his vision will never be the same. If anything, it's going to decline.'

Patty is responsible for taking her parents to their respective doctors' appointments, or for procedures. She also plays interpreter because their first language is Greek. 'I don't actually identify as being Greek,' she clarifies. 'My parents are Greek. I am Australian.'

I ask Patty how she makes time for the appointments, and how it all affects her mentally.

'I don't want to sound arrogant, but it doesn't,' she says simply. While it's a stress on her life, it's also just a part of her life. 'If I have to take my parents to a doctor's appointment, it's simply slotted in. I speak to them every day, or at least every second day, and I'll see them every week, or at least every second week minimum.'

For Patty, a philosophical approach helps. 'There have been times this year when my professional career has really skyrocketed and been absolutely amazing. On the flip side, I've had to hold space for some pretty intense family transitions that have been a little bit negative and stressful. I am a firm believer in when you hold one extreme type of energy you have the capacity to hold the equal but opposite polarity. It's like when people say they had the best year of their life and also the worst.'

Patty knows that her responsibilities towards her parents will increase. She is at peace with this eventuality. 'I think it's a natural extension of what's already going on. If anything would happen, they would move in with me. I see that as inevitable.'

Not everyone finds relief in spiritual pathways. But Patty is someone who makes a lot of sense when talking about life and human behaviours. If anyone can offer some nuggets of wisdom, I'm convinced it's her. And maybe there's something else in my request for toolkit tips; a persistent desire to feel plugged in to a sense of something *more* in this strange, heaving universe.

Patty says that some 'creative adjustment' was needed when she had to start accommodating her parents' needs, but 'now it's, for lack of a better word to describe it, normal'.

A new normal. We spiral upwards, I have realised somewhere along the way. Much of what existed before remains, but it all looks different from this new angle.

'That's really beautiful that you can manage those things,' I say, glancing at a forlorn-looking RuRu. We're in Patty's small, cosy apartment in a Sydney suburb not far from the beach. She does her healing work from home; shares vibrant sunrises and melting, vivid sunsets on Facebook, taken beside the ocean or from a cliff she's meditating on. She is intuitive but practical, the kind of person who knows there's a 'woo woo' spectrum of spirituality and won't try to slide you too far towards one end of it if you're not interested.

So it's not surprising how matter-of-factly she speaks of caring for her ageing parents, both of whom are in their seventies. Not that her spiritual beliefs and adherence to Chinese medicine slip into her thinking. On her father's diabetes, for example, she talks about the liver meridian. 'When you're a diabetic [the liver] gets impacted; the meridian stops at the liver and starts at the eye,' she explains.

Patty lives alone, maintaining her professional life, and a personal one that's separate to her responsibilities as daughter. 'I feel very blessed, very lucky that this happened at this particular juncture in my professional life.'

But also, as she points out, there's nobody else who can care for her parents. It's Patty who has the capacity to be the helper. Capacity more than patience, she emphasises. 'It doesn't drain me. It's not upsetting. I still get a chance to spend time with my family. It doesn't stretch my patience. But I have to say, I'm not a patient person by nature. I'm very quick thinking, I'm a very pragmatic person. One of my flaws is that I'm highly intolerant, but this doesn't stretch my patience.'

I know enough about Patty to agree – having worked with her on my own personal journey. She's the take-no-prisoners, no-nonsense, keep-it-real type. But I also wonder if there was a defining moment when she realised, like I did, that a new reality was forming. That the coordinates were shifting and life was transitioning into something unfamiliar.

'The one defining moment was that I stopped getting shocked when something would happen with my parents' health. When it first starts happening it sends a bit of a jolt of shock in your system. "Oh my god, oh my god," – because it's so unusual. Then I got to the stage where I just went, this is actually going to be normal, so I have to stop getting shocked about it. Not necessarily expect that they're going to die any second, but I have to be realistic that this is my life at the moment, and stop sending stress into my nervous system. When I made that decision, that's when I stopped getting impacted. I think what impacts us as people is the element of shock.'

I had been thinking about this very realisation earlier. How I used to assume Dad would go back to 'normal' following a hospital visit. But now I am no longer looking for a way out of it. I'm existing in it.

I'm subscribed to Patty's private Facebook group, a following interested in self-improvement to whom she sends out messages of encouragement. Patty is often wise and funny, and very generous in doling out spiritual comforts. She has told me more than once that I need to accept the new reality of my life. But more than that – to not expect more from a person than they can give, or are willing to give.

'I think – and I don't know if it's a Buddhist philosophy or an ancient Yogic philosophy – that the greatest cause of suffering is the desire for things to be different,' says Patty. 'And I certainly know from my own personal experiences in the past, where I've moved through difficult transitions both personally and professionally, I amplified my own sense of suffering by constantly wishing that things were different.'

Patty says she no longer succumbs to this instinct. 'It's not that I accept I can't change things, but with certain things I just accept them as they are because then I'm not constantly wishing. I don't plug into something that's intangible, like, if only he were better then this wouldn't happen.'

Moreover, she makes a pertinent point about personalities. 'I see my dad dealing, or maybe a lack thereof in terms of dealing, as a simple extension of his personality. So it's not like he's vastly different. They're exactly the same people and they're dealing or not dealing with it, just like they dealt with or didn't deal with life's ups and downs previously.'

I am reminded of a similar realisation of my own: that my father has two competing sides, never in alignment. The old Dad I have known my whole life is there, but he's competing with new Dad, the one who struggles to understand the rapid, uncontrollable unravelling of his life. They don't always get along; it's like he's fighting himself. Preferring to sink than swim. Is it always Yin and Yang? Two selves that battle it out?

Then I have to remind myself that he's not simply my father – he has his own identity, story, needs and desires.

Friday

On Fridays, I become a collector of memories. A story-keeper. These wandering conversations, like excavations, shift things in all of us.

My mother, Samia, was born in Jenin in 1951, when the city was part of Jordan. But her passport says Arrabeh, the town in which my father grew up. An error made by a worker at the citizenship office in Australia, who didn't want to change it. 'What's the difference?' he asked my mother.

'Sometimes I want to scratch it out and replace it,' she tells me.

'Why does it bother you so much?'

'I don't know. It doesn't feel right.'

Another day, Mum puts it simply: 'I love Jenin.'

My mother moved to Kuwait at the age of fifteen; she was married a few years later to my father, who had been living in Australia for two years before returning to the Middle East to find his bride.

My mother's memories of her early years in Sydney are razor-sharp, her commentary acerbic and, at times, loaded with regret. Her grievances are understandable given the settings and circumstances. A stranger in a foreign land, without her family, without friends, piecing together fragments of a new language by watching television. My parents arrived literally without a single Australian dollar to their name (the Jordanian currency would take months to exchange, via London). Kind airport staff enlisted the assistance of a stranger to give them a lift – in a limousine no less. Mum recalls her introduction to cheese on toast; the Anglo-Australian couple she and Dad shared a flat with for a year and a half. She remembers the woman's name – Jenny. She says she wishes she could thank her. 'She was my dearest Jenny.'

Mum took on work in Australia a few days after her arrival, despite a lack of English, wrapping ice creams in a factory assembly line (where she paid 20 cents for a home-cooked hot lunch, like stuffed chicken and vegetables). Her second job was as a seamstress, employed by two old Greek ladies. She got sacked when she was too pregnant. (It wasn't planned.) Before that, for eight to twelve dollars a week, because she wasn't yet twenty-one, she sewed buttons on clothing. Underpaid in a foreign country, learning the language by watching television, connecting to her dearest Jenny while Dad took on more than one job, and a portion of their earnings went overseas to support my uncle, Dad's younger brother, in his university studies.

✦

I knew my father's story but in patches; anecdotes shared along the way, emotional remembrances of his time in Germany in 1963, the first country he migrated to when he left his town in Palestine, the recollections of which seem to have shifted over the years.

Dad can rattle off the name of every German town he lived and worked in, tales of strangers he encountered who provided assistance, how these moments of kismet shaped his experiences of loneliness and solitude. But tonally there is a deeper resonance, one drenched in the reality of isolation, the fear that came with the new, particularly in a country where the language, culture and people were all foreign.

Dad thought, in fact, that he had made a mistake upon first arriving in Germany. 'It was very, very hard.'

But he grew stronger. He found work, which helped him settle a bit. Immigrants congregate and ghettoise, and this was true for my father to an extent. He recalls with emotion how fate landed him in the right place in Germany – a town called Speyer – just as he was ready to give up, to be taken under the wings of other Palestinian men who were a bit older and familiar with their new home.

But to understand my father as he is now, it helps to have knowledge of the effort he's put into achievement and living a full life, one that has seen him attract much love and praise from friends, customers, even the waiters at the local café. In fact, it's interesting how individually my father has lived. He worked hard to support his family, but it was my mother who was present, who raised us.

As a child, living in the small mountainous town of Arrabeh, disconnected from the rest of the world, on the cusp of conflict, my father dreamed big. He was an ordinary student, achieving pass grades in school. But there was no limit to his imagination and potential, and in his final year of high school he concocted a plan to travel beyond the borders he'd known his entire life.

Upon sharing his plans to leave Palestine, my grandfather – a severe, brusque man – expressed doubt. 'My father used to say, "How are you going to survive?"' Dad tells us. 'I said, "No, Dad, you should think about me in a positive way." He always put me down.'

It was June 1963. Dad obtained a passport, then a visa to get him out of Jordan into Syria. 'I took care of it all myself. My father didn't know, I only told my mother.'

Dad replays the conversation that bewildered his loving and dedicated mother: 'I have to leave very, very soon.'

'You want to go? Where?' came the alarmed response.

'Germany.'

His mother reported this to his father.

I ask Dad why he wanted to leave so urgently, and he explains that he felt an immense amount of pressure. Were he to stay in Arrabeh, his future would have been limited to teaching or farming, neither of which appealed to the wanderlust in him.

'I was dreaming about Canada,' he recalls. 'I applied for Canada and Germany.'

Later, he had to choose between Canada and Australia, the latter of which he picked upon advice from a friend.

'Australia is a pot of gold,' he advised my father. Another man instructed my grandfather not to let his son move to Canada. Its weather was intolerable – 'It's freezing. Don't even think about it.'

My father recounts his departure from Arrabeh with tempered emotion. There he stood in the street outside his father's home, my grandfather calling out to God. 'I've tried everything to stop him and it's not in my hands.'

Dad tears up as he recounts this. 'He tried to get me into higher education or to open a shop. I said no. I was very determined to leave.' His inner workings, hidden for so long, perhaps even hidden from himself. My father is like many people in this world who strive not only for purpose, but also acceptance from others. For Dad, his father's approval held significant weight. 'I wanted my father to be proud of me,' he says, simply.

Eventually he would be.

A person, not a person and patient

When I meet with Patty, I admit to her that, in general, I've switched off. I feel things, yet somehow I also feel detached, like I'm untethered and at any moment could float away. Maybe it's a coping mechanism.

'People respond very differently to illness,' says Patty. 'Some are very "I can beat this." Some are very "This has beaten me." I think that irrespective of which spectrum your parent is in, it's important not to wish something different for them than what they want for themselves.

'Meet them where they're at because it's more respect-ful. The amount of times my dad has been told to cut out drinking and smoking and he's resorted to trying to hide it or to lie about it, bless his cotton socks. He's got the good sense to self-medicate, and that's how I see it as well. I just think, well, he's not going to take organic wheat-grass shots at this time. He's not going to go on a vegan diet. He's not going to make himself smoothies. I think what's also helped me is just meeting him where he's at, so that when he does leave, he'll leave feeling content and full of what he wanted, not necessarily what I imposed on him.'

That Patty talks about her father lying and hiding indiscretions isn't surprising: many carers share similar experiences. My own father seems to wrestle with the truth of his situation at times. I don't think he lies to us; I'm just not convinced he is always seeing the truth for himself.

And so many others have told me stories like this: parents who are getting older, but they know how to get their own way. They will obfuscate; 'forget' appointments; sit in denial when something becomes difficult; outright lie about when the aged care worker is coming over; insist that the worker not work – just talk. They want company – no need to vacuum, just sit down and chat. Isolation is a killer. One woman I speak to, Carla*, who used to be an aged care worker, felt conflicted: she had a job to do, but she also appreciated the client's craving for human company. If Carla was lucky, she would have time to make her client a cup of tea. She says they always had a cache of good stories to tell. Deep, and sometimes dark, histories they wanted preserved or passed on. One woman, Carla told me, spoke about her parents putting her on a train to flee a conflict zone during World War Two. Some of the older women I met with, who lived alone but had full lives, reflected wistfully on their experiences as females in a world centred on men. They had their stories to tell for the sake of posterity, too.

Patty's insight offered a fresh and useful perspective.

'It's not about me, nor is it about what I want,' she emphasises. An important point, given how badly we feel when someone close to us is affected by illness. How desperately we try to fix it all, offering opinions and advice.

Yes, advice. Don't be a know-it-all because you've spoken to a few people, read a few books and listened to doctors on *Conversations with Richard Fidler.* I might feel like a counsellor, but I'm not one. I don't want to be militant, hounding Dad every time I see him. You can read an article or two but what do you know, really?

But it's hope, I realise. Every possible solution is a moment of hope. We become experts in solutions that don't apply to us because we are invested in the outcome and we think we see things more clearly, unaffected, not so emotional.

'Sometimes it's important to think about your family member away from their illness,' says Candace*, a registered nurse. 'It's really nice to have that dedicated time where you're just sitting with them; just having that time with your dad, having that bonding. Because I think often you can get really hung up in worrying about how effective the treatment is, and what's going to happen in the long term. But it's nice to feel that you can just be with him.'

'And they just want a normal day,' adds Diane*, her colleague.

I'm getting better at seeing Dad as a person, not a person and patient. I'm better at reminding myself, when I look at him and my mother, that 'I'm not going to let you feel this every moment of the day.'

Sometimes being there is about knowing when to pull back. I like Patty's advice to 'meet them where they're at'. It resonates, it's practical, it's fair, even when life feels completely unfair. 'I meet them with no judgement, with my perspective that isn't imposed on them, with my views and values that are respectfully exchanged, without compromising my own personal integrity.'

But surely – capacity, empathy and patience aside – challenges lie in this? Like where they've wanted something of you and you're unwilling to offer it? I am thinking of all the times my father wants to do something impractical and, despite my advice against it, insists, and I, not wishing to upset him, give in.

Patty says she chooses her battles. 'I don't walk on eggshells, but also I've seen a different facet of my parents, because their capacity to tolerate chaos has diminished significantly as their health has.'

My close friend Marcela has similarly described a shift in intensity. She has spoken to me of her father's limitless love for food and wine, a bountiful table being core to the family's Chilean culture. But she hopes that her father will some day come to sufficiently appreciate the gravity of his situation to abstain from indulgent treats. And she's acknowledged a reshaped relationship between two very similar characters – feisty, stubborn, headstrong. Neither can ever win the argument. He was very much the father, but as his health ebbs away, there are changes both to the life he knows and the way she relates to him.

'My dad was always the man to turn to when you were in trouble, as was my grandfather. He's overseas, but they were very similar in that sense. Between those two, nothing could ever touch you. To have them both on my side, it was like I was invincible.'

Marcela got along well with her grandfather but she and her father clashed a lot. But he's not well now, and the dynamic has shifted. 'I let him get away with it. I wouldn't get into those arguments with him again. It turns around a little bit. You become the parent and they become the children, right?'

It affects us all, this gradual, or sudden, role swap. Em*, a healthcare support worker who provides at-home services

21

to the elderly, offered an important perspective on cognitive and physical decline. 'It's said that when people get old, they start regressing into being children. However, from what I can gather and understand, if you have a child, you're feeding the child with knowledge and doing things. When you have an adult that's losing it, and you're taking more things away from them, you're not feeding them. You're actually making them feel worse.'

This deprivation leads to apathy, he says. 'So they'll go, "Why should I get out of my pyjamas? I'm not going anywhere. Why should I shave? Why should I shower?"'

Em is fifty-eight, and working in home services for the elderly is a world away from his previous life in the finance industry. He says it's eye-opening. His observations are sobering.

'People have said to me, "Jeez, it must be very rewarding." And [the first time it happened] I had to sit back and think about that for a few days, actually . . . to see how I was going to respond to that question next time. And the response is, from where I came from, yes, it's rewarding to see people succeed and do well in their health and all that. But what's rewarding about watching people die, being disabled, continually going to see doctors, and watching their life deteriorate right in front of their eyes? And then watching their family trying to cope with it all. So, is there anything rewarding about it? No.'

'What does it take to do what you're doing, do you think?' I ask, curious about his move from finance to a helper profession.

'It goes back to empathy . . . It's all about giving the other person a feel-good story for that moment in time, whether you've got them for one hour, or four hours, or thirty minutes.'

Em says he becomes a storyteller on the job; he's always been one, even when dealing with clients in the finance realm.

In a way, he is doing what Patty has talked about – meeting the person where they're at, without putting pressure on them to be other than who they wish to be.

It complements what I hear from an Arab-Australian couple, Charlie* and Laura*, about drawing up a new dynamic. From children to friends. An approach that allows you to monitor your parents' wellbeing while also strengthening bonds.

Charlie and Laura are parents themselves, in their thirties, and fit comfortably within the 'sandwich generation' – looking after parents and their own children, though they are not full-time carers. They fully expect to take on that role when the need arises, but for now it's about keeping their parents active and engaged. Both believe caring demands 'the feminine touch', but as the eldest boy in his family Charlie feels compelled to step up. His attitude is a practical, easygoing one: there's no sense of obligation or burden. 'As a best mate would do . . . being there for one another, that's what you're trying to get to.'

This means, for Charlie, making sure his parents don't fall victim to scammers who call them at home; that their bills are paid on time; and that they are engaged in a very ordinary way in each other's days. He angles for a friendly conversation that will expose any issues. Asking direct questions is too much like a transaction. Inclusivity is also important for Charlie. Not belittling his parents and their ideas and opinions.

Charlie is seeing a greater need for this now. His mother is still fit and healthy; she can go about her daily business. 'Health is a concern but easily measurable,' he says.

Charlie lived with his parents until he married a few years ago. But the transition in their relationship from 'transactional parenting' to 'friendship' began about ten years ago, before he left home. His father, who is now in his seventies, worked as long as he could; his mother, who is in her sixties, was trying to re-skill herself, but also have hobbies, so she took

TAFE courses in arts and crafts. But the reality of 'some form of cycle of life that I don't really understand' was starting to dawn upon Charlie. 'Parents are parents, but they've got to be friends [with their kids].'

He tried to boost their social life – dinners, get-togethers, travelling as a family, all foreign to his parents, who were focused on work and family duties, saving a future inheritance. It was a challenge to get them to engage in these social activities – to Charlie's mind, his parents had already set their children up for the future by ensuring they had a good education. He's not worried about inheriting their savings; he would rather his parents spend their money on themselves, taking well-earned holidays.

Charlie says, 'My mum loves that sort of stuff, but the reality is she's not going to do it by herself.' His father wouldn't stop her, he just wouldn't join her and she would worry about him.

Charlie's father experienced a late onset of diabetes in his forties. Then, twenty years ago, he underwent heart surgery. And now, he says, 'You just start seeing things . . . my dad's starting to notice it.'

A difficult thing to ignore is the death of people in your generation, or close to it. His father had several siblings and only one is still alive. 'And he won't admit it because he'll stay strong . . . but I think there's an element of him where . . . you can see it affects him.'

Laura expresses sadness that Charlie's father jokes about not being around when their daughter gets married. 'I'll be long gone by then,' he'll say lightly.

'That hurts me, so I don't know how hard it would be for his own kids to hear things like that.'

'And they thrive on still wanting to help us, as in the parenting 101,' says Charlie.

'They're hanging for us to say, "Can you pick up the kids from school today? Can you take them to soccer? Can you take them to swimming?" And literally their calendars free up even if they had something on.'

'Because they feel needed again,' says Laura.

Meanwhile, Charlie's dad is handy, cluey – an engineer, he was a business owner. If Charlie ever has something that needs repair, his father remains his go-to man. He wants to nurture a sense of ownership in his father's life – when he comes over, Charlie wants his father to feel comfortable, like Charlie's home is his own. It can be something as simple as watering the plants in their garden before Charlie and Laura have even got up for the day. Laura pipes up with more examples of Charlie making requests of his father – 'A builder's coming over tomorrow and I need you to do something'; 'Can you please do my banking?'

Laura was horrified at first when she heard these requests from Charlie, and called him on it. 'But the way he explained that to me was, "I need to do that for my dad because it's good for him. I can do all this myself, but Dad now feels important." And that was a lightbulb moment for me. I was like, "Oh, that makes sense now," because he does feel important – he's like, "Oh, my kids still need me, I'm still doing things that help them."'

Being friends with their children means parents aren't diminished in their child's eyes. They are not obligations. They are parents, and although the dynamics between them and their children are shifting with their changing needs, Charlie's approach to underplay that shift seems a constructive and positive approach.

'I've done my part'

For some people, 'meeting them where they're at' or being a friend to a parent is loaded with the troubling necessity to be there, period. There are threads to this. A dissonance of chords that can compound into a screech, far from a harmonic melody. The idea of obligation is a bloated one.

People I speak to reveal commonalities in their coping with parents' frailty, with a body ravaged, a mind overcome by grief. In the same way doctors like to know exactly what conditions they're dealing with in order to address them, carers seek information as a form of relief. If we know what we're dealing with, we can do better.

Though knowing may offer a sliver of relief – symptoms can be addressed, and so on – what you arrive at is often merely an acknowledgement of the surface grief you feel. There might be something more sinister and sad circulating inside. It's the loss of a person as they knew themselves. The freedom of being you as you knew yourself. The unpicking of past hurt and pain, of needing sometimes to brush aside interventions and truces. And what can rush to the surface is family tension, often between siblings who, as adults, are linked simply through their parents. This tension is like a rubber band. It has a certain amount of elasticity to it, which can be stretched to a limit but then snap, and the death of one or both parents can be the cause of that snap. If a parent is ill or gone, things can unravel swiftly in families. What is family love and what does it look like?

Some reflections from people seem like meditations on a peaceful acceptance. Others are like outbursts, accusations to lob at the nebulous, all-seeing cosmos.

For one of my interviewees, Julia, the angst is plentiful. At times her anger overflows. But mainly in our discussion Julia taps into a reserve of resentment, which some people find difficult to open up about.

Julia grew up the responsible one, working with her parents in a shop. 'From the age of eleven to twenty-five years old,

I worked seven days a week, helping these people accumulate their wealth. And so now I resent having to do more, because all these financial discussions, and money and wealth and how you divide it, come into play. And I feel resentful because I think, I've done my bit. I've given to you, I've helped you, I've worked. And you haven't acknowledged my efforts.'

Julia would like her brother and sister to 'step up to do this part'. The problem is, they haven't. 'And so I've got resentment toward my brother and my sister,' she says.

Julia is in her fifties, the eldest of three siblings. She's divorced with adult children. She lives with a partner, and is also a grandmother. Her brother, who is close to Julia in age, has assumed financial responsibility for their parents' assets and the like. Her sister, meanwhile, plays 'the dynamic of being the youngest in the family'.

'And so the dynamics are that I'm the oldest, I'm the most responsible, I'm the one to help with the running around.'

It frustrates Julia. She feels she's subject to the gender bias that afflicts other women like her – she has friends in similar situations. She offers examples: a woman who's never married quit her job to help care for her high-needs parents, but made the choice to continue living on her own. However, her extended family pressures her to move in with her parents, both of whom require 24/7 care. There is a story of two siblings who asked their eldest sister to quit her job; they would pay her to be a quasi-carer because they run a business full-time. She said no. 'She's not comfortable dealing with sickness. She doesn't want to deal with old people.'

Julia is trying to put in place boundaries, to say, 'I'm only prepared to do X.'

'So I've got to work out what that X is for me.' She describes her partner, from Greece, like she is, as a very caring man, who cooks food and takes it to Julia's mother. 'He does things that I haven't seen other men do. It's nice. But he's forcing me to do more than I want to.'

She admits that left to her own devices – and she realises it may sound harsh – she would rather walk away from the situation, say, 'No, I'm not prepared to do anything more for you. I can't. Because I'll resent you too much.'

She describes a father who was very focused on himself; generational favouritism towards males in her family. 'My grandmother loved her sons more than her daughters. I was twenty-one years old when I turned up on my grandmother's doorstep and she looked at me and said, "Why didn't they send your brother?"' Julia was disappointed and hurt; she'd only seen her grandmother a few times in her life.

A deeper source of trouble is in her parents' attempts to marry her off at seventeen. 'I resented that so badly. Because I kept on thinking in my head, "I'm not a burden to you." I got into university and I didn't even tell them because I knew that they wouldn't value that.'

But instead of walking away, she is trying to let past hurts go. Not completely forget, but find a way to help her parents without sacrificing her own serenity and lifestyle. She is brokering an inner peace deal in order to be there for parents whom she feels were not there for her. Attempting to dilute the strange power of regret.

Both of her parents have health problems. Her father was recently involved in a major car accident in Greece, where Julia's parents spend six months every year, a more social and enlivening place for them than Sydney, where they're relatively socially isolated. And before travelling overseas, they were both involved in minor car accidents. 'So the decision not to drive, it will be upon us,' she says.

Her father, in his eighties, doesn't want to lose his independence. 'He's been driving since he was sixteen years old. So to mentally acknowledge that he can't drive, that's going to be a big deal for him. And I think he will struggle with it.'

Julia says her father is physically strong but is starting to exhibit possible signs of dementia. Her mother has an ongoing cancer issue, which won't be fatal for her, but debilitates the family. 'She's been battling it for at least the last twenty years.' It's a blood cancer that exhibits itself on the skin. 'But I think the impact of her disease has made her quite tired, and . . . whenever we bring up the fact that Dad should go and see a doctor about his getting older, she's very reluctant to do that, because she's tired of seeing doctors, and tired of constantly doing that doctor dance and routine. I think that that's the wrong choice, because that's been detrimental to my dad . . .'

She doesn't think fear is the only inhibitor. Rather, her mother assumes this is just how people get old. 'So, forgetfulness – this is just people getting old. There's nothing you can do about it. And truly she's tired. She's tired of seeing doctors. She goes to the doctor once a week to get her bloods done. She's tired of the check-up [at the hospital] every quarter. So she doesn't want to start that with my dad. She's scared of the unknown, in that she doesn't want to have to deal with it. So she fobs it off, saying he's just getting old. He is just getting old, but we could help him just get old. We could potentially slow that down.'

In all of this, Julia's struggle is to find and maintain some peace. She realises a missing key to serenity is letting go of her resentment and frustration, because her parents won't always be here. Years of therapy have helped Julia on this path, while being a mother and grandmother herself has also contributed to a gradual shift in tone.

'It's easy for me to say, "Oh, my parents weren't the best and didn't do the right thing by me." But I think my parents did whatever they knew. They were the best parents they could be. Now, whether they made mistakes or did things wrong, well, they're only human. So I've had to learn to live with that and accept that . . .'

'Do you?' I ask.

'Well, I try to. And I've got good days and I've got bad days.'

Experience isn't a straight line. This peeling away, it's painful. Parents getting older forces something upon you. You can no longer carry your grievances in the same way.

'It's like, "I have to be the better person, and I don't want to,"' I observe lightly.

We both laugh, even though it's not really that funny.

With my folks

We're at the hospital again.

'We're going to polish him up a bit.' That's what Dr A*, my father's specialist, said a few years ago when Dad was in for a stay.

'Has he been here before?' a nurse asks me today.

'Yes.' He should get one of those loyalty cards that gets stamped every visit.

Forms to fill out. 'Where was he born?' asks another.

'Palestine.'

He frowns. 'It doesn't exist,' he mutters.

'We're going to take a photo of your brain, Mr Mahud . . .'

It's Mahmud, I want to say, but don't because they are only here to help.

✝

The emergency room at St Vincent's is small. Two vending machines stand to one side, a TV looks down on those waiting. The plastic chairs are uncomfortable.

In the same way an airport can be a third space – neutral, disarming – a hospital waiting room dissolves differences. It can be strangely unifying – within a family and more collectively. It can also break you open and put on display the inner workings of a family in distress. This is the place that invites reconciliation or a fight. Where things are exposed or laid bare. It's like a checkpoint. Something important and more significant than your everyday issues is taking place here, where nurses and doctors triage patients, plug them in and reassure them, try to solve the challenges they present. It's a place of life, but the waiting room forces something in those waiting: a reminder of how battles rage daily, how none of us are completely free. It's not exactly neutral. But it doesn't have a dog in the fight. It just holds you in a cold space, drained of emotion – practical, real, a buzzkill, in a way. Buy some crisps and watch the football on silent.

Inside the ward, there is more of everything. Opinions, emotions, activity. This is the real world unfiltered. You hear things, sometimes funny. The whir of machines, the low chatter of nurses and doctors.

I'm there every day with Mum. We become familiar with the hospital again, pressing the buttons on the lift for Dad's floor in an automated way. You get used to this.

Friday

Mum is perched on a chair in Dad's room as though she's expecting a reason to get up at any moment. An arrival or news. We spend a long day with Dad, who is taken in for a procedure in the afternoon. You lose all sense of normal time on days like this, when you're drifting in and out.

I see a shift during this particular hospital visit in how Dad deals with it. When he was in earlier this year for the catheter procedure, he couldn't leave fast enough. The day he was to be discharged, he was heavy with frustration – he wanted to go. And when the nurse finally announced that he could leave, Dad whipped off the blanket to reveal he was fully dressed under his robe. The nurse had a chuckle, but she looked quite startled.

'Goodness,' she said. 'You're in a bit of a hurry.'

I wanted to laugh – Dad acting like a teenager whose parent had just left the room. Dad about to sneak out the window.

During a previous stay, I would wander into Dad's ward only to find his bed empty. Once, when I questioned a nurse, she broke out into a knowing grin, attempting a scolding tone: 'Your dad's a bit cheeky. He just disappears.'

This time there's no fight in him. It's not defeat though, either. It's some form of acceptance. Maybe he needs to stay longer, he even acknowledges at one point.

When they prep Dad for a procedure to check his heart, I wait for them to wheel him off, always beside Mum, and my heart feels heavy. I have never found it easy to see Dad taken away like this. I can help him eat, adjust his bed, make sure he's comfortable, ease him through a dip in his mood. But when I see him in a bed being led away, my calm almost slips.

I'm not sure what it is about this that lands so hard in me. The day before, his angiogram seemed far more worrisome. This simple procedure requires only a local anesthetic. But the tears threaten to erupt at seeing Dad's vulnerability. Fresh sadness.

'The hope of human connectedness'

Emma*, forty-three, jokes early on in our exchange that it's not age that makes her feel old, it's some of her life experiences. 'Especially this year, I've definitely felt older.'

The recent death of a young relative sent the older generation in her extended family spiralling. Emma says that was when the reality of her growing responsibilities hit her. She and another relative had to take care of the funeral. 'We suddenly realised that the adults were falling apart. We had to do all the adulting stuff to look after the adults.'

The moment held a currency of surprise – when did *she* become the adult?

Not that Emma is a stranger to grief and loss. In her early twenties she lost her mother to cancer, relatively quickly. It was traumatic. Emma, a mother herself, observes, 'Grief as a parent is different because you've got to contain and manage, because you've got to be a parent first – you can't just break down when [the children] are around. Because that impacts on them, so that was a real adult experience compared to my early grief. With Mum, where you just broke down, you could do whatever you wanted in that sense.'

Emma is a counsellor. She understands the workings of grief, how it afflicts people, and what coping mechanisms they may latch onto to find relief. It's different when it's happening to you, though; nothing can inoculate you from feeling the full strength of the anguish. 'There's a lot of grief in a lot of people's lives that I deal with. You lose health, older people are grieving the loss of their independence and then their health, the loss of their youth.'

'Has dealing with other people's grief taught you anything about grief?' I query.

'Yes. That people are resilient. A lot of people are way more resilient than I am, or will ever be, probably . . . And people's ability to survive, and their will to survive. And the hope of human connectedness.'

Emma is 'sandwich generation' – a mother who helps care for her ageing father, Michael*. At one point they shared a home, but she has since moved out to accommodate her growing family. She has regular contact with her dad, who, like most men in their eighties, still potters about but endures health challenges. She wouldn't define herself as a 'carer', though (too official). 'I define it as helping him out, and I think that probably he wouldn't like seeing it as that.'

It doesn't help that he's stubborn. Emma says that Michael doesn't consider himself old. 'I mean, it's a relative thing, age, isn't it?' She laughs, recounts an exchange with him to demonstrate. 'He used to go down to his old pub, and I said, "You haven't been down there for a while," and I thought it was because he couldn't get up the stairs. And he said, "Oh no . . . there's too many old people down there."'

Emma is amused at her father's inability to transition gracefully into older age. At the same time, his stubbornness and resistance to change can be irritating and frustrating. 'I think it's just a clinging on to youth and [avoiding] a loss of independence, which would be quite scary, I think, for someone who's very independent.'

Her father lives alone, and he still drives. She expresses relief at not being given the responsibility of deciding whether or not he should continue to do so: 'I think not driving would be massive for him.'

On the whole, Emma demonstrates a practical attitude. She doesn't live with her father, but she's not so far that she can't be there for him. And she's reflective about what her father's age represents. 'I think ageing, to a degree, is a privilege, and I'll be very grateful if I get to my dad's age,' she says, reflecting on the relative youth of her mother when she died.

Like many people I met with, Emma isn't necessarily afraid of her own death; she worries more about the impact it would have on her children and partner. Nor did her mother's premature death inoculate her. 'There's the pros of it, because I think all people's experiences are different, but I think it gives you the heads-up on what a grieving process looks like.

Your first one's a bit like anything – you don't really know what you're in for, and once you've had that experience, and then you have another death, I think you're a bit more experienced in what the waves of grief might look like,' she says. 'It's like a dipping. I think you dip in and out of grief.'

Emma's work is in the area of interpersonal violence, including against older people. 'There's lots of aged people in personal-violence relationships. Absolutely. Whether there's domestic violence, whether there's family violence, from the children, sexual assault . . .'

But, she says, publicly people never talk about it. 'The fact that people don't even think about, but one of the things that's coming up for me is that I'm seeing people in aged care homes quite vulnerable to violence.'

Elder abuse is massive, Emma says.

'Who's committing the violence against them? Are they strangers or are they family?' I ask.

'Children, caregivers, professionals potentially, partners,' Emma responds. 'Certainly I think there's an idea that your children wouldn't necessarily do that, but that's coming from the perspective that the family unit's functional. And not everybody has their parents' best interests at heart.'

Elder abuse can occur through violence or mental abuse, or take the form of financial abuse. Emma points to a common imbalance of power, where a parent has signed power-of-attorney over to a child, who is then empowered to make financial and legal decisions on their behalf when the parent is deemed unfit to do so. 'I think the vast majority of people who make decisions do so genuinely in that person's best interest, but there would absolutely be people who would abuse that.'

Lesley, a retired nurse with decades of experience, saw how abuse played out in ways that affected the daily lives of people in nursing homes.

'I was a matron in a nursing home when I was studying in the nineteen-seventies. People, couples, would form friendships, and sometimes they wanted to get married, even though they were eighty. But you would find, not uncommonly, relatives moved their relative into another nursing home, and that was clearly about inheritance. They didn't want them to marry again because that would halve the inheritance and cause big problems,' she says.

'We had that in the nursing home I was working at, where the family immediately separated [the couple] – usually the person with the most money. Moved that mother or father to another nursing home and broke up the relationship, which was very sad when they'd found a great companion.'

I spoke to numerous aged care workers, and most suggested that the days of elder abuse were past. However, in 2018 damning media investigations uncovered terrible abuse in some aged care facilities. While there have been reports in the past of financial abuse, and aged care workers operating under extremely difficult conditions, an ABC *Four Corners* investigation revealed the extent of physical and verbal abuse elder residents and patients can suffer.

In the weeks after the program went to air, with many families opening up to media about their experiences with aged care and nursing home facilities, the Federal Government announced a Royal Commission into Aged Care Quality and Safety. 'This follows more than 5000 submissions received from aged care consumers, families, carers, aged care workers, health professionals and providers,' the Australian Government's Department of Health posted on its website.

Of the aged care workers I spoke to, some indeed indicated that elder abuse does still occur due to numerous potential factors: stress on the job, lack of training, difficult residents. Carla* said that accusations against staff of theft are common from family members of dementia patients. And they were specific, in her experience. 'I was never accused of it,' she told me, pointedly.

Emma ventures into another important aspect of how we age – social interaction. Michael is still a social person, but the dynamics of this have changed – he relies more on people visiting him rather than him going out to meet friends.

'When you think of your dad, what are your concerns at the moment, and what are your hopes?'

'My concern for him is that his health would deteriorate and his quality of life would decline, and for him that would be really frustrating and isolating.'

You lose your friends as you become older, Emma notes. You go to a few funerals and the circle diminishes. 'I remember [Dad] saying to me, not recently but a few years ago, that it hit him when he'd heard of someone else that died. He kind of realised, "Ah, well, I can't call any of the people to tell them because they're all dead too."'

Connections severed by the natural course of life. It can be distressing. Emma believes the loneliness is even more debilitating for men. 'Because I think men, their sense of relativeness to others, maybe friendships, may be different than women.'

She feels that her father may garner less sympathy or attention from people because 'he's aged so well', relatively speaking. 'I've been guilty of that, too,' she says. 'Recently that's changed, but up until probably a few years ago, you're kind of like, "Oh, come on, Dad," because he's so well and capable. You forget that he's actually older and things do take longer and . . . it's only when there was the decline, I suddenly went, oh shit, that's right, he probably can't walk that fast anymore, or he probably needs to start doing all these things differently.'

When Emma and her family lived with her father, she says he was quite independent. It was a neutral space – she wasn't a carer as such, but she identified potential 'needs in disguise'. Emma says there is often a focus on looking at how much a person can physically do on their own – things like house-hold chores, shopping and cooking – and seeing that they can get around on their own. Visible things. But perhaps more focus is needed on how many people someone has to talk to, on not being isolated. 'And I wonder sometimes whether requests for help, not that it's framed like that, and who they're to, are actually not about the request, but some kind of need.'

She makes a pertinent point. You become fluent in a new language when you spend more time with your parents; you look for signs of embedded issues, things that perhaps they are not even aware are issues. Often you're not going to need to dig deep to discover what might be more obvious to an external observer, like a request for shopping and a visit equating to a desire for greater connection.

'But it's a huge need – connecting to humans, and having a sense of worth and value and purpose, and all those things change as you get older.'

My own father's self-worth is so deeply entwined with his career, so connected to his role as a breadwinner. How many people have I spoken to who offer similar observations?

'I suppose if they've been working full time, then a lot of their value or purpose falls around them being a bread-winner and then providing for their family,' says Emma, 'so retiring is probably a significant let-down, because what does life mean? What's the purpose and value now? This is what I valued for the last forty years of my life, it gave me purpose and drive – but what's that now?'

Emma doesn't rule out living with her father again, but it's complicated, a situation laced with certain challenges because, as a woman, she has competing interests, 'a tug of war' between her role as a mother and her place as a daughter. She has a sibling who helps, but in less visible ways. 'I go over there and I'll see how many meals my father's got in the fridge and just stuff like that, or empty the bin if it needs emptying . . .'

For now, she's focused on her father receiving help. She recently registered Michael for a comprehensive assessment by the Aged Care Assessment Team (ACAT), a government initiative to determine eligibility for funding assistance. 'They do an assessment, and it's for overall functioning and what potential support the person may need – whether it's at home or in a nursing home – so for any kind of transition to more supportive housing or needs.'

The ACAT is an important function for the elderly and their family, carers included. It involves an assessment of physical and psychological needs before a funding package can be assigned. But the process is riddled with issues, including long waits. Applying might not take an inordinate amount of time, but you can literally wait years.

Em advocates government intervention – systems and processes that are easier and much friendlier to work with – to allow people to look after their parents or the elderly. He says the elderly people he deals with are at a very vulnerable stage of their lives. 'They don't know what's going to happen to them tomorrow. They don't know what's going to happen to their spouse. They don't know if they're going to be alone, and for how long, and when. There's a whole lot of things that enter their lives, that for some people [are] very difficult to understand.'

He circles back to a crucial point: the importance of empathy. He is talking generally here. Empathy on a wider scale, across society, not just by carers or within families. As a carer, Em says his job is not to be a therapist. But, as he did in his finance days, he approaches his work ready to offer emotional support. 'I'm here to listen,' he says.

'It's like the well's empty'

'You just reminded me that I'm supposed to ring my mother,' Danielle* tells me when we sit down for coffee in a bustling Sydney café on a weekday morning. It's a busy time for her, a writer whose career is expanding in all the right ways. She's stressed – a lot of work, a lot of balls in the air. 'I'm also a mother, and I'm the breadwinner in my family, so all the things that are happening to me work-wise and career-wise have a knock-on effect on my partner, who's just been made redundant. And because she's much older, she's sixty-five, she won't be able to easily get a new job, so . . .'

Danielle is also dealing with her mother being unwell; she's dying of metastasised ovarian cancer. The initial shock has worn off. 'But my mother's perspective was, "Oh, great, I'm dying. I'm so happy because I've got cancer, now I don't have to kill myself." So, the next emotion that I have out of it is, "How terrible that my mother's got such a sad and awful life that she would rather die of cancer than . . ." That she's happy that she's dying of cancer – that is so awful. But what do you do with that?'

'Is it true?'

'I think she's been in a bit of denial, and also she's an attention seeker, but . . . She has been claiming to be suicidal for a long time, and she was cutting herself.'

Before the diagnosis Danielle's mother was cutting her arms, which led to two hospital visits and more than fifty stitches each time. 'She's had emotional and mental issues her whole life because she was abused by her father.'

Danielle has recently returned from London – an 'amazing experience', the kind that makes dreams a reality, but which also requires the sacrifice of being separated from her family, particularly if a longer-term stay in the UK is later required. 'And there is no way I can say no to that because of all the other factors in my life, but of course I'm already thinking that my Mum is dying . . .'

She describes a somewhat topsy-turvy life. She left school in Year 10 to become an actress. 'In those days, nobody stayed at school unless they were really super-academic. So, I was fifteen years old and I got a job, so I was basically self-sufficient. My parents never pushed me to do anything career-wise . . . Dad used to say, "Dream on," but my mother in particular was always encouraging of me to do my writing and to do anything that made me happy.'

Their relationship has its share of troubles, but Danielle's mother is supportive. Danielle recalls an emotional moment when she got back from London.

'I've had this wonderful trip and these wonderful things happening, and of course my mum was very excited, and the first day we all had breakfast together so that we could see each other, and my mum hugged me in the restaurant. Now, she's actually not a crier. She seldom cries, but when she hugged me in the restaurant, she said, "Oh, I'm so proud of you," and then she burst into tears, and I did, too.'

Danielle takes a moment. 'I cried on and off for the rest of that day, because even though I very rarely have any feelings about my mum in that way – any feelings that I actually have an emotional response to – I knew she was crying because she was never going to see my book made into a TV series. It's one of the great pleasures of her life to share my work, and one of the only areas we connect in, so the sadness around the fact that it was something we could share and genuinely enjoy with each other was never going to be.'

In that moment, Danielle says, her mother suddenly felt scared and upset. 'That was the trigger point for her to suddenly realise, maybe I'm not happy I'm dying.'

'She wants to live.'

'And she had to get there . . . That would have had to happen, I think, at some point, because you can't hang on to that, the denial. Maybe some people can all the way through, but I don't think she would . . . That was sad.' But Danielle confesses she's glad to have felt that strong burst of emotion.

What worries her, though, is her mother's desire that Danielle join her at doctor's appointments. She doesn't have the time, and doesn't believe she needs to be there. Her mother, she thinks, just wants an audience. 'So when I can't come she takes her best friend or an aunt or whatever – to every doctor's appointment, of which there are many. Her pleasure is in talking about herself and all of her bowel movements and all these sorts of grotesque physical things that she can talk about, and have someone there who's listening. I don't have a lot of patience with that because I just feel like it's indulgent, and yet I'm trying to be present for it as often as I can because it means so much to her and it is the only thing that I can give her.'

Still, Danielle spends more time with her mother now, and rings her more often as well, while carefully maintaining her boundaries around her time.

'I feel guilty, but I never let it get in my way. My mum wants me to do stuff, but she is really understanding. I just always have that boundary, and at a certain point . . . I am the sole income earner in my family. So I can't sacrifice my family's wellbeing for my mother's. Going back to that, she didn't sacrifice hers for me,' says Danielle. 'I think that's what happens to people. You get out of your children what you put in early.'

Still, Danielle's mother's diagnosis put a new spin on everything – she doesn't get the twenty extra years she expected to have with her mother, who is seventy-five. 'Even when she breaks her leg, she'll just keep walking. She's a very strong person. So, to have her at quite a young age be dying – it was a shock.'

For Danielle, childhood was a difficult period. When she was a baby her mother sent her to a foster family, taking her back when she was four and a half. 'That was an incredibly traumatic experience, both ends of that, and from that, over the years I've discovered that I have a lot of damage from it, and our relationship was damaged by it.'

Danielle's mother is in the top 1 per cent of the population in her IQ; she's intelligent, but on an emotional scale less so. 'What can I say? She's applied her intelligence into learning how to act in the world and do the right things by watching everybody else, but she isn't very good at actually having true emotions. So, she's been a tricky mum.'

Danielle's parents' marriage didn't last long. 'They really didn't like each other. Then he married her sister, which is weird.'

When her mother took Danielle out of the foster home, she remarried, to a man who became Danielle's stepfather. He was a lovely man, Danielle says, and it was a lovely marriage. 'But he died twelve years ago and she's never recovered because . . . They didn't have any friends, they just had each other, and he was her audience. So, without an audience in your house it's very difficult because all of your madness comes to the fore in public. She goes out attention-seeking in every possible way she can because she's not getting anything at home.'

Danielle indicates two positive prongs to her relationship with her mother: she could always rely upon her; and 'a very good and positive relationship' existed in her mother's support of Danielle in her career. 'She is nothing but support-ive, enthusiastic, proud, and positive. Also, incredibly unselfish in terms of wanting me to achieve my goals, regardless of what that means for her.'

However, when Danielle was a child her mother wasn't able to provide emotional support. And now, Danielle admits she struggles to offer it in return. 'I don't have a well or a reservoir of emotional support for her, and I really have felt empty of it. She couldn't be sympathetic of anything. If I cut myself or hurt myself, she'd go, "Oh, you're so lucky." She was never able to just sympathise. If I was sick, she'd be gritting her teeth and doing the housework because she would be really upset that she hadn't gone to work. She wasn't a warm, sympathetic, genuinely emotionally attached mum.'

I remark that her mother sounds like someone who was uncomfortable being a mother.

'She didn't know how to . . . she was just acting. She was role-playing Mother the best she could, and she actually wasn't capable of anything more. What I have thought over the years is that, because she didn't pour anything in, there's nothing there to draw from. It's like the well's empty . . . I can do what any human being would do for another human being, and someone that they love and care about, but there's not a lot there that I could draw on to go, "I want to give up and sacri-fice everything of mine to help my mum." I don't have that.'

But her emotional supply is otherwise plentiful. Danielle hasn't emerged from these scarring experiences devoid of emotion. She says she is bonded to her child.

'I may be repeating my mother's mistakes, but I really wanted to stay home with my child, and I did as much as I could, and I was heartbroken when I had to go back to work. I never really got over it. That first breaking of the bond when I had to go back to work was really hard.'

Danielle's plan to spend more time with her mother involves outings to the movies every Thursday night. Her mother has recently come out of a respite period in palliative care, and at the cinema they can talk together freely. Danielle can even talk to her mum about death, ask her questions about how she's feeling, what she believes about an afterlife, her fears.

'So you can do that now?'

'I've been doing it from the moment we started going to movies. I always ask her outright, "How are you feeling? Are you afraid of dying?" I think that helps the process because there's nothing hidden and nothing unsaid, and I don't feel like, oh, I wonder if Mum's scared or upset. I know when she's scared and I know when she's okay.'

Having open communication means being able to actually ask those terrible questions, but also talk about practical matters, even money and inheritance. Danielle, for example, was able to discuss her mother's plan to split her estate unevenly, in favour of her brother. Danielle's brother stayed with his and Danielle's biological father from the age of three. Danielle says her mother and brother 'had a personality clash . . . She gave him to my father because they didn't get on. And so, this is the sort of mother she was.'

Danielle's brother has been an alcoholic, and he also has complications from chronic illness. 'But he's been . . . very supportive and trying to be much more part of this situation with Mum. But he's quite pompous, and he's not very insightful to our mother because he didn't grow up with her. He hates it when she says she just wants to die and she's not having any treatment. I've had to kind of counsel him around to say that it's not his position to stomp and stamp and say what he thinks is right; he has to respect what Mum wants.'

Danielle says he's a nice man but, 'I have a lot of emotional separation from my family . . . It's an effort for me to put in time and energy to them, with the exception of my aunt.'

Danielle calling her mother on the disparity in her split of her mum's estate delivered a fair result. Her mother has decided to divide everything evenly. 'I don't want more. I just want an absolute split.'

'Is there anything you wish you could say to her that might give you peace with the past?' I venture.

'I've already said all those things before she was dying. We've had a lot of conversations about all of the things that she did, but also understanding that she did what she did at the time because she believed it was the best thing to do. I have never had any doubt of that. She was never malicious . . .

'But, there are things that she can't take on because she's just not got the strength of character. She's not got the self-insight to do it, but also, there's a point at which you have to stop beating your mother up for her mistakes and just realise what was, was. But, luckily, I have had conversations that have been enough about that. I don't feel I ever have to accuse her again of anything.'

Friday

Groundhog day: we are back in the hospital. This time there's a fracture in Dad's lower back in addition to the kidney failure. He can barely move without wincing. They want to figure out how well his heart is ticking along, as well. The doctor doesn't think Dad needs a pacemaker, but there will be tests. Dad seems unperturbed. 'We're famous for our hearts,' he says, matter-of-fact.

A doctor is cheerful, sweet with Dad. There's something almost jovial about Dr B*. He's young and doesn't look worn down like others we've encountered.

I don't want to seem like an annoying family member when he comes in, but then I think, why not? It's okay to care. I'm mindful of not sounding accusatory or entitled. I focus on articulating as clearly as I can what he should know. I keep my questions, I hope, entirely relevant.

When Dad is resting, I sit with Mum in the cafeteria and we split a bagel and drink coffee. I generally only eat bagels at the hospital. It has kind of become a thing. I see a bagel and the hospital cafeteria comes to mind. Other scenes, now common, are burned into my brain. Familiar faces, like the old lady, so hunched over that from behind you can't see her head, who is there every single day. The chatter. The snaking line of nurses and doctors in scrubs getting their lunch. The woman behind the counter who talks to me like a friend after she's seen me every day for a week, and shares her own stories of dealing with illness and death, and the mounting grief that follows.

I used to find hospitals depressing. They used to pull me apart and stretch me out. But they've lost their power over me. I'm more grounded now. No longer feeling like a visitor, someone who has accidentally landed in the wrong spot. I don't know how often I have come, nor what is to come. I know the guy at the parking station ticket window. If it's been a while between visits, he looks surprised then delighted to see me.

And in these waiting periods, while Dad repairs, I sit with Mum and we talk.

Arabs are a superstitious lot. In the absence of a foreboding dream, we consult the residue of a coffee cup, scanning for clues in the thick mud that covers the interior. My mother does it out of habit. But she's taken to reading the shapes in the foam of a latte, rather than the industrial coffee Arabs, Turks and Greeks like.

Some days she points out a fish leaping up out of the water – a good sign. Other days, it's heads knitted together. A gathering?

Today, it's a fighting kangaroo. 'That's me,' Mum says, half-joking.

Mum and I talk about Dad. We talk about his resistance to what his body is trying to tell him. The way his mind seems to be in one place, his physical state another. The way it's common. The differences between how women and men deal.

'Women are more practical and resilient,' declares Mum. 'They can manage. They've spent their lives cooking and cleaning, looking after the family. So they know how to cope.'

I ponder this for a moment and recognise that there's some truth to it. Often I've heard people talk about how quickly men, broadly speaking, move on after a divorce and remarry. 'They can't be alone' is how it's described.

Then again, when you're ill I wonder if there's any way to surmount the loneliness of it. This is what I try to help my father with. He has my mother's companionship, her care, but he lights up when I arrive to take them out.

'I love having breakfast with you,' he tells me one Friday. 'I wish you could join us every day.'

'You are never putting me in a nursing home'

Gillian* is a married woman in her forties, with children and a full-time job. She is also sharing a new house with her ageing parents – they're on the bottom floor, her family occupies the second one. She's another in the 'sandwich generation', but though she's a mother to her own children, she jokingly complains that she is still being mothered. Sitting at a large wooden dining table in this new shared home, Gillian gives a relatable example of being lectured to 'wear a jacket' when she was on her way out with the kids. She erupts into laughter at the recollection.

Gillian's parents are ageing but have had no major health scares. Some aches and pains with her mother and a major procedure that affects her mobility. Her father's had two procedures. But her father is 'a man's man'. He thinks he's a twenty-year-old and will recover like one, Gillian says with a laugh.

Meanwhile he's been diagnosed with industrial deafness and won't do anything about it. Because of his poor hearing, minor things can become arguments. 'That's what frustrates me,' she says, a nerviness to her narrative emerging.

Still, living with her parents means she can be more alert to shifts in their health. She can already see that, in future, she will be on call for them more, particularly regarding their mobility. Gillian says there's no denial about this on her parents' part. They can look after themselves, but they need help. Her mother doesn't drive and when her father was in hospital she needed to take time off work to help her mum. Nor does she like her father to drive at night. 'If we go some-where, even before I lived here I would pick them up.'

Central to the decision to create a home together is her parents' desire not to move into a nursing home. Her paternal grandmother saw the end of her life in one and Gillian grew up with the refrain 'You are never putting me in a nursing home.'

Gillian doesn't have the best of relationships with her brother. He speaks to his parents, but the burden rests on her to look after them. It helps that her family is supportive and engaged – her husband even helps with shepherding her parents to appointments when she can't, thanks to a flexible job. He helps with cooking for the family.

Certainly there were teething problems. Her father, a sociable man with a bit of a temper, had difficulty handling the construction phase. He wanted a whole new house without the effort.

'Basically didn't lift a finger to pack and . . . my mother is a hoarder. Like, I found an envelope . . . "Gillian's teeth". That was just the start.'

So it wasn't simply about constructing a new home, but sifting through a jam-packed former one. 'That was quite traumatic . . . and Mum was crying all the time, memories and this and that and finding things . . .'

Her mother was only just a World War Two baby, but Gillian says she's like a child of the Great Depression. 'Nothing can go to waste.'

For some, childhood issues rise to the surface the more we deal with our parents. These issues may appear differently, diluted in some ways: you might feel forced into a new relationship with parents whom you have unresolved issues with, and a new understanding is formed. It can invite resolution.

'There's a lot of running up the stairs,' says Gillian of how she releases the angst. A way to flatten out the tension. 'But I need to not personalise it all the time, and then try and think about it from their point of view as well.'

She confesses to feeling guilt about her parents' sacrifice in building the house. She tears up. I suggest that with her presence she's giving her parents something valuable in return, and she agrees, recalling how her father has always liked his kids being around, to know where they are, what they're doing. 'That doesn't necessarily mean he wants to talk to us all the time,' she says, laughing. 'He just wants us there.'

Gillian's pathway is packed with commitments to others. She has many people and needs to manage. I ask her how she ensures she doesn't lose sight of herself completely in this new stretch of life.

'I'm working towards that,' she says in a small voice. She has taken up yoga – just a beginner course that runs for six weeks – and completed postgraduate studies last year. 'I've started to read a lot more. It has been quite good with everyone's little spaces to go into that I can do that.'

'If I start working, what's going to happen to my parents?'

Carla* doesn't live with her parents, but she has become the equivalent of their full-time carer. Married, with a teenage son, she suffered a workplace injury around the same time as her parents retired. 'It's very busy and stressful,' she tells me over dinner. She's enjoying the warm summer night, her relaxed posture like a massive exhalation. She's treating herself to a drink or two; it's been a long . . . well, few years.

Carla was an aged care worker who visited the elderly in their homes and helped with chores – taking them to the shops or for a walk in the park. She says it became more of a domestic cleaning job than caring, and after her warnings that she was unable to carry the weight of a client who needed help getting in and out of the car fell on deaf ears, she was injured. Carla was beset by the stress of insurance negotiations and ultimately didn't get workers' compensation for her chronic pain condition. She's on painkillers.

That she's under pressure is evident. She drives her parents to doctor appointments, specialists, the hospital. She's had to reorganise certain things – arranging a clinic visit because her mother hasn't provided the right information, or hasn't understood the doctor because English is her second language.

Carla has a good relationship with her siblings, but both work full time and can't assist in the way she can. She has a supportive husband, who will step up to help ferry her parents to appointments if she can't do it. Her son also takes responsibility, something she encourages. But still the burden is primarily on Carla. She tells me she was exhausted after a specialist appointment two days ago, 'like I was running a marathon'.

'My mum doesn't help much.' Her mother talks a lot, moves a lot. On a forty-five-minute drive, her mother didn't stop talking or fidgeting. Carla put it down to nerves. 'Because she's suffering from anxiety and depression at a really high level. She has medication.'

Carla is also prone to depression and is taking medication to manage it, as well as anxiety. But she has to put all this behind her, she says, and keep going. She's postponed looking for work. 'If I start working, what's going to happen to my parents? Who's going to take them to the hospital? Who's going to take them to their doctor's appointments? Who's going to take them? Nobody's going to take them.'

She's also a bit of a boss. What she says stands, and being a carer for the elderly has plumped up her authority in that respect. Her parents have no choice but to listen. And they do listen to her advice. They're a bit forgetful, though. They repeat stories. 'That's the time I feel like, "Oh god, they're getting old." It scares me and I feel a little bit sad. You don't want your parents to get old, because when they're getting old you know what's going to happen, and you never want that to happen to your parents. At least not me.'

She understands 'it's life', but she feels tired at times, too tired to attend to her own life. The feeling that occasionally rises of determination – that she's going to stop neglecting herself – doesn't last. She feels stuck.

Carla finds relief in activity. She does Zumba. 'It's the only time I feel I'm doing something for me. Just me. And because I enjoy it . . . for two hours I don't think about anybody else . . .' She first embraced it because she was overweight and not in a good mental state. 'I didn't want to end up like Mum with depression or like my dad with his chronic conditions.'

Grief. Hope. Coping mechanisms. How to deal.

Reflecting on Carla's simple solution, I am reminded that humans have an admirable capacity to manage the storms of life. But it is more than that. How many of us who are caring for others are actually on a quest to progress beyond their stories? To dissolve the hold our parents' struggles have on us, and how they shape our own experiences? Alongside our caring duties, how many of us believe we can have a peaceful, content life?

'Our parents get sick and in the end, subconsciously, it disrupts our lives'

Karen Hitchcock, a doctor and writer, has written stirringly on the idea of the elderly being burdens to family. I never see my parents this way, and it bothers me to think they might ever consider that I would. But there's no denying that, sudden or not, a shift in dynamics brought about by illness and age will alter people's lives.

Dr Vasi Naganathan, a geriatrician at Concord Hospital in Sydney, spoke to me about the impact of such upended lives. 'Certainly in the western world – this includes me as a son – part of our angst is we've been put out, subconsciously . . . our parents get sick and in the end, subconsciously, it disrupts our lives.'

But really, it's intense guilt that plagues me. I can't do enough. I admit this to my brother Alex one day, who seems often to inspect me for signs of fatigue or distress. He stares back at me, surprised. 'I thought you were more intelligent than that, sis.'

I'm a bit insulted. Maybe he has a point. But what does intelligence have to do with emotion anyway? I'm swimming in unpredictable seas as I try to navigate my new normal. I'm losing myself in all of this. I don't know who has emerged and if I like her better.

I notice how the shape of life changes. You think differently about the smallest things, perhaps because everything feels more amplified. A meal changes its form when it's taken in the hospital cafeteria. A burst of sun after a day in a hospital ward is more than a flood of light, it's a reminder of beauty. Memories form differently. Nothing is the same, even in ordinariness. Everything is heightened. I wonder sometimes if melancholy in a high concentration floods other people like it does me. Maybe it's the opposite of projection, but at times I see more acceptance in other people. Like they have unlocked the secret to dealing with the shitty parts of life. I wonder if my emotional response is normal.

Then I remember how often interviews have led to tears from the interviewee, a ripping open of the façade. How circumstances of difficulty vary but are everywhere. My favourite hairdresser casually mentions that her mother recently had an experience with bowel cancer.

'Was it hard?'

Sally shrugs. 'Yeah, but you have to stay positive. You can't let it take over. It only makes things worse for the person it's happening to.'

I am reminded of how common illness, in the context of ageing, is among families. How frequently I am talking to someone about my book, only to be told that they, too, are in a similar position with a parent. Recently, in a writers' room for a TV drama, I befriended playwright Suzie Miller. She is a rare human, immensely generous and open, quick to encourage and demystify the road of the creative. Her three days in the room are crowded with family troubles – two sick parents, a father who is particularly unwell. I feel deeply for her. I admire her resilience. I realise how thick-skinned and leathery we become when dealing with this sort of thing.

Practical. Grounded. But with a soul untethered in a sea of lonely fear. This melancholy, it floods us all. That's why we shut it down. We have to survive.

'Without me, she dies'

John, fifty-one, blames a great deal on Irish-Catholic guilt. He'd like to say that years of caring for his ill mother are born of love, but in truth, he says, it's more Irish family obligation, a robust energy force that runs through his life. 'I swear it's bred into us,' he tells me.

John has been a caretaker for his mother, Linda*, since 2009, his sturdy life plans upended when she developed abdominal problems and had her gall bladder removed in what should have been a straightforward surgery.

'The surgeon made a few mistakes, ending up with my mother losing most of her bowel and lower intestine to post-operative infection,' John says. 'SBS, that's the acronym for her new condition. Short Bowel Syndrome. It means five times a week someone has to hook her up to a TPN [total parenteral nutrition] bag. Think of it like three meals a day, liquid, in a bag that is jacked into your body through a PICC [peripherally inserted central catheter] line or Hickman port.'

John's sister paid him a visit to discuss their options. They either had to put their mother in an assisted living facility or someone had to move in with her. Given the amount of damage – she was left with an 8-inch gaping hole in her lower abdomen where faeces and waste poured out at a regular rate – her prognosis wasn't strong. They were told she likely had twelve to eighteen months to live.

'My sister was immediately ruled out as she was married with three young boys. Four if you count her husband,' John tells me. John stepped up. He sold his beach property ('My german shepherd has still not forgiven me') and moved in to be his mother's carer.

However, John's commitment is greater than most sacrifices of this kind. His relationship with his mother was almost non-existent when he took on the role. A little back story is necessary. John's mother was seventeen when she married his father. It was 1966, and his mother's young age wasn't an impediment to their union. John's mother dropped out of high school – at that time, it was against school policy to have pregnant students – and became a secretary for a large defence contractor. John's father worked there in middle management.

'The early years seemed great to me,' John recalls. 'We may have been poor, but my parents and grandparents never let me know. We're a one hundred per cent Irish family. Pure bloods and, it goes without saying, Catholic, too.'

He has a sense of humour about this. 'If my sister or I are the culmination of a thousand years of Irish inbreeding, then the Irish have some serious genetic shortcomings,' he jokes.

John's sister, Meredith, was born six years later. 'I asked for a puppy. I got a whining, crying sister.'

John says Meredith was clearly his mother's favourite; John was his father's partner in crime. They went hunting and fishing together while his mother and sister went shopping.

Following the divorce of his parents, John and Meredith split up along with them – he went with his father, Meredith with their mother. 'To say that my mother and I were not close would be an understatement. With only seventeen years between us, we developed more of a friend relationship than a normal parent–child association. We liked the same music, movies, cars. She was like an older sister.'

Their relationship grew more distant when John joined the army for a stretch. Linda later remarried – to a hunting buddy of John and his father – and the gap between her and her son widened.

'Fast forward twenty-plus years, [my mother's] husband committed suicide by gun while battling cancer. I tried to be supportive. It's hard to console someone who, through time, became almost a stranger.'

Life continued. John says his mother had Meredith in her life, who was by now married with children, and her work. 'She had gone back to school and was the assistant dean of a community college.'

Four years later, John's father died of a heart attack. John grieved and went through a period of healing, then re-emerged to a generous inheritance of two large houses and a large beach-front property with several cottages. John's work meant he was on the road a lot, so he decided the cottages were the ideal home for him. He gave Meredith one of the houses (their childhood home) and left the other empty for future renovation.

John devised a 'grand plan'. 'I would renovate the empty house, put my mother and her mother in it (my grandmother was edging up on eighty-five) and my mother would have a place to live, free, and she would look after my grandmother.'

The renovations came along nicely, and after a year his mother and grandmother moved in together. Then his mum became ill and the damaging surgery followed. At this point, John made the sacrifices – selling the property and moving in with his mother.

'No amount of warning could have prepared me for what was to follow. Cleaning up her body, bed, bathroom, and anything else she touched if she had a leak. Administering IV and injection medication daily. Treating infections, trying to find food that she could eat and actually absorb [because] the

SBS doesn't allow enough digestion time for normal foods to break down. Often, I would give her pill medication orally, only to find the pill completely intact in her "output" two hours later.'

And that twelve-to-eighteen month diagnosis? 'Well, I moved in in January 2009. It's now August 2017. Somebody is terrible at estimates.'

John doesn't feel that he and his mother have grown closer. 'She still sees my father every time she looks at me. But we do have an understanding. Without me, she dies.'

His life has changed dramatically. Before becoming a carer to his mother, he had a successful career as a project manager. He travelled throughout the US. All of this has been scaled back. He now owns a small high-end wood-working business. 'I still travel to Eastern Europe and such, but instead of three- and four-month trips, now I am limited to two to four weeks, and it takes months of preparation to make sure a family member can care for my mother while I'm gone.'

John says that some day soon his mother will receive her multi-million-dollar settlement from the surgical group. 'Financially she'll be well off. But to be honest, physically she's ruined.'

He takes another poke at his Irish ancestry and their tendency towards guilt. 'And to add insult to injury, my dog now loves her more than he loves me. Damn traitor.'

Friday

A screenwriting project requires some family history research. However, it's not stories I'm after but the imagery of the past. Mum delivers a large plastic box full of memories. They need sorting, decades of life.

Mum looks beautiful in these old photos. What a mystery she was; a feeling that only deepens as I stare at the black and white images that document shreds of her life. And Dad, handsome, fresh-faced, smiling, well turned out in a nice suit, surrounded by friends. There he is behind a counter at the Royal Easter Show, ridiculously young and trim. My mother in a skirt I couldn't get away with, her hair long and dark. My parents on the pedestrian walkway of the Harbour Bridge. Then, a graduation of experiences . . . the pictures become more colourful with more children.

The photos are ageing the way you would expect of decades-old cardboard. Crinkled, dank-smelling, torn around the edges, creased throughout, patches of fading colour. It occurs to me that old photographs are nostalgic and haunting. They tease you from a distance, a memory drenched in golden perspective. Those were the good old days . . .

'I never thought this would happen to me.'

I'm astounded at how little I know about my mother. I know her quirks. What fires up her temper (a lot of things); her strengths, her weaknesses, her predilection for being suspicious. She has a wicked sense of humour. But I don't *know* her. She has kept many parts of herself hidden. Or maybe I just never bothered to look more deeply, or ask the right questions?

Dad often reflects favourably on his experiences, but there is always a disclaimer: building his life and providing for his family was very hard. They are the words he always uses. 'Very hard.' No embellishment, just impenetrable fact. But he will come back a moment later to balance it out. 'I enjoyed every moment of it.' And what he enjoyed was a variety of job titles – landscaper, phone technician, video rental store owner. Dad took up many occupations over the years, landing on travel agent before he retired several years ago.

When my parents speak about the past their memories, based on experiences, are vastly different. Dad's memory bank is populated with people, experiences, opportunities, hard work and travel. Mum has some of those things, but she also lived a more isolated life, focused on raising her children. I don't know if she felt then how hard it was, how lonely and soul-crushing. I don't know if it's all just catching up to her now. She didn't show us this pain when we were children.

I think Mum wants acknowledgement that she too has battled – there is no denying that she has. And one day Dad makes a point of how hard my mother worked. 'Five kids. People struggle with one.' But there are other shades of colour to her experiences. Australia was more isolated four decades ago. Phone calls were an expensive indulgence. Nowadays, social media, apps allowing free calls, and cheap international calling cards are abundant.

Most Fridays I take my parents out, I try to do a weather reading on Dad's mood. But I also wonder what stories my mother will tell. At one stage it felt like she was finally addressing her grievances as a migrant woman, emptying out a stream of complaints about her sacrifices. But I've wondered often what she longed for, not what ailed her.

One Friday, Mum obliges. There are no lamentations, just heartwarming remembrances. She recalls how she used to sing out loud when she had to walk somewhere in the dark as a child. She would belt out Arabic love songs to combat her fear of walking alone, even though she knew she was safe. There is something heartbreaking but compelling about this moment of nostalgia. A glimpse of my mother as a child, innocent and untouched by the harshness of life. She proudly tells me that she took care of grocery shopping aged ten when her father moved to Kuwait for work. 'I didn't just buy anything. I knew where to go for the best meat, the fairest prices. When the women sold yoghurt in clay pots, I looked for the ones with a yellow crust, because it meant that it was creamy.'

2.

I'LL GET BY WITH A LITTLE HELP FROM . . . THE PROFESSIONALS

*It's not a language divide that troubles us, **it's a dissonance between what is and what can be.***

Dr A's patience seems to be running thin. At one point he starts muttering in his mother tongue. I'm not Greek, but I get the gist of what he's saying.

'You're lucky I like you,' he tells Dad. About three times.

I believe him. Perhaps he's not gentle per se, or nurturing, but I sense genuine concern and frustration. It's the frustration born of helplessness – knowing you can help someone, but not being convinced they want to help themselves. But, because I go to each quarterly appointment with my parents, I detect a shift – gradual but noticeable. We all know each other now.

Occasionally I will act as an interpreter of sorts. It's not a language divide that troubles us, it's a dissonance between what is and what can be. Dr A wants Dad to use a Webster pack; Dad doesn't like them. He has his way of doing things. Then, on one blessed visit, Dr A is congenial, seemingly pleased with Dad, whose mood has substantially improved, though he is still quiet.

'He seems better today,' he remarks to me as we leave. I simply smile, unsure if Dad is better or we're just getting used to the difference.

'Depression and independence go hand in hand'

My interviews are a window on to a world of drama. Ageing and illness, family troubles simmering away. Emotions ready to spill over, everyone feeling the strain. But there are perspectives I'm finding useful, which are not often heard. Professionals who help usher people through their elderly years form an expansive universe of specialties and concerns. And while I meet with doctors, geriatricians, pharmacists, and even a psychiatrist, I find that some of the most practical information comes from carers themselves.

Martin Warner is director of Home Instead Senior Care in Australia, an organisation with thirty-five franchisees in Australia. It's a US business, founded in 1994 by a couple called Paul and Lori Hogan. Martin says the business is expanding in twelve different countries, with 1100 franchises around the world.

These facts are important. The significance of offerings such as Home Instead's lies in its very name: people who are ageing and ill generally wish to maintain, to the best of their ability, the life they enjoy.

'Instead of being elsewhere, that is to say a residential care home, nursing home or whatever,' Martin says, 'the traditional thinking has always been [that] when people get older, they go into a home. They go to a retirement home or old people's home.'

We're speaking in advance of National Carers' Week, an initiative designed to highlight the contributions and sacrifices of carers. Such campaigns are increasingly common. Multicultural Health Week's annual event in 2017 centred on the theme 'Caring for Carers'. The campaign aimed to direct carers to culturally and linguistically appropriate support services. Meanwhile, Deakin University researchers, in association with service provider Australian Unity, developed the StressLess app, to help non-professional carers manage their stress.

Carers are gaining attention because there are so many of them. In today's fast-paced, sandwich-generation world, needing extra help for ageing parents who live alone is not uncommon. And Home Instead is like many providers that offer in-home, non-medical services to the elderly – assistance with personal care, light domestic duties, meal preparation, medication reminders. 'We take people to appointments, we take them shopping, we take them to social outings . . . Our role is very much about enhancing their lives and allowing them to have that independence in their own life by being with them to stay at home whenever they want that.'

Martin points to a prevailing mindset in Australia: the dominance of the government system. 'First of all, the heritage of this is institutional care, which is then broadened out into community care.' The community care model the government ran previously saw providers funded to deliver services for a client. There was very little choice, Martin says. 'The clients had pretty much no control over the services they were receiving.'

The whole model, in terms of care, has been skewed towards tasks and providers delivering services according to their own schedules. 'That's a very different mindset, in terms of being able to allow people to live a genuinely independent life on their own terms, which is what we've done. We've given that complete choice.'

And Martin makes an important point: the government's move into a new online portal and system with My Aged Care is an exercise in protecting those who are in need of services; it's an attempt on the government's part to see how well the money's spent. '[But] they can't measure things such as relationships, companionship, social isolation,' he says.

My Aged Care is certainly not a portal that addresses such issues. It provides information about aged care services and, importantly, how to apply for and receive them. Like the National Disability Insurance Scheme (NDIS), it has been designed to empower the recipient of services, enabling them to select their providers, and indeed which services they require at all.

I've heard that in Britain a minister for loneliness was appointed to tackle the isolation experienced by more than one in ten people in the UK. Elsewhere, headlines scream that loneliness can be fatal: 'Loneliness kills; Former surgeon general sounds alarm on emotional wellbeing' (*Boston Globe*); 'Loneliness could kill you' (The Conversation in the US); 'What loneliness does to the human body' (The Cut). A pharmacist I spoke to, Gerald Quigley, affirmed this: 'People die of social isolation. That's been clinically proven.'

Having been told by several aged care workers that conversation and company were unofficial duties, it was interesting to hear Martin talk about their approach – one that focuses on the qualities of the person who will work for them. 'We're looking for people who can actually build relationships with their clients. Clients have that social isolation. They want to converse, they want a relationship, they want trust, and so we train our own caregivers . . . We take them right the way through to a national qualification.'

And this is another significant point: often, when elder abuse arises in conversations, workers blame inadequate training, not helped by a poor salary.

I appreciate that Martin is running a private business in 'consumer-directed care', but he makes a lot of sense. And what he talks about is generally in line with what other people I spoke to said about the delivery of aged care services. It's a complex area.

Martin considers Home Instead as rare in the industry. 'We have been very different to other organisations. When we came into the industry, we deliberately chose not to get involved in government services.'

He says the organisation has never taken funding from the government. 'It's all been through two areas. One is private services. The other one has been through those organisations who are funded by the government. They come to us and say, "Home Instead, can you please deliver these services to our clients?"'

As of February 2017, the government system was deregulated. No longer do providers tender to government for funding; money goes directly to the client, in a similar system to that of the NDIS. 'The client now has the choice. The client is now controlling those funds. The client can determine which organisation they want to have delivering those services. The client can say, "No. I now want you round at four in the afternoon. I want you at three in the morning," and all these sorts of things. The client is in control. It's completely turned the industry upside down. As a result of that, the industry is having to respond.'

Em, the healthcare support worker, believes a privatised system filters out flagrant abusers. Private businesses, he says, have an interest in doing well. However, with government, it's about ticking boxes, and things fall through the cracks. Martin agrees (though his bias should be noted). 'The government system was broken. It was absolutely broken,' he says. 'I've done everything in my power to meet with every person possible, at ministerial, prime ministerial level, to say to them, "It's broken." I've presented at conferences to say, "It's broken." As a result, not myself, but certainly coming into the market, we could see as clear as could be that there was a problem.'

The industry lobbied, advocated, Martin says, and should be commended. As an approved provider, Home Instead benefits. People receiving government assistance can now elect for care from Home Instead.

It will take time for the system to really work for those in it. But there is a sense of expansion and possibility, the hope that recipients will have greater control of how they live.

✦

Dimi Vourliotis is the senior manager for Aged and Disability Services at Advance Diversity Services (ADS), a non-profit organisation that provides support for CALD (culturally and linguistically diverse) people who wish to remain living independently at home. She is more reserved than Martin about the changed funding apparatus.

'We used to receive our funding in a pool,' she says. That is, one hundred clients meant ADS received one hundred clients' money in a pool every month. In 2010, a pilot program was launched around consumer-directed care. In 2015, anybody who came into aged care had to have their money as consumer-directed care, which meant that the client managed the funding that the government gave to ADS, plus a small contribution. This enabled them to have access to the services they wanted.

'We may have thought that they wanted showering five days a week, but the client's said, "No, I've never showered five days a week. I want a shower Monday, Wednesday and Friday, and I want to use my other two days to go somewhere else, to do something else; prepare a meal for me." So they've got a lot more control.'

And they can buy other services and products – lawn mowing, incontinence pads, equipment, things that previously were restricted. 'Now they can use that money for their health.'

Dimi isn't dismissing the system. It has its strengths, and it functions. It does mean, however, that ADS is more limited because the money isn't pooled. 'You're restricted and limited to the money that you get from the government. But consumer-directed care is working, and that's the way of the future.'

Beside Dimi is Mikall Chong, chairman of the ADS board, whom I first met at a talk given by the Age Discrimination Commissioner, the Honourable Dr Kay Patterson AO – 'Will you still need me?' – for Affinity, an interfaith group, in which she pointed to three primary areas of concern: elder abuse, older women at risk of homelessness, and the ageism that impacts employment opportunities for older people. When I asked the commissioner during question time about CALD communities' needs, Mikall raised his hand and explained how ADS services CALD communities. 'We have a whole spectrum of services, and each department deals with a specific area,' Mikall says.

ADS supplies personal-care services to people over sixty-five. Social support is also an important part of ADS's offerings. The organisation caters to multicultural communities. Senior day centre programs are ethno-specific and run weekly to fortnightly. They cater to Arabic, Greek, Italian, Macedonian, Chinese, Bangladeshi, Maltese and Nepalese communities, to name a few. 'We deal with thirteen languages. We provide a day out for them,' explains Dimi, who herself is from a CALD background – her parents are Greek. It's a respite day for carers. '[But it's] also as a social interaction for the client, who gets to be with another person who speaks their language, are similar age and culture, of course, and they get to make friends. What it does is diminish social isolation in a short space.'

Access to these days out, as with any other service, depends on the client's funding, meaning their condition and what they're eligible for. Activities are purely social: buffet lunches (the most popular outing) or, weather permitting, morning tea in the park. 'A couple of weeks ago we went to Bowral for the flower festival,' says Dimi.

When discussing the role of families managing ageing parents' needs, it's here, often, that conversations diverge into cultural and gender factors at play in the lives of the elderly.

Aged care workers I spoke to talked about the strength of Asian communities' robust family ties – it's simply accepted that parents will age in place, surrounded and supported by family. Other people, medical professionals included, told me that you see the whole spectrum of behaviour, across cultures.

Dimi, however, says that while there may be language-related issues, culture isn't the obstacle to peace: she reiterates that the major challenges for people in old age relate to their freedom and state of mind. 'Depression and [lack of] independence go hand in hand,' she says firmly.

She elaborates: 'People don't access these services because they want to, it's because they have to. They've come to a stage in their life where they're no longer able to look after themselves a hundred per cent, so they have to access services . . . People get sick, people go into residential care, people are separated from their friends, their community, their contacts. With that comes some sort of loss and grief, and from that stems illness. So if the grief is not dealt with, it festers, where then a person is unwell.'

I'm not alone in believing that this downward spiral of emptiness begins as people wind down their working lives, during which, regardless of the politics of the workplace and the commutes they once complained about, they were forced into more social settings, and probably benefited from them. A recent VOX video piece talked about how people who travel on public transport for their commutes generally live longer than people sitting in their cars, alone with their thoughts. People, people, people – and remaining active. These are everything in a time of life that may feel increasingly isolated, with a future clouded by uncertainty.

But Dimi notes that it's not ADS's job to manage their clients. 'When people come to us they've already been seen by psychologists, aged care assessment teams.' ADS will, however, help people from CALD backgrounds to navigate the My Aged Care portal if they face language barriers. An assessor for ACAT continues the process. '[The] original assessment person goes out and sees them. They do about a two-hour assessment with them, where they talk about what their illnesses are, what their medication is, why they contacted My Aged Care, and it could be as simple as maybe they only want there to be the social support. They're lonely. Their best friend can't drive them anywhere anymore, and they want help with a trip up to the shops, and they can't go on their own because they can't get on and off the steps of the bus. That's a simple case.'

More complicated cases see greater needs around the home, and for the person undertaking simple tasks. 'There's so many things that we take for granted every single day that we do automatically. You get up in the morning, you make your bed. You go and make your breakfast. Some people can't do that anymore. They can no longer manage.'

Following an assessment, applicants are placed in a queue. 'But you could be waiting in a queue for three years,' says Dimi.

Not only can it take years to get assistance, the funding is spread thin. Dimi quotes a government estimate of 11,000 packages since the deregulation in February 2017 – across the whole country. 'It's a user-pay system now, where the government says, "If you can afford it and you're a self-funded retiree, go buy it."'

Mikall and Dimi say these are things the government doesn't talk about. It's a competitive business, and the big providers are in a better position for survival. 'We don't have three thousand packages. We've only got a hundred,' says Dimi.

It doesn't help that sometimes family expectations can be unrealistic around what My Aged Care can provide an elderly person. And, she adds, My Aged Care itself is a difficult system, burdened by inconsistencies, too cumbersome for many of the people it's designed to assist.

'We're supposed to be medicine managers'

Increasing responsibilities as a carer, or of any kind, can feel intimidating and even lonely. But there is an inordinate number of services and people who can provide helpful guidance to improve everyone's quality of life. As a former journalist in the pharmacy industry (and a frequent visitor to a local one with my folks), I believe pharmacists are an untapped resource.

'I'm talking to elderly people all of the time,' says Sarah, a co-owner of a suburban pharmacy. 'And I'm seeing sickness; I'm seeing people becoming unwell; I'm seeing children looking after their mothers and fathers, and the toll it takes on their family, on their life, on their marriages, on themselves; and it's always in the forefront of my mind.'

As a pharmacist, Sarah is attuned to the way ageing and illness change people's lives, the burdens they can involve, and what solutions exist to ease the situation.

Sarah is also in a business that allows her to form long-term relationships with her patrons. 'I lost two patients last week and it was very sad, but because I'm in pharmacy I see the children coming in and getting the medications for their dad. One with a newborn baby, and her dad had cancer and the child is only three weeks old and she had to move in with her dad and spend six months looking after him. And then he has died and she has just given birth and it's very hard.'

Pharmacy is different to other professions, continues Sarah. 'When you go to see a doctor, or when you see a specialist, or when you see a solicitor, or when you see a speech pathologist, or when you see a physiotherapist – all these people, you are paying them for their time. So they can set aside half an hour, one hour of their paid time and you can see them. A pharmacist isn't like that – we get paid according to what I sell you.'

It means that they're time poor, but they are available. Sarah talks about Home Medicines Review (HMR), where patients are referred by a doctor to a pharmacist. Pharmacists go into people's homes. 'We go through their cupboards, we throw out all of the expired medications. We say, "Bring out all of your medications . . . Oh, you're not on that, you're not on that, you're on this, how are you taking that, do you know what that's for?" [They tell us] "I'm getting up five times a night to wee." "[We say] That's because you're taking your diuretic at night – you should be taking it in the morning."'

Pharmacists are paid for this service, but it's a role that requires extra training, staying up to date with Continuing Professional Development points and getting accreditation. The pharmacist will then send a report to the referring doctor, which will include any recommendations. There are also MedsChecks, which can be done in the pharmacy itself. An initiative from the government, it doesn't require accreditation or a doctor's referral. 'So it's almost like a mini HMR,' says Sarah. A patient will go into the pharmacy armed with their medications and, in a special area of the pharmacy, will have a discussion with the pharmacist. It's not as in-depth as an HMR, Sarah explains; it takes about fifteen minutes.

'I go through their medications; I confirm that they know what they are taking their medicines for, they know how they are taking their medications. I am having a quick look to make sure that there are no interactions, they are not taking vitamins that I don't know about, vitamins that can potentially interact with their medication.'

Sarah identifies clashes. For example, someone on antidepressants went to a health food shop and came out with St John's Wort. St John's Wort is a vitamin and can be effective as an antidepressant, but it interacts with many things.

Given how much medication some people are on, it's a valuable service. Another one on offer is the provision of Dose Administration Aids (DAAs), popularly known as the 'Webster pack' (a patented product). The government is pushing for greater use of the packs, subsidising pharmacists to provide them. They take time – Sarah employs a pharmacist to work on those alone. She's seen all sorts of situations with the DAA – there are people taking it up, others being encouraged by their children but the parents refusing it. 'So all scenarios are not unusual, if that makes sense.'

The reluctance can stem from the desire not to relinquish control. A patient knows exactly what they're taking, when and why. 'I am often recommending Webster packs to the elderly, especially when they can't remember if they have taken a medication, or if they get very confused.'

For Gerald Quigley, pharmacist, master herbalist and health commentator, the relationship with patients is where pharmacists are too often failing. 'There's two aspects of visiting a pharmacy. You go and buy something, you might even go and have a medication being dispensed. But it puzzles me that the dispensing process has become just that. A process . . . We're supposed to be medicine managers. Medication management is one of our big things we hang our ticket on. Come to us, we're free, we're available, we will help you manage your medication. I don't see that happening.'

'Why do you think that is, though? Is it just time?' I query.

'No. Time is an excuse. You make time. If you value your career [and] you've chosen pharmacy or medicine or any of those things, part of that is responsibility. To first of all do no harm, that's a little Hippocratic oath the medicals take. You do no harm and you encourage the person to become a partner in their ongoing choice to be as well or as sick as they want to be. And I think there's a whole cohort of Australians who don't know what it's like to feel well anymore.'

Health has become very clinical and very medicalised, Gerald argues. 'Now, when a person talks about health, the implication is that there's a problem. And that problem needs to be treated immediately with something.' A headache, for example, shouldn't simply invite a dose of Ibuprofen. Questions should be asked: like, is it today, or day after day?

'Because the simplest solution for headache is just to drink some water. The most common reason people get headaches is just dehydration. Often it can be the fact that they're magnesium deficient [which can cause muscle cramps], so they tense up because they might be humped over a steering wheel, humped over a computer screen, in a position that they don't really move from, and they get a headache. But then you put dehydration in there as well. So no one has the time in engaging.'

Engagement is especially relevant with an older person, Gerald says. 'Older people don't think as quickly, they don't understand as quickly. Names are so long, medications they take have got such long, unpronounceable names, and everyone's in a hurry. People speak quickly, they want to give instant solutions. The pharmacy these days has gone from an opportunity for a pharmacist to engage with a person and enquire as to their ongoing wish to be as well as they can, to now being, "Here's your prescription, it's going be three or four minutes, there it is, take it down the front and pay, please, before you go." And that's the process.'

Gerald takes his criticism a step further. He suggests that the lack of personal connection has severed the traditional relationship between pharmacist and local customer. 'I'll give you an example. You can probably tell me the name of your hairdresser. You can probably tell me the name of your nail technician if you go and have your nails done. What's the name of your local pharmacist?'

I have no idea of mine, but, to be fair, my parents know theirs well. They're on a first-name basis.

Gerald would like to see pharmacists take a more pro-active role in identifying changes in their customers, to ask more probing questions. He blames a lack of communication skills. 'I just remember in pharmacies I've owned we would have people dispensing at a great rate of knots, and people sitting in chairs waiting. And I would often spend hours just sitting in those chairs. "What's going on?" "Who do you follow in the footy?" Having a discussion about something other than the illness that they are convinced is running their lives.'

He likes to see how his patients are tracking; whether family or others are coming to visit them; what they might have had for breakfast. 'I've got a GP friend of mine who greets' – Gerald shakes my right hand with his right hand, and touches my shoulder with his left hand – 'He greets you like that, he says "Hello" and he says that from the muscle tone in their shoulder he can tell how physically robust they are.'

The doctor Atul Gawande, author of *Being Mortal*, regards a geriatrician who checks feet. The feet will tell you everything about this person: how well they're being taken care of, how clean they are, the health of their body as well. You can tell a lot from a person's feet.

'This whole engagement thing could revolutionise pharmacy,' Gerald says.

'Do you think pharmacists should be doing more on home visits?' I ask him.

'Absolutely, but someone's got to pay.'

Gerald says that at one time, he would take three people for afternoon tea once a month, through his clinic. 'I would say first in, best dressed. I don't care whether you're a patient or not. If you want to join me for an hour, I'll give you a cup of tea and a sandwich at a local restaurant . . . This isn't a consultation one on one, remember – there are other people there, but you all each have fifteen minutes . . .".'

Indeed it wasn't a clinical intervention – just a chat about their health, and it was offered at no cost to the person participating in it. They could tell Gerald things like, 'I've got blood pressure and it's badly managed, and I do everything the doctor says and I do everything the pharmacist says and I'm still out of control.'

Gerald would offer his views, including advice to discuss things with their doctor.

'I've had people tell me that the letter I've written to their doctor is just torn up. In front of them. And one of those ladies said to me, "I don't go to that doctor anymore." Interestingly, what I suggested in the letter was done. But never acknowledged.'

I think a lot about this later. Help – simple in its need, sometimes difficult in its accessibility. And it takes me back to Gawande, talking about feet. Of all things, feet. I think of how diabetics should be extra vigilant. I don't push Dad on a lot of things, but I book him in with a podiatrist. I don't ask, I just do it. As luck would have it, she's a sweet lady – she calls dad 'sweetheart', and is always smiling. Dad is comfortable with her. It's a small thing, but it's significant.

'Serious clash'

Medications can certainly be a minefield. Professor Richard Lindley, a devotee of computer-assisted medicine, has a series of medical applications on his phone so a database is but a touch away. He logs into an app. 'We were last looking up vaginal cream for oestrogen, for atrophic vaginitis, so there you go,' he says cheerfully. 'But I've got all this full data on my computer.'

We're at the George Institute, located in one of the several buildings that constitute the Royal Prince Alfred Hospital (RPA), where Professor Lindley is a professorial fellow. He is also professor of geriatric medicine at the University of Sydney, and a clinical geriatrician at Blacktown Hospital, with an office based at Westmead. And somewhere along the way, he found time to pen the book *Stroke: The Facts*, the contents of which he describes as a 'sort of stroke for the intelligent layman'.

Professor Lindley continues selling me on the advancements of technology. 'I'm a great believer for dangerous stuff like medication that if the professor has to look up the side effects or interactions of medications, it's not embarrassing for the resident to look it up. Because I'd much rather people be safe.'

He leaps up to offer a quick example. 'We've got a drug interaction and I can just . . .' he types in the names of two drugs. 'Old people are often on far too many medications, so . . . you can see people that are on this drug and they're not very well.'

If there's a clash, it comes up red.

This match comes up red on the screen. 'Serious clash,' Professor Lindley declares. 'And you can't possibly learn all the interactions of every medication because there'd be millions and millions of combinations, but as I've just demonstrated in five seconds, I've got the answer.'

He looks pleased, understandably chuffed at the swiftness of modern advancements. I think of how many people I've met with who have fridges filled with medicine boxes; of all the children of ageing parents who worry about how many medications their parents are on; of the pharmacists who tell me they are but a question away, if only people would ask.

'Well, you know if you're on six or more, the chances are you've got an adverse drug reaction,' says Professor Lindley. 'Statistically.'

'We don't see our role as extending life'

'If you practise Western medicine, unless you're a paediatrician, everybody's doing geriatric medicine – they just don't realise it,' says Dr Naganathan. 'They all are. The average age of people in an acute hospital in Sydney is roughly about seventy-eight, seventy-nine. So everyone is doing geriatric medicine.'

A hospital full of old people is a sign your medical system is good.

'People are living longer, and not many young people are getting infectious diseases. In countries like Australia we have little HIV, TB; we haven't got malaria.'

As the head of the Concord Clinical School, Dr Naganathan has worked as a consultant geriatrician for seventeen years. He is also an associate professor at the University of Sydney, where he teaches and is involved in research. I'm keen to draw out his perspectives on extending a life when it's not necessarily a fulfilling one.

We discuss the frequent refrain 'I don't want to be a burden to anyone when I lose my independence.' Unquestionably people are living longer. One of the big questions being asked about ageing is: at what cost? What quality of life follows life-saving procedures? 'I can speak for geriatricians . . . we don't see our role as extending life,' replies Dr Naganathan. 'We see our role as trying to help people . . . meet what they want. What I do know is that until you're older and potentially frail and have got medical problems, you don't really know what you'll think about it. And you may look at yourself when you're young, and you look and you go, "No way. There's no way I want to live with that." And then when you reach that stage, you go, "Actually, you know what? I've got a lot to live for."'

People have a higher threshold than they thought. People also change their minds.

'I've had people who've been sick, who when they're sick will say, "I don't want to live anymore." And then they get through it anyway, right? Then you see them three months later in clinic, and they're enjoying time with their grand-children. And then you ask them, "Was it worth it?" And they go, "Yes, it was." But they got through because they got through. We might not have done anything to help them get through, but they got through. We human beings change our minds even on life and death decisions.'

It's indeed worrying how definitive people are when idealising their own death, or drinking the miracle-solution-to-stave-off-ageing Kool Aid.

'What do you do with that when somebody's convinced of one thing?' I asked Dr Naganthan. 'If you have this patient who says, "I'm sick and I don't want to be here"? And then three weeks later they're like, "Well, I'm glad I got through." What role do you play in that?'

'We play a big role . . . Not just the doctor, the whole team plays a big role in working out how far you go, what the limits in treatment are.'

He explains the concept of limits of treatments when someone is sick in hospital. 'There are levels of treatments from . . . maybe we'll go from simple to harder, right? Someone comes in with an infection. The simplest levels of treatment are antibiotics and fluids. [What if that person has] end-stage dementia and has, what most people would think, no quality of life. Well, they can't tell us, so we will ask the family, "If they could talk to me, do you think they would want antibiotics and fluids for their pneumonia or urinary tract infection?" Something that is very simple to treat, right? So we do our best to give people a choice, even if it's asking their family.'

Dr Naganathan says that not being given a choice on treatments like antibiotics and fluids is an issue. He gives the example of a nursing home patient coming in to hospital with end-stage dementia. With quality of life in mind, the patient's family is consulted about possible treatment scenarios – and after discussion with the medical team decide that no CPR, ICU, intense treatment or dialysis should be given.

'Then I might ask, "But did you give them a choice in anti-biotics and fluids?" And there's silence on the other end of the phone. And sometimes if I feel they don't get it, I go, "Well, if that was you, would you want fluids and antibiotics?" And they go, "No." And I go, "Yeah, neither would I."'

It raises an interesting ethical question for doctors about initiating active treatment which they themselves in the same situation would not want. Dr Naganathan says that care must be taken with how the choice is presented to the family.

'Is there an emotional edge to this, though, for you?' I ask him.

'Oh, no. No, no, no. It's a very simple question. And the way to do this is to say to the family, "Tell me about your father's quality of life." And then you'd say, "Now, if your father could speak to me, what do you think he would say about being given fluids and antibiotics to help him pull through this pneumonia?" Take that as an example. And sometimes family will say, "Actually, now that you've put it as a question of what my dad would want, I think I know. Usually people ask me what I want, and I want you to give the fluids and antibiotics, but now that you've put it from Dad's perspective . . ."'

Dr Naganathan offers up a statistic: that in such a situation involving fluids and antibiotics, 50 per cent of families would agree to it; the other half would say no. He hopes that point provides reassurance to the family that whichever choice they make is a 'perfectly reasonable' one.

Friday

My father never expresses regret about coming to Australia. He always says, 'It's a beautiful country.' He appreciates its landscapes; he's travelled far and wide, exploring with my mother. He has built himself into the success he always wanted to be, and he links his achievements to the country he chose as his new home.

It was supposed to be a temporary move.

'When I told my father I was coming here, he asked where it was. A friend had told him that once I take Australian citizenship, I won't come back. I was planning to stay five years.'

A year later, the Six-Day War erupted. Dad is no longer a citizen of Palestine. In order to remain one, my parents would have had to return there every year.

Dad remembers his first return to Palestine following his move to Australia. It was 1975. 'The Israelis were waiting for me.' He was strip-searched on entry. 'I asked them: "What did I do?" Their response: "Nothing."'

'Did it hurt to have to answer to them?'

'Yes.'

Checking my father's ID for 'security' reasons, an officer queried him on Arrabeh, his hometown. 'Where is it?' the guard asked Dad.

He provided its exact location, short of coordinates.

'Are you trying to tell me that you came all the way here from Australia to *this* place?'

Dad's instant response was an emotional one. Arrabeh was his home. He tells me the soldier, in an unusual move, apologised for offending him. Such interrogations aren't unusual. As Dad says plainly, 'We Palestinians have suffered a lot.'

En route to Palestine in 1975, Dad was subjected to similar questioning in Egypt, for three hours.

Dad has always been the helper kind. He quickly made friends in Australia, men like him – Arabs who had left behind families, a homeland, a culture as familiar as their reflection. I piece together a sense of the excitement and confusion of this eruption of new life – uncharted territory, a new language, a fresh way of being.

Dad tells me stories. Of what he did for these friends – helping them with language difficulties; his finding work; getting a driver's licence; finding a partner. He's not anchored to the past, he's able to relive it in bursts, to recapture his youthfulness and ambition, his appetite to help everyone he knows.

That was Dad. In some ways a different person to the breadwinner I grew up with. The same but different. It is an aspect of his character that takes on new meaning when he speaks of my grandfather, a man who didn't express love easily; fierce, a survivor. Dad was always a dutiful son, always good to my grandparents. His every visit became more than a reunion, it was an offering. My father had left his family to build a life elsewhere, a sacrifice that began when he first moved to Germany. And with every return home, he would invest in his family's security and comfort, each act of generosity an affirmation of loyalty and love.

3.

A THRONE FOR
THE CRONE

*People's stories are lessons **in humanity.***

Among pagans, there is a tradition called 'croning'.

'If we think about our society now, it's not cool to be old,' says Stacey Demarco, self-titled 'modern witch'. 'Especially women.'

Croning occurs later in a woman's life, after she has stopped menstruating – in her fifties, sixties, seventies, eighties. 'I think one of the best cronings I have ever been to was for someone in their nineties, and it was *the* best. So what happens is, you invite all your friends, and at first it's only women. So this is all your friends and their kids who are female.'

They decorate what is called 'a throne for the crone'. In the old days, when throning a crone was tradition, she would be carried in. There are refreshments, and the guests gather around the crone in a semicircle on the floor. 'She is the wise woman, the archetypal wise woman. How many times do we do that in our society now, when we look at an older woman and go, "I want a bit of that"?'

Stories told are not sentimental reminiscences. They're brief and designed to impart experience, the primary lessons of this woman's life. 'Here's my wisdom I'm going to pass on to you, right? So, "I learned early that it's best to do this, and you young ones out there, try to do this."'

Some of the women present will stand up and share positive memories of the crone. '"You have given me this"; "I remember you said this to me and it changed my life." And to just hear that. To hear, at maybe ninety, that someone's life has changed because of you – and it might have been simply, "You made me the best biscuits I ever had and I needed that at the time because I was going through this terrible situation and I hated myself."'

The fun part, Stacey says, is that questions are written down for the crone to pull out of a box. 'And she answers them like an oracle. One of the questions might be "What's your advice about men?" Or, "I have a boyfriend who does *this,* what should I do?" And generally the answers are hysterically funny or just beautiful. There's laughter, there's tears. And then everyone is allowed in, so the men in the family. And a few of the key people there talk again about what they've learned from this woman.

'Then comes the feasting. The woman walks a spiral, the labyrinth, but she walks inwards. A maiden would walk a labyrinth out. But the crone is signalling that she is keeping her wise blood within and her wisdom is held tightly. And she's signalling that it's time – "I don't know how much I have left, but I'm giving it back to where it came from." It's transformation. And I can tell you every woman who's been to a croning – a very positive croning – has gone, "I want one of those, I want that for myself."'

It's not that common in Australia, but Stacey thinks it's done in the US. She'd love to see it take hold here. 'It's something I've got on my big list that I'd like to organise for people, because I think it helps with ageing; it helps with your self-esteem as you age. The women I know who have had a croning, oh my god, they're on a high.'

It's a practice at odds with the modern view of ageing – that it's punishment, or an anomaly; it wasn't meant to happen. But it's the natural way of things. Like the change of seasons, and the cycles they represent, our bodies go through these stages, and we seem to grapple with each one.

Nobody wants their body to fall apart, to lose its rhythm, to struggle with the toll of years of life. But, as Stacey suggests, 'We've got to have a pay-off. To me, the pay-off is [that] you're collecting wisdom, you're collecting perspective. I'm getting to this age now where I say, oh, I've seen that before. Do you know what I mean? I've seen people do that before, or, wow, I've seen a pattern there. I know how to handle it.

'So as a pagan woman, looking at cycles, working the cycles intimately, from the lunar cycle to the seasonal cycles . . . you don't even have to be spiritual about it. [You can decide], okay, it's winter, probably smart for me to go a little bit more introverted, for me to do my planning now – I don't have to be so extroverted. We have biorhythms in our body. We have all kinds of cycles – as women with menstrual cycles, that's a really easy thing to see.'

Croning appears to stem from Celtic tradition, but Stacey says there are a lot of pagan cultures that celebrate 'the wise time' – that is, being an elder. Native Americans have medicine men and women, elders who sit on a council. 'So every one of them does it very differently. But if we look at the Celtic model or the witchcraft model . . . cronings [were] a rite of passage. Men, too – a lot of theirs is around the transfer of strength.'

Think of the father running with his son, faster than his child, but who will one day be overtaken. But rather than express sorrow at being surpassed, it will signal a time of celebration. The son will be given a gift.

Men as warriors and protectors is a similar idea. 'The fact that men are losing what they see as their strength or their ability to protect, that's a big deal in our society.'

Indeed, for many of my interviewees dealing with a father who is ageing and unwell, a response of mute shame is not uncommon.

'My father right now hates being weak,' says Melanie*. 'He sees himself as being weak. It's only yesterday that he has accepted a walking stick.' Her father's condition she describes as the 'classic bad knees, which led to him not doing so much exercise, which led to him becoming overweight, which led to him being diabetic, having kidney problems'.

A kind of trickle-on effect.

'It's what my husband calls "the cascade" – one thing goes wrong, then everything goes wrong.'

Melanie's mother, however, hasn't allowed anything to stop her physically. Balance issues are addressed by going to a dance class – and if she falls against the wall, who cares? 'It's a completely different headspace.'

Her mother has also maintained her commitments to volunteer work and a social life. Perhaps it's as my mother suggested: some women are more resilient for all they have endured and managed – a life-long balancing act, less free and wild than those of so many husbands and breadwinners of a certain generation, who may love their families but do not always have the same everyday presence within them. Old age, and the illness bundled with it, renders them less independent, free and strong. For Melanie, it also goes back to the masculine desire to be a protector. Keeping him engaged. She does the same with her mother, who has strong knitting skills. Her mother complains if Melanie requests her help knitting, but a few days later will ask whether she has the wool.

'Is your dad sad or angry?' Melanie asks me.

I tell her it's more sadness. Anger requires too much energy. And what's the pay-off? You can get angry, but it won't change the problem.

'My dad's angry,' says Melanie definitively.

He wasn't always angry, though. She describes him as someone who has always been 'the calm one'. Playful even. And now her mother is dealing with a different man.

A map of experiences

Throughout my research, it became clear that few men were willing to share stories, whether as carers, or as people ageing and perhaps experiencing a decline in health. I lack empirical evidence as to why, but perhaps something can be gleaned from the willingness of women to share their stories. Because when I interviewed certain women, another important realisation struck me: not only were they more willing to express their fears, vulnerabilities and strengths as their mortality stretched out before them, but many women age capably alone.

Certainly, I have read harrowing reports on the rise of homelessness and grave poverty among ageing women in Australia. Indeed, among the women I spoke to, some were comfortable but others relied on inheritances, government support, access to cheap services and affordable rent. Some were in debt. Others expressed worry about how their circumstances would change once their savings were diminished, particularly if they were supporting a partner in a nursing home, or how their wellbeing would suffer if they were fated to reside in one themselves.

Yet in my many conversations, women appeared to me as resilient and determined as my mother thinks they tend to be. And none had any intention of one day being fully dependent, whether it be on a family member, or in the care of a faceless nursing home. Many also indicated a new breath of life that was peaceful, self-accepting and authentic. They were not troubled by societal pressure to be youthful, beautiful and ageless.

It's an important point. In my search for books on ageing, the section that houses the topic in a large bookstore in the city is paltry, easily eclipsed by the bulging cancer section. Most of the titles aren't about the realities of ageing, they are guides on how to prolong youth and stave off the decay of your body, the loss of your vitality. The loss of you. Ageing isn't 'sexy', many tell me, health professionals included. People wish to deny it, as though ignoring its signs can stop it in its tracks.

I detected two primary trails of thought on preserving youth and beauty. On one hand were the women who, mid-life, were teetering between that youth and a future that held no certainty but the potential for more wrinkles and saggy skin. (There's an elasticity test to determine your ageing process. Pull up your skin into a tent, somewhere around your wrist, and watch how quickly it springs back into place. The quicker it does, the younger you are – or the 'better' you're ageing.)

Yet other women talked about the relief of age – they no longer worry about how they look, and, more importantly, they feel free to be themselves, to speak their truths, to do away with the nonsensical need to please. One woman spoke of her fears of getting old and losing her looks: having had a gnarled relationship with them throughout her life, she was only now coming to a place of appreciation for her natural beauty. Another woman expressed regret for the years she lost as a young woman in a headscarf. She still wears one, but she's taken other measures to celebrate her womanhood. She had a big females-only bash for her birthday. She does botox regularly, and she also had a boob job.

For my part, I'm taking my cue from Isabel Allende. Now in her seventies, the renowned author declared her intention before a TED audience to 'live passionately', no matter her age. 'You know, for a vain female like myself, it's very hard to age in this culture. Inside, I feel good, I feel charming, seductive, sexy. Nobody else sees that,' she says to laughter. 'I'm invisible. I want to be the centre of attention. I hate to be invisible.'

But Allende also asserts her freedom in older age. She doesn't have to prove anything anymore, isn't stuck in an idea of who she was, or wanted to be, or what others expected her to be. She says her body might be falling apart, but her brain is still first-rate. She observes how great it is to let go: 'I should have started sooner.' Nor is she scared of being vulnerable, saying that no longer does she see it as weakness. Allende admits that now 'death is next door, or in my house', but this knowledge simply means she tries to be present in the moment. She makes me smile when she says, 'The Dalai Lama is someone who has aged beautifully, but who wants to be vegetarian and celibate?'

'I've been through the wringer'

'When my older friends and I get together, we have what is called the "organ recital". It's like, "Let's get our health out of the way, and then we'll get on to ideas and thoughts and philosophy,"' says Lindel, an author, tea-leaf reader and astrologer. The humour helps. 'It does because all of us are cracking up in different ways.'

Cracking up, falling to bits. Having a sense of humour is important among friends who are all dealing with the challenges of old age. And having friends, period, is core to a good quality of life.

Lindel is in her late sixties and lives alone but for a faithful cat, who has proven useful more than once when it comes to monitoring Lindel's blood sugar, frantically prodding her awake when her eyes closed and she began to slump in her seat. Lindel has chronic illness, and her eyesight has suffered. She's an example of someone who is determined to live the best life she can without being dependent on anyone.

Limitations, like not being able to drive at night, have prompted her to be vigilant about her social life. 'Just making sure that I have lunch with friends or having regular contact, and I have a couple of friends that I ring regularly, really old friends.' It eases her loneliness and anxiety. 'I've made that a priority.'

Following the organ recital, Lindel and her companions discuss children and grandchildren. Lindel doesn't have any of her own but she has beloved nieces and nephews, and has watched children of friends grow up. She's invested in their lives and wellbeing, and counts long-term friends among her group. 'What I think is that all of us are highly intelligent, educated women. We saw our mothers, what happened with our mothers. My mum, she had the church. I don't have the church.'

Rather, as a tea-leaf reader and astrologer, Lindel finds community among like-minded people. 'Whenever I get together with tea friends, we always have a little peek [in our tea cups], and people from the past ring me and ask me to do a reading. I don't actively seek it but it's always nice, and it's lovely to see people I've read for before.'

And on her dedication to astrology: 'I've made a really academic study of this stuff as well, but also my own chart continues to reveal itself. I do charts for people if they ask me, and I have good astrology friends – we discuss world events mainly.'

Meanwhile, social media is also significant to her wellbeing. 'A lot of people say, "I don't need Facebook." They don't live alone and it's a way I can see what you're doing. I might not be able to get up and out because sometimes, in this year, I've had quite a few months where I haven't been able to get up off the bed.'

'You've been through the wringer?'

'I've been through the wringer.'

Lindel's ill health began when she was a baby, suffering multiple pneumonias – three times before she was eighteen months old. 'That basically ripped my lungs. I have severe lung disease,' she tells me. She would get bronchitis as a kid and spend at least three months each year at home. 'I never really went to school in winter.'

She grew up in Tasmania, a place notorious for its unforgiving weather. The house was freezing, the air cold, a poor setting for someone with damaged lungs. Lindel was always a bit weaker than other people. 'I couldn't run, but I did swim and that helped me as a young person to keep my lung function up. We grew up on the beach, and I was a great walker and I used to go horse riding. Because I was born blind in one eye . . . I couldn't see ball games. You can imagine, I was always the last little girl to be picked on the softball team and to play tennis. Everybody would stand around and laugh because I could throw the ball up but I couldn't see it to hit it.'

Lindel only came to understand her condition when she was around fourteen.

'I have bumped into things all my life; I run sideways. It's just been awful.'

At least, however, she can decipher images in a tea cup. Lindel has a great love affair with tea. She divines information from the leaves she pours from pretty pots. She shares images of beautiful tea cups and saucers on Facebook.

'I see very well with my right eye and I do believe that I have second sight.'

Lindel was a teacher before she found her new path. First, symbols began to fascinate her. Second, she was diagnosed with Type-1 diabetes at forty-three. 'It's not usual to get it at that age, [Type 1 is] the childhood one. The doctors said to me that I had a predisposition to it and lucky I didn't get it as a kid.'

The treatments for her two conditions – the lung condition (an adult form of cystic fibrosis, 'bronchiectasis') and diabetes – fight each other and cause further problems.

'It's got worse over the last few years. I have had many pneumonias,' says Lindel. 'My doctor reckons I'm her most complex patient, but it's just because [my conditions are] not very usual things. I have a thing called autoimmune hepatitis, which is a sister disease of Type-1 diabetes.'

It impacts her interactions in the world. 'I only have to go to the movies and I get pneumonia, what they call community-acquired pneumonia. I can't go out into public places; I can't go where there are lots of people,' Lindel explains. 'I cannot be near anyone who has a cold . . . Most of my friends know that [but], some people don't get it. It's not like I get a cold for a week; I'm sick for eight weeks.'

But Lindel is a pragmatist. If her eyesight is poor, she can still enjoy audiobooks through the Vision Australia Library. After suffering nerve damage to her hands she underwent a hand operation, and then installed new taps. 'I'm a problem solver and I'm quite proactive. I had a fall earlier this year, so I went to a fall prevention clinic for a six-week course.'

She relies on an inheritance from an old friend, whom she looked after in her dying years. 'She said to me, "This money is for your health."' Lindel was in her fifties at the time. 'I didn't live with her but I was her main supporter. It was a real privilege, actually. I lived far from my mum, and my sister did the caring for my mum, and I felt because my friend . . . didn't have any children; I could support her. She was a fascinating person.'

When her friend had to move into care, Lindel would visit her at least twice a week, in addition to long phone conversations, sometimes several a day. 'I remember going into the hospital, and when she was sick they put a tube in her stomach. I was there, but she couldn't speak to me or anything. I was rubbing her feet gently, massaging her arms, putting oils and creams around her face. The nurse came and she said, "Is this your mother?" I said, "No, this is my friend." She said, "I hope I have other friends like you when I'm at end stage."'

While her friend was very sick by that point, almost semi-conscious, a bit confused, she knew who Lindel was to the end.

'Do you find comfort in your astrology, in your tea-leaf reading?' I ask her.

'I do. I don't read the tea leaves for myself, but I find great comfort in astrology.'

'What does it give you?'

'Well, it gives me a framework to understand the world . . . It's like a religion, but I rejected religion very young. It's a way of understanding the world, it's so ancient.'

Lindel has written a book on goddess myths, a guide to tea-leaf reading, and a book on tarot. She also invented an astrology game and, more recently, a tea-leaf-reading app.

'I'm a highly creative person, so I love that. What I feel really sad about with ageing and illness is that I haven't been able to type because of my right hand. I'm working on a novel. I've been working on this novel for years and I just can't physically do it. I've been thinking about voice and then I try to edit after I've spoken it into a recorder.'

You get the feeling that if anyone can persevere and find a way, it will be Lindel.

'It's almost like you aged young,' I tell her.

'I aged very young and that's written in my chart. I turned grey when I got diabetes. My hair went grey, it was such a shock.'

'What does the chart say about someone ageing young? What does it look like?'

'It's usually a certain strong Saturn aspect. In astrology Saturn rules ageing, so that's what it was.'

'When you look at your life now – and you live alone, you're independent still – do you have concerns about the day you *can't* be independent? Do you get care at all right now?'

'Yes, I have home care . . . I have one hour a week, and then every second week I have another hour because I can't do ordinary things – like I can't clean windows because of my hands. They clean one week, and then the second week they'll do whatever I ask, and they always do the floors because of the dust. They'll clean the bathroom every two weeks, but it's not as much as I would like.'

Lindel observes that such help has been privatised. But she believes that ageing, ill people will have greater choice once the NDIS is rolled out. 'I think this is important,' she says. 'And as a going-blind person, I will have more access.'

She's very concerned about what happens when she can no longer drive. 'You hate to ask for help, even though people are so kind, but it's those little things you need and think of. I've been in touch with the community bus, but it's difficult. They leave you waiting there for hours and if you can't afford a cab . . .'

Luckily, Lindel can afford to take care of her health through the inheritance. When her hand went numb, she purchased an automatic bottle opener. 'I have a jar opener, so I don't have to ask. I've got a tipping kettle because I couldn't pick the kettle up. Can you imagine? I couldn't make tea.'

As we finish, Lindel say, 'I know it sounds crazy, but I'm happy. I'm happy with who I am, who I've become through these challenges. That's the truth of it. You come to a distilled version of yourself.'

'If there's something there, I'm not interested in it'

Ruth, aged seventy-six, a retired nurse with thirty years' experience in infectious diseases, and drug and alcohol detox, describes her life as very peaceful. But she harbours gripes about the past – growing up female in a world that favoured males, for example. She gets emotional when she begins talking about her father, whose worldview was limited: in his opinion, women got married and had children. This attitude has influenced her life trajectory. This is why, at the age of fourteen, she decided to be a nurse. But Ruth's father didn't encourage her. 'He just said no because I wasn't a boy.'

All of this floats to the surface early in our conversation. We're in Ruth's apartment, one in a large block of low-rent flats run by a religious organisation, in a leafy, quiet suburb of Sydney close to public transport. Rent is about to go up, she tells me, so she's readying herself to move out. She has issues with religious organisations profiting from people in need.

Her apartment is spacious and uncluttered. Ruth is an avid reader: 'I've always got books everywhere because all I do is read, because I still think there's so much I haven't learned, that I want to know everything.'

Ruth is English; her family migrated to Australia after World War Two. Ruth remembers the voyage over. 'It was wonderful. It was such an adventure because we went through the Suez Canal before they closed it, so we saw the Pyramids; we saw so much. We went to Aden, we went to places we never would have gone to. And then, coming to Australia, because I really love animals, it was like coming to heaven for me because there were animals everywhere. And fruit trees – we didn't get much fruit in England because the Germans were bombing all the ships that were bringing supplies through.'

Her family relationship is important in our discussion. Ruth says she struggled to forgive her father for his lack of support. She had a tense relationship with him. 'I was always angry at him.' But she believes his own conditioning locked him in to his way of thinking and acting. It softened her towards him a bit, she says, tearing up. She grabs a tissue. We talk about how common it is to have parents encourage pathways that aren't necessarily the ones their children desire.

'I've got another friend who always wanted to be a doctor, and still does, and couldn't be because she was a girl,' Ruth says.

Ruth's father was a teenager in England in the early 1930s, when they had the hunger marches due to a lack of food. 'The government turned the army and the fire department and the police on to them, and they arrested everybody. My father was seventeen, and they gave him the choice: he could either go to jail or join the British army and go to India. So he went to India because he didn't want to have a police record.'

Ruth believes this influenced his character. 'But the thing is, he loved India. He learned to speak the language. He loved it, he loved the colour, because we come from Manchester, which is such a dreary, grey place. And they had this beautiful tasty food . . .'

Ruth says she had a better relationship with her mother than her father. 'My mother was a bit emotionally not well. I think she was clinically depressed most of her life . . . She had a really hard life because her mother died when she was nine, and I think there were ten kids in those days. And then her sister, who she was next to and really close to, got burned to death in front of her.'

While Ruth is attuned to hardship, particularly the struggles of women, she is buoyed by progress. She is excited by the freedoms women enjoy today. 'I think it's fabulous. I was really in the feminist movement, and I wanted women to have the opportunities that we couldn't have.'

She tells me she was inspired to speak to me after her neighbour put out the call, attracted to the idea of 'the young ones writing a book'.

'I think whatever we do outside of what we're expected to do is wonderful.'

Her feminist years were during the Vietnam War. 'And we succeeded there, and we were the ones that got "Ms", you know? We were the ones that got that through, instead of Mrs or Miss. I use that a lot, actually.'

'So do I,' I tell her, I suppose as a compliment.

Ruth speaks in a low voice, her tone matter-of-fact, thick with certainty. She tells me she's a lot more peaceful now than she has ever been. 'I don't mind getting older. I don't have all the turmoil I had when I was younger.'

'What's that like?'

'It's gorgeous.'

'What do you think was the turning point for you in getting to that?'

'Accepting.'

+

Ruth lives alone. She is the last of her siblings; her sisters have all passed away. But she is enjoying her life. For her, the most difficult period happened twenty years ago, when she had a brain haemorrhage and lay in a coma for ten days.

'I've been there, and survived it. They didn't think I would and they thought if I came out of it I might be brain damaged, or deaf, or blind. I decided myself that I was going to get well.

And I realised that it was between me and my brain to get well, nobody could do it for us. They could assist us, but they couldn't do it.'

Being in a coma 'was pretty interesting', says Ruth. 'If you're ever around anybody who's in a coma, be careful what you say, because I could hear everything.'

She remembers it all clearly. 'I could hear everything, but I just couldn't talk back, because my sister was saying, "Say something," and I was lying there and I was thinking, "Well, I would if I could."'

Ruth emphasises that she remembers the whole experience. She couldn't move or speak, but at her sister's request to squeeze her hand if she could hear her, she obliged. 'She said, "Oh, she's squeezing my hand." I thought, you silly bugger. Even people in comas can hear.'

It was an incredible experience, says Ruth. 'I was in a valley and I thought, it's so cold, so at least I'm not in hell.' She was walking through the valley with other souls, she recalls. It was an afterlife kind of place. 'Everybody was wailing and I thought, oh hell, what's everybody wailing about? Then I realised I was wailing too, and I wondered what are we wailing about? And I thought, well, this is what we do on earth, we whinge all the time, we just wail and moan and complain, and this is what was happening there, but we took it with us.'

There were other visions, which Ruth believes were reflective of the evolution of life.

Ruth is a spiritual person, and she says the experience didn't change this. 'I don't believe in religion, and I think most of it's made up by mankind to make you feel good . . . but I believe there's something that's way beyond anything that we can comprehend.'

Given her turbulent experiences, it's heartening to see that Ruth has taken their lessons to carve a more peaceful pathway for herself. She's determined in how she lives her life; even the way she speaks is that of a person who does not brook fools. She has always craved freedom and independence. To cement her point, she tells me about her short-lived marriage to a nice man, declaring it was a mistake. She had never wanted to be a wife.

Ruth and her husband had two kids, whom she ultimately raised herself. Then she got sterilised. She wanted more joy, more sex, but no more children. 'I felt trapped. I felt like my wings were sort of cramped, so I had to go.

'It was a bit like selling yourself to prison. So I decided that I didn't want to be married any longer, so I divorced him. And I did say to him, "Seriously, this is not you, you're a lovely man. You could be the king of England and I'd divorce you because I want to be free."'

'Did you feel better after that?' I ask.

'Absolutely.'

'Did you have that free life that you wanted?'

'I did, yeah.'

'Did you ever come close to being with someone who you really thought, well, no, this is not temporary, I want to be with this person?'

'Yeah, he was really lovely, too, but he got killed in a car accident, so that sorted that out.'

They were together for twelve years.

Her resolve filters into how she deals with her body. She believes everything comes from the mind. 'I decided that I was going to keep as healthy as I could. You can fall into being an ailing old woman, but I decided that's not what's going to happen.'

It's a continuous commitment to herself. When she had to have an X-ray and ultrasound a couple of weeks earlier, she instructed her doctor that she wasn't interested in a diagnosis.

'If there's something there, I'm not interested in it,' she told him. 'Because I've seen people have cancer implanted into their brain, and once they've got it in there, they obligingly die.'

She saw it when she was a nurse, but also with friends, one of whom was given six months to live, told to get his affairs in order. 'When he told me that, I said, "Don't listen, [the doctor's] only another man, he just happens to be a doctor, he's not bloody God Almighty. You don't have to die in six months." But he did,' Ruth recalls. 'If somebody says to you and your mind's a bit weak, you accept it like that.'

As for getting older and needing assistance, Ruth doesn't think about it. 'It's not to let it in, because sometimes if you let it in, it's like a worm and it burrows in there, you know?'

She ensures she remains active. She goes out every day. She takes walks. She is critical of those who put every ailment down to getting older. She continues a love affair with life, a devotion to animals. When talking about the prospect of death, she demonstrates no fear. 'It's going to happen. If I'm afraid of it, it's not going to change it,' she says, adding that if there is an afterlife, she hopes there are animals there, too.

'I had a laugh with my son because I really like everything – all things, I think. All things love their life, nobody wants to be killed. I don't know if you've ever tried to hunt an ant down – it runs like hell because it doesn't want to be squashed.

'So I feel like that about everything. When I was visiting my son, he's got ants in the kitchen, and so I told him his family weren't allowed to kill them. They had to clean the kitchen sink before they went to bed at night, and that way there was no food or anything on it so the ants won't come looking, and I'll put food out the back for them.'

Ruth made a deal with the trespassing ants. 'I said, "Look, if you'll go outside, I will feed you regularly while I'm here, and when I leave, I will get one of the children to do it." So I had a little saucer that I would just put food on and put it out the back. It worked.

'And then my son . . . because I used to [knock] on the wall when they started coming, to give them a warning that there's danger around, he said, "God, you've even got me standing here knocking on the kitchen wall if I see an ant."'

Later, Ruth shows me a laminated photo of a drop of water, magnified, and beside it an ant suckling from it. She's fascinated by the image – the small made large, a fresh perspective, a reminder of how we're all connected.

'There's an essence of who you really are'

Charlotte*, seventy-two, says she's never 'totally retired'. She runs through her work history like we're in a job interview. She taught business, took on a bunch of training and management roles at a local college, holds accounting qualifications. It took her a while to get there, though. 'When I first left school I started to study accounting, but didn't finish it. And typical of that time when I got married . . . I stayed at home with the children but I always had part-time bookkeeping jobs.'

She has three children. Somewhere along the way she got divorced, in the 1980s, escaping a marriage she describes as traumatic. Trauma, she tells me, is the 'hot topic' in psychology, an area of interest she eventually pursued in her later years. A diploma in the history of psychotherapy in the 1990s, then enrolment in university to complete a masters of mental health in art therapy. When she couldn't find work, she got into real estate.

Charlotte herself went into therapy a couple of decades ago with a Jungian analyst (someone who subscribes to a school of psychotherapy that had its origins in Carl Jung's ideology). She found herself going to the art gallery a lot. 'Art became very much a part of my process, just going there and learning about art. I do go to the exhibitions and get the headphones, and I started to really just allow myself to stand in front of artworks and absorb them. I'm not an artist. Although I dabble.'

Art therapy combines her love of art and fascination with Jungian psychotherapy. 'Originally I wanted to be a doctor, but I was at a ladies' boarding school and they didn't teach physics and chemistry . . . and my father didn't want to pay the extra money for me to learn that because I was a girl.

'So I always meant to be more in the helping professions, I think, rather than business. Business horrifies me with the game-playing, it's just unbelievable. And teaching – I quite enjoyed really getting to know the students and everything, but government departments frustrate me.'

Charlotte keeps busy. She lives alone, in a similar situation to Ruth – low rent, run by a charity, everyone in the building is over sixty-five. She's happy to be in a good location, close to public transport.

Ask Charlotte about her average day, and she'll tell you methodically: early riser. Diabetic medication. Breakfast, followed by two loads of washing, which she hangs on the line. Visits her daughter. And she's active – she exercises, swims. She likes watching the ABC. On her mind is setting up an art therapy business (she's previously practised on the Gold Coast), an endeavour that's encountered delays due to personal circumstances in her family.

Like many people her age, Charlotte has various ailments and conditions to manage on a daily basis. Once again, she rattles off a list. 'Diabetes, you don't forget about it almost ever . . . it's constantly in your life. And I have asthma. I only have one kidney. I have a lot of arthritis degeneration. I have hearing aids. I have glasses. I have false teeth – only two. I've just gone through a bad winter with about six urinary tract infections . . . A heavy cold and a month or two after that a flu. So I ended up taking eight lots of antibiotics, but it's only in the last week or two that I got myself back on track,' she finishes, without flinching.

'So there's this conscious, constant need to exercise, eat healthily, get your social connections happening, relaxation.'

Charlotte has ended up with nothing financially, she says, the result of a lifetime of being a helper. She's in debt, a loan that is about to run out. But she has the pension, and the debt is only to the bank. She's expecting it to be written off as a bad debt. 'I'm quite happy, though. I've got the lovely trees to look at and enough space.' Although she has no money, she says, 'I feel very secure. I'm incredibly grateful that I live in Australia.' She offers me an itemised gratitude list – her luck in finding a good place to live and the like. She just doesn't want to be dependent on anyone, she says with a laugh.

Charlotte certainly makes the effort to be social. She has friends in Sydney, women she's known for years. And when she goes to the pool, she is friendly with the regulars. She doesn't have a 'bestie' in Sydney, but she has a lot of family. 'I'm one of seven children, so I'm on the phone to my sisters and brothers. I'm connected on Facebook to all my nieces and nephews, so I have massive amounts of connections with people.'

It helps to stave off loneliness and isolation. 'And it just gives you an interest. What are they up to in their life, so to speak.'

Importantly for Charlotte, she tries not to allow her health to be a burden. Attitude is everything. 'And my kids just say, "Oh, you're not old yet, Mum!" They're not going to take up this role that you're taking up, I think, ever,' she tells me.

Her family in general doesn't allow anyone to sink into an attitude of dependency. There are parties and get-togethers. 'I spent last weekend with my sister on the Central Coast.

Three and a half weeks on the Gold Coast a month ago. I've got a lot of friends and family up there.

'But . . . like the fellow next door, he's in hospital, he's got diabetes, had his toe cut off last week and we're waiting to hear the results today. If it's gone to the bone he'll have to have his foot cut off. But I jolly him along. I say, "Stop all this learned helplessness!" And his son loves it.

'And I think he sort of listened to me . . . He said he got a new tablet and that's really helped him, and I can see a big change.

'Don't make it worse than it is. That's the big problem. I'm not unfeeling. I don't go along with this "snap out of it" when they haven't heard what the problem is,' she adds. 'I don't like the idea of real pain and cancer and Alzheimer's, and I gave up sugar last week because eighty-five per cent of diabetics get Alzheimer's, and the big thing to help is to stop eating sugar.'

Charlotte has her own issues to unpack, though. Her studies on trauma have led to past issues rising to the surface. She's scheduled to meet with a psychiatrist the day after we speak. She says such therapy has been helpful in the past. And, now, the imprint of an unhappy marriage has led her to recognise it as a traumatic experience. '[My ex-husband] was sexually abused by a school teacher . . . I used to say things like, "It's like he's not connected to his own inner person." And I can't get him to discuss anything. He just says, "We'll do it your way." But then he goes out and does it his way.

'And it's very unsatisfactory when he gives me a hug. It's just like nothing. And everything seems to be all about him. There's just no matter what happens, even when I gave birth to twin babies, ten weeks prematurely, and one was stillborn, and the other one lived for twenty-one hours, and I came out of hospital and I turned to him and he just looked at me and said, "Well, they were mine too, you know."'

Charlotte goes deeper on trauma and how it affects people. 'They lose the ability to trust anyone . . . They find it extremely difficult to be intimate. They're anxious all the time.

'And it's overwhelmingly sad, because it's not their fault. But the effect on me and the children was horrific, and I can still see how the effects on the children are still playing out in all our relationships. What can we do about it? How can we deal with it? That's the question I'll take tomorrow [to the psychiatrist], and we'll see where that takes us.'

Charlotte has been on a winding journey for some time. In 1964 she was struck by chronic fatigue syndrome. She got on with her life. She kept working. She says that for years she didn't feel well. But suddenly in 2014 the chronic fatigue dissipated. 'Nobody knows what it is and I don't know if they ever will. I definitely believe that psychology and physical illnesses are all mixed up together.

'And so at sixty-nine I started to feel like I felt at forty-nine. Now I'm much more able to plan ahead. And I just sort of have a passing thought: I hope I live long enough to get through all that.'

Charlotte's apartment is small and full. Not exactly cluttered, but there's evidence of a variety of interests and experiences. Most striking is her hunger for knowledge and greater understanding. She invokes well-known philosophers and spiritualists such as Rudolph Steiner. She's open-minded. When we meet, she is full of praise for an online course she's completing on the human's evolutionary relationship to life.

'Good therapists tend to believe that there's an essence of who you really are that never gets damaged no matter how much trauma or bad health . . . which can be trauma, too . . .

There seems to be this part of you that is always protected. And actually in protecting that part, sometimes you can be destructive to other people.'

Charlotte is comfortable not quite belonging in any one tribe, but recognises that she too behaves in a certain way to keep social connections. She likes socialising with like-minded people. 'I still think sometimes how lovely it would be if I were sharing my life with a deeply loving man. I'm heterosexual. But I actually think it's impossible. I'm not sure,' she laughs. 'When I'm with married people, I think, why do they put up with all this, even though they're presenting as reasonably happily married.'

Friday

The renal ward waiting room on a day of tests. Dad falls asleep on the chair, close to my mother and me. He won't take a bed. I think he likes having us around. I don't think he's comfortable, but we're close, he's at peace, and that makes me feel better.

Infomercials light up a flat-screen TV mounted on the wall by the reception desk. Karen Moregold prescribes astrological forecasts. I think of Lindel. She told me she'd seen two major illnesses in her own chart when she was in her mid-forties, not that she'd understood it at the time. 'Astrology is a drip-feed thing. You think you know it, but you can't necessarily take in the deeper meaning straight away, especially for yourself. But you can help others.' I think of how little I would like to know what life could have in store for me one day. Tempered serenity is all I have. I don't need to disrupt it with inevitability.

The waiting room is full of humorous moments. When Dad goes back in to see the nurses, it's Mum and me and a couple of regulars. Sometimes a familiar face passes us by and we nod in acknowledgment, like we belong to the same team now. Today a full-blown domestic unfolds as a woman zips around in a wheelchair yelling into her phone. The man beside me has a face mask on (he thinks he may have a cold), but he wonders out loud to me 'Why can't she take it outside?' What I can deduce from the shouting is that inside the ward her husband is undergoing dialysis, but she's mad as hell about something happening outside the ward. The collective energy of the room shifts. We're all drawn in. We're reading, sure, but her tone and decibel level are bound to pull an audience. She winds up and heads back into the ward, staring down the room. As she whizzes past us, she throws the man with a face mask a dirty look. I hold back laughter. Life can be so absurd.

There's temporary escape between the pokes and prods. We steal a moment in the sun at Centennial Park, buy coffee from a vintage model cart. Mum takes photos of the lake. Then we return to the hospital for a visit from the dietician. Her attempts to offer Dad advice become comical; Mum interjects before she can finish a sentence.

Dad does need the diet advice. He sometimes lacks an appetite. I find myself urging him to eat. One time he gave in, eating a sandwich then declaring, 'I ate it for you. I didn't want it.'

He used to be the type to eat the garnish off the plate.

But it's really Mum who plays food cop. I call it the Battle of the Capsicum, the tense to-and-fro that is also, quite frankly, amusing to watch. Mealtimes are all about negotiation. Mum monitoring Dad's funny eating habits. At times, he seems to get full just looking at his plate. Mum will harass him until he's eaten enough. Dad will resist, but Mum's a warrior: she knows that eventually Dad will go for the slice of capsicum on her plate that she's been haranguing him to eat. Meanwhile, Mum's plate sits away from her, towards the middle of the table, like she's waiting for someone else to finish her food. Some days she's better about enjoying her food. I wonder why she does this, but I suppose Mum's nature means she's not happy unless she's feeding people.

When we're finished with the dietician, we're done for the day. As we leave, Dad calls out to the nurse, almost cheekily, 'See you next year!' I don't know that he's used to the hospital visits, but he seems less surprised by them now.

Moods uplifted because we're done, it's quieting walking though the renal ward, to see all these people in beds, immobile, not resistant. Some of them hollow-eyed, defeated. A three-times-a-week, five-hours-long reminder of your body's challenges. A farm of cords and whirring machines transmitting life. Keeping them alive.

I recognise some of them by now. I nod a hello to a sweet Arab man I briefly spoke to during Dad's hospital dialysis stint a month earlier. 'I've been misdiagnosed,' he told me knowingly, before launching into a conspiracy theory and his plans to travel overseas. 'I can do dialysis there.'

Maybe I was tired, maybe I was amused, but I called him on it. 'But you just said you don't think you have kidney failure.'

I smiled as he shrugged. I guess we just need something to hold on to sometimes.

'I think the hardest thing for the patients, particularly our patients and also the patients in haemodialysis, is that it's so relentless, like there's no escape,' says Candace*, who's registered as a nurse in peritoneal dialysis, a type of fluid swap when the blood is filtered and cleaned not through an outside dialyser but in the body. 'It's not an option not to come in for dialysis. That's really hard, particularly for some young ones that we've had. It's a big disruption in their life . . . The challenge is developing a good rapport so that they want to take your advice. Because they trust your opinion, that you wouldn't suggest it if it wasn't appropriate.'

Diane*, a clinical nurse for peritoneal dialysis, identifies the difference between the two types of patients they see in the renal ward: the ones who come in three times a week for the five-hour-long dialysis treatment, and the home patients (peritoneal or machine). For the regulars at the ward, the frequency is a burden. 'When they leave, they're quite exhausted.'

Some patients at home use a dialysis machine that runs all night; others, like my father, undertake peritoneal dialysis, which gets done four times a day. You're dealing with a bag of solution, a catheter sticking out of your belly, not a drop of blood to be seen. Later Dad will switch to the machine that runs overnight.

Home patients are responsible for their own treatment and management. 'So, different ends of the spectrum, I guess. A lot of the patients that do home dialysis get very sick of doing it themselves.'

Candace and Diane say that persistence and developing a good rapport pay off; they have seen improvements in patients. They can refer patients to an appropriate counsellor – if, for example, they can't come to terms with the treatment. Young patients on dialysis may experience difficulties differently from older patients. 'I guess with the younger ones, it's a lot of body image things, difficulty with partners, and how they're going to deal with it, as well. Whereas if you get somebody that's older, who's maybe been in a relationship for much longer, it's different,' says Diane. 'Someone older – they've got this assumed support person, and there's never any debate that their husband or wife is going to be beside them,' says Candace. 'Whereas I think younger people . . . there's so much guilt tied up in it. That you're bringing that other person down to your dialysis every day.'

4.

THE MEDICINE OF LIFE

'The giants of geriatric medicine'

Being ill is not normal in old age, says Professor Richard Lindley.

'I see some people who say to me, "Doctor, you shouldn't be bothering with me, you should concentrate on the younger people." And I have the pleasure of telling them, "I'm only employed to look after people like you. I'm a doctor for older people and I think we can help." So I think there needs to be advocacy that if you're getting sick and you're old, you should get medical attention because it could be things that we could improve – that's the whole point of geriatric medicine. Diagnose; treat the treatable.'

There are a few key questions you want to know of your parents, he says. 'What's more important: is it curative treatment, is it palliative treatment? Is it comfort care or do they really, really want to get rid of that tumour and have all the ghastly chemo and injection therapy known to man? Or would they rather just be kept comfortable and let nature take its course?'

There are also key questions for the doctors: how is this treatment going to help? Are all these tablets really necessary? 'I think that's a great question to ask, because it can concentrate the mind. Some people end up on tablets because they were started on them a few years ago and no one's ever stopped them.'

It's also important for families to check in with elderly family members about their wishes for the future. That is, advanced-care planning. Consider some 'what if' scenarios, Professor Lindley suggests. '"Mum, what if your breathing got so bad you ended up in the intensive care unit on a ventilator? Is that something you'd want?" And you might find they'd say, "Of course. But if it was something they couldn't treat, get me off the ventilator quickly." Some people are very surprising. They say, "Oh heaven's sakes, no, I don't want any tube treatment. I don't want to be kept alive on a machine. If God wants to take me, I'm ready."'

Lesley, a former nurse, recounts how her mother had rheumatic fever when she was about seven, a condition that is known to damage the mitral valve in your heart. 'When Mum's heart specialist said to her, "Well, we can do a mitral valve replacement," Mum's response was, "For heaven's sake, you have to die of something." . . . And it's true.'

Professor Lindley argues that, as they age, we don't know our parents' wishes well enough. 'And these conversations are difficult, but you can bring them up at appropriate times. Like older parents often have stories about their friends: "The neighbour died the other day; she had a terrible time in hospital." And that might be an opportunity to bring up a discussion. "Mum, I've worried that might happen to you. If you got that sick, what would you want in hospital? Would you want them to resuscitate you? Would you want to go on a ventilator? What would you want, because you won't be able to tell me when the time comes." And that could be a way of starting a conversation.'

Professor Lindley appreciates how difficult these conversations can be for all involved. I think of the medical professional who told me that he's broached the subject with his mother in the past with mixed results. 'The first conversation went very well – she surprised me by saying she wanted everything. When I tried to reaffirm that this year, I had an adverse reaction and we changed the subject.'

He put this down to a few scares: 'It became all too difficult. But at least I can have a conversation with the intensive care unit that the last time my mother gave me guidance she did want everything done. And that I think's very helpful.'

In terms of how Australia is dealing with its ageing population and treatment of their ailments, Professor Lindley says, 'It's complicated. That's the first thing.' 'At medical school, you're taught about the classical medical problems. Let's think of a heart attack. So you're taught classical heart-attack people get central crushing chest pain, radiating down the left arm; they get grey, clammy, sweaty; they feel a sense of impending doom. So you know if you see people like this, you immediately do an ECG, check their blood pressure, get them to the coronary care unit, give them emergency treatment. And there's thousands and thousands of conditions that have a classical presentation.

'The problem when you get old and frail is that the heart attack might show itself as someone falling over, or one day they can't get out of bed. And unfortunately there are hundreds and hundreds of reasons for falling over or not getting out of bed, and in a younger person it wouldn't possibly be a heart attack – or very rarely – but in an old person it could be, because they have atypical presentation.'

Professor Lindley invokes Occam's razor, the famous problem-solving principle of medicine. 'What is the simplest explanation that can account for all the patient's symptoms?

Google is very good with Occam's razor. If you put in the symptoms, it will tell you.'

I express surprise. Isn't Dr Google responsible for a million brain tumours? Doesn't plugging in a bunch of symptoms always land on cancer or other frightening conditions?

'It will tell you,' he insists. 'However, if you're old and frail, Occam's razor fails spectacularly, because you've got an infinite number of ways people have degenerated; an infinite number of combinations of diseases; an infinite number of combinations of medications. So they've got huge complexity. Now, the reason I start with that preamble is that medicine has got so complicated that in every speciality – like haematology, gastroenterology, neurology – you need super specialists who understand the diseases in that system, the modern treatments, and the huge complexity that's under-lying this now with our knowledge of genes, proteomics, genomics.

'If I get a melanoma, I don't want to see a geriatrician, I want to see a melanoma-specialised oncologist . . . They've got these fantastic new treatments for melanoma, and it's complicated. The problem is that only about half of emergency or important medicine is in that simple problem–solution specialist.'

Professor Lindley says, 'With every medical success, we add to the queue of the frail elderly.'

People with melanoma are a good example. 'Australians were dying of melanoma in middle age, never getting old. There's now these spectacular treatments, which mean people are going to get older, and they're going to be frailer – because the treatments are not without their problems. So twenty years ago we never saw the survivors of melanoma. Now we see them and they're old and frail, and they're going to have different problems.'

Professor Lindley says we need the super specialists but we also need an army of geriatricians and other professions – nursing, general practice, you name it – people who understand the complexity of the frail elderly.

'Do we have an army of them?'

'We're getting an army of geriatricians in the hospital sector, which is the bit I know. But we're an ever-expanding speciality and we are seeing people choosing geriatric medicine – it's good. I think all sorts of things are helping with that. The fact that there is a large department of geriatric medicine in most Australian big hospitals is important. There's a critical mass of us now, to demonstrate that you can have a good life, a good career, being a geriatrician. I hope that some of us can be seen as good role models. There's a lot of nice things you get out of the profession because it's holistic, you have an excuse, you have an important reason to get to know your patients well – what sort of people are they? What did they do? What are their family circumstances? You have to know all that to know how best to treat them, and that's actually quite rewarding.'

'You're a people person.'

'Well, you've got to be. You can't look after a poor, frail, incontinent older person if you don't like that sort of person. Some people would just throw their hands up in disgust having to deal with such a patient. But you've also got to be a good general physician, know your way around all the systems with a certain degree of expertise. It's putting it all together, that's our role.'

He doesn't think we have a particularly frail-friendly hospital system. 'The emergency department is diabolical for older people, because it's designed to resuscitate and save lives from severe injury and severe emergencies like heart attacks and strokes, trauma. So the little old lady in the corner might have a similar death rate to the heart-attack patient, but because they're old and frail, people don't realise they may have a twenty per cent chance of dying in the hospital as well.'

The triage system in the emergency department does not help, Professor Lindley says. 'An older frail person could be very sick and be triage category three or four, which is not a priority in the emergency department. And emergency departments are hectic, they're very noisy, they're the worst environments for people with delirium, which is a very common way of older people showing they're sick.'

Professor Lindley raises the name of a geriatrician in the UK, the late Bernard Isaacs, who coined the term 'the giants of geriatric medicine' – syndromes that older frail people tend to present with when they get sick, which are 'giants' because of the gigantic effect they have on the patient and their family. 'His syndromes were falls, inability, incontinence, iatrogenesis – things like medication's adverse effects, the stuff that doctors do to people. Incontinence, stroke, and delirium, confusion.'

Professor Lindley says these syndromes were reviewed at Westmead Hospital – he thought they required an update. '[And now] we've got three new ones for old people . . . sepsis, pain, and breathlessness. They're very common syndromes that old people present with when they get sick.'

The family is key, says Professor Lindley. 'There's an infinite variety of families. In the last few months I've had examples of some of the nicest possible families you could imagine, and some of the worst. All life is out there.

'The thing about medicine is that it exposes you to all of life . . . The media and society may not like what is out there. I can give you an example. I'm personally against euthanasia because I see so much abuse of older people. And a good example is Sydney. If you've got a rundown fibro shack in Blacktown, you're still looking at half a million to a million dollars of property. When you start having that sort of money dangled in front of relatives, they misbehave. And a surprising number of older people have estranged children, for all sorts of reasons. And we see evidence of potential emotional abuse and financial abuse all the time, [so] the thought of euthanasia fills me with horror because for all the Andrew Dentons of the world, for every ten of the Andrew Dentons, there will be one unfortunate person who's got a family who just wants to get rid of them to get their hands on the cash. So I think it's a very . . . It's like all these things – fantastic for the many but extremely dangerous for the few.'

He believes people assume too much about human resilience. 'I think the thing that a lot of people misunderstand is when you are disabled you can still have quite a good life. If you've talked to older people and you say, "Would you rather be disabled or dead?" the majority say, "I'd rather be dead; I don't want to be disabled. I don't want to have someone have to wipe my bottom in the toilet." If you talk to a disabled old person and say, "Would you rather stay as you are or die?" the majority of them said, "Oh, I'd rather stay as I am."'

However, he makes a significant point about personal choice. 'Now it gets to a stage where . . . The burden individually is such that they say to me, "I'm ready to go. I've had a good life but I'm ready to go." And they often die unexpectedly because I think the psyche and the soma are connected.'

'I believe this, too,' I tell him.

'Yeah, yeah, I see it, I see it. Once or twice a year someone tells me on a ward round, "I'm ready to go, doctor, I've had enough." And the next ward round they're not there. It's quite interesting.'

'We're all about fixing the problem'

Dr Adam Rehak is a doctor and anaesthetist in Sydney. In addition, he teaches in a simulation centre, which involves instructing on crisis management. He estimates that ninety per cent of his patients are over the age of fifty. 'They need more surgery than anyone else. But certainly in the environment I'm in, which is surgery, we're all about fixing the immediate problem. This, in fact, reflects the broader medical paradigm, where we've learned to identify ill-health and then fix the problem, we've learned to keep people alive, we've learned to reverse pain, suffering, whatever else. And most of us really don't deal well when we're presented with a patient where you can't fix the problem or you can't reverse the suffering, or you can't make things better.'

It's particularly hard in surgery and anesthesia, where there's a factory-line procession of patients to deal with, even though most are really in need of better continuity of care. 'That's why I have nothing but the utmost respect for people who go into geriatrics and palliative care, and those areas which are so necessary with our ageing population. They don't just deal in fixing the problem, they deal with getting to know who the person is and doing what's best for them. Which is not really what we do in acute medicine: it is, as I've said, more about seeing a problem and fixing it. And the fact that there's a person attached to that problem is neither here nor there.'

With older patients, chronically ill patients, and those with terminal issues, it's not the conditions that doctors need to deal with, says Dr Rehak. 'It's about what management plans are going to give them the best quality of life. And really, is that just about fixing a condition?

'How are we doing on the job? It's such a complex issue. I mean, on one very basic level we're doing a terrible job at it, because what is the single biggest cause of suffering for many of our ageing population? It is lifestyle diseases such as obesity, diabetes, smoking-related disorders and problems relating to immobility, which people have acquired through-out a life where not enough has been done to prevent them.'

Dr Rehak poses a hypothetical: if we were to take away 50 per cent of the funding that goes into solving acute problems in the hospital, accepting that it would lead to many deaths in the next two years, but with all the money going into primary health care, in turn that would lead to a massive improvement in death and suffering in twenty years' time. 'In retrospect it would end up looking like the best-value diversion of funds ever, but no four-year-term politician is ever going to be able to say that, nor are they ever going to say, "Okay, we'll keep paying for all the acute care, and we're going to double, or triple, or quadruple primary health-care costs, because we know in the long term it will lead to massive savings in health expenditure and an improvement in health outcomes." No politician will take that initial hit for the long-term gain. They're unelectable if they do that.'

We're locked in. There are hugely escalating healthcare costs, related in part to growing older, and growing older more unhealthily. 'A proportion of the population are very unhealthy and previously would never have survived this long. So in terms of prevention and maintaining health, we're doing very badly. Are we doing any better in caring for those people who are already unhealthy, unwell and suf-fering? I suspect not, because their numbers are growing so quickly that there's just not the money, or the appeal, to get the necessary doctors involved in palliative care, geriatrics, chronic pain management and other such areas.'

Meanwhile, Dr Naganathan says that it's true that it's costly to treat older people, but technology, and newer, expensive drugs also contribute to the high cost of the health system, and these are usually spent on younger people.

'There is no evidence that an eighty-year-old now is unhealthier than an eighty-year-old from times past. In fact, as a group they are probably healthier. The issue is that since there are more older people, if a proportion are unhealthy it can have an impact on the health system.'

Even adopting the necessary public health measures won't stop the costs. 'That is, the same things happen to people at a later age. You can't have it both ways. A good public health system means that people live longer and therefore we have the luxury of a lot of older people in our hospital,' says Dr Naganathan. 'Many poor countries would like to be in that position.'

Dr Rehak says, 'It's not just doctors. It's nurses, and more than that it's infrastructure. And if you look at the systems that have made a difference in chronic pain or in back pain, or in any of these complex, chronic processes, it's never just the way a doctor works that makes it better. It's when a doctor and a number of other services, including psychologists and occupational therapists, work together to develop complex solutions for complex patients. Then you start to see differences.'

A call for coordination. 'There's also a big disconnect between delivery of family healthcare in the community and the care delivered in the ivory towers of large tertiary-level care hospitals where much of the acute care is delivered. There's not enough coordination and communication between the people who are supposed to be healthcare coordinators, the GPs, and all the other services.'

'That's come up elsewhere,' I tell Dr Rehak. A lot of medical professionals I've spoken to have said they want greater cooperation and communication. Dr Naganathan is one of them.

He believes the problem that needs to be challenged now is 'too much medicine'. He says that he's had patients for whom, in order to coordinate care, he's had to cc eight specialists in correspondence. 'Sometimes I'll even say on the bottom of that letter, "I don't think there's any value in me being the ninth specialist seeing this patient."'

The renal nurse I spoke to, Candace, worries that people get hooked into the hospital system. 'We wait until people get sick, and they're treated . . . [Then] it's really hard to get out.'

She has undertaken studies in primary healthcare based on preventative care, and based on expanding the health-care provided in the community, to avoid people coming to hospital. 'I think that's probably the biggest problem with our healthcare system – is that there's not enough focus on prevention,' she says.

But there have been improvements: blanket guidelines about a healthy weight and exercising, around lifestyle choices – to stave off Type-2 diabetes risk factors and the like. Heart disease kills more women than breast cancer, a nugget of information I recall from my time as a health writer in the pharmacy industry.

Elderly people 'cruise along until they get sick, and that's just the way it's always been,' says Candace. 'So I think the cultural [lifestyle] thing is quite hard to change.'

'You've got to be a special person to do geriatrics'

Sophie* is a registered nurse in her late thirties and she's currently doing the rounds in the geriatric ward of a Sydney hospital. It's a leap from her previous job in an office, dealing with numbers. A visit to her mother in hospital years ago left her in awe of nurses' work. It looked relatively exciting, and following some soul searching and 'find your purpose' inner work, Sophie was led to the profession.

'When I did the quiz, my strengths were communication, harmony, intellect, empathy.' Several motivational quotes later ('Just do it', 'Life is too short', etc.), Sophie shifted her career trajectory. Recently she was assigned to a geriatric ward, one of two rotations all new graduates have to undertake when they're fresh out of university.

'My first one was a busy surgical ward. And now I'm in a sub-acute . . . meaning they're not dying. They've got the all-clear from surgery, but they still need a little bit of support, and mine is sub-acute rehabilitation [specifically geriatric].'

This involves working with physiotherapists to improve patients' mobility. 'So, getting them ready to get back into society, because that's what they want at the end of the day. They want them to be able to go back to the lives they had before, say, the fall they had. And a majority of our patients have had a fall on concrete. You know, they've been lying there; no one's seen them and . . . yeah, it's quite sad.'

Sophie admits that she wasn't keen on geriatrics because of her experience as a student. 'I knew it was tough work,' she explains. 'Tough work in the sense that a lot of them aren't really communicating as much as someone who's, say, in their forties or fifties. They're often quite miserable, which is fair enough . . . they've just broken their hip and they've been stuck in a hospital.

'When you're in the surgical ward and dealing with forty- or fifty-year-old women, they get it . . . you ask them a question and get a simple answer. I think you've got to be a special person to do geriatrics.'

Geriatric patients require more care, and they're slow, even in how they speak. There's an added challenge if the patient is overweight. It's also laborious, Sophie says. 'Too laborious . . . these people have zero strength and I am expected – of course, with the assistance of someone else – to help [them] mobilise.'

She points out that geriatric patients are treated like babies. 'They're in nappies. They have zero control over their bowels. And these people, they contributed so much to society and now they're just so dependent on that care.'

I ask her about the reported predisposition of some medical professionals to talk down to elderly patients. In *Dear Life*, a *Quarterly Essay* by Karen Hitchcock, she observes that speaking of patients in limited ways – usually 'cute' or 'difficult' – is not appropriate.

'I hear that all the time and it annoys me as well,' says Sophie. 'I think it's really condescending.' During her studies, they were advised not to use the terms 'darling' or 'love'. They were told to use the patients' names. 'Once you get talking to them, they were engineers back in their day, they were mayors. They really contributed so much to society and now, you're right, we do hear them being referred to as "cute".'

'Do you feel that sometimes that's all they want, to share their experiences? Or just to speak to someone?'

'Most definitely they do. Unfortunately, though, nurses are so busy that we can't. We cannot spend any time with them. In the public health system, there are a lot of four-bedded rooms and these four-bedded rooms, as much as you'd think, oh, I want my own private room, for the elderly, my personal opinion is [the four-bedded rooms are] great because [the elderly] see these other patients, they see the family of other patients.'

Sophie cites the example of patients who are relegated to a single room because they might be infectious. Such patients will call out in distress, desperate for some attention, some company. Sophie finds it difficult not to be able to support these patients. It was partly what led her into the profession, after all. 'Some of these stories are bloody amazing, what they've been through. Someone just the other day was telling me about how she went through that whole Royal Commission and the whole sexual abuse scandal back in the day. And she just wanted to talk to someone.'

But time is the issue. 'In the acute hospital setting . . . [the ratio is] supposed to be four patients to one nurse. But, in the sub-acute aged care of the nursing homes, there's no quotas as far as I'm aware. So you've got one nurse to twenty patients, forty patients – I'm not sure – and that's where the problems start to occur. Things such as neglect, elder abuse, all of that sort of stuff.'

A major issue for some older patients is that if they don't have visitors to assist them, they won't eat properly. Sophie says that although the hospital ratios aren't too bad, meals will often go cold before a nurse can reach the patient to feed them. And hospital protocol doesn't allow them to warm food up in a microwave because of the risk of bacteria and germs. 'When there's family, we are so grateful. Some people have family who stay the whole day; they'll shower them for us, and we're just so happy that they're there. Then you have other members of families screaming at you, "Why didn't you feed them before the food went cold?"'

Feeding a patient is part of the job if a patient is marked as someone who requires 'full care'. 'That's the term we use, full care. And it's just a matter of getting to it. We definitely have to help them set up, open the packages. Because a lot of the packages, they're just too weak to do it. So we know which ones. We'd never just leave them there.'

Sophie feels patients are generally treated well, partly because there are laws in place to ensure they are. 'If you get a pressure area sore, which is an avoidable sore – so somebody's sacrum, because they've been sitting in bed too long – there's a $100,000 fine. I don't know if that's the exact figure. So it's taken seriously, so that's one good thing.'

Family and friends paying a visit delivers another benefit for the elderly. 'Their faces just light up because they're bored. And I think, if anything, I mean obviously these people are really sick, they're not mobile. But the biggest problem is they're so bored in this hospital. They're not interested in TV. Usually their eyesight's too bad so they can't read anymore. So they're just sitting there, and it's especially things like . . . someone brings in a little baby into the hospital. Their faces, oh my god. They just light up.'

On the other side is the patient who has given up. 'And I get it, I get why they don't care. There's a man at the moment, he's got some sort of emphysema and he's in pain. He's wheezing the whole time. He can't catch his breath. He keeps saying, "I just want to die." And I don't blame him. Like, he's in pain, there's nothing really more they can do.'

'Is he being artificially kept alive?'

'No, he's not that bad yet . . . They haven't referred to him as palliative. He's just on his way out. He's not going to get any better. There's nothing you can do for him.'

'What do you do when a patient keeps saying that? What are you meant to say? What are you allowed to say? Have you been trained in what to say?' I ask.

'Yeah. The way we're trained is that you don't have to say much at all. You just have to listen, and I'm a big believer in that. Most of these people want to talk and they want to hear – often just holding someone's hand, which unfortunately we don't have a lot of time to do. They like that touch.'

Such moments usually occur when it's just the patient at the hospital. 'I wouldn't probably touch their hand when their family is around, just because they've already got that support. It's always welcome. These are these European old men, who would've come from the school of hard knocks.'

They need the gesture of kindness.

'If I put my hand on their hand they will not let go. Who knows what they're imagining? Maybe in their head they think I'm their wife, but even if they do, for that couple of minutes or seconds I've given a bit of happiness.

'You can feel their calm. You can feel their body and they're calm.' And, adds Sophie, 'Some of them are scared. Some of them have accepted and they're like, "I want to die" . . . Some of them you can just tell that the family is wanting them to die.'

'The families are waiting for them to die?'

'Yeah, because they are so grumpy and they're burdens on them. Not burdens – that's the wrong word. But you can just tell. They're fed up.'

'They're over it.'

'Yeah.'

Friday

Every Friday my father attends the obligatory midday prayer at the mosque. This leaves me and Mum with forty-five minutes alone, and we might sit on a bench in a tiny park, or we'll go for a walk. Sometimes it's a short drive to find coffee or a drink. We talk. This is usually a time for sharing, or unloading, depending on the mood of the day. I would say it's mutual. We both have a lot to say. I'm just there, trying to be present though. To really *be* there.

An opportunity to reflect, it's also increasingly a time for passing on wisdom rather than grief. One Friday I ask my mother what she expected of Australia, as a young woman, newly married.

'It was exciting,' she says. 'All this land, and sheep and people.'

Always the sheep. Or kangaroos.

My parents knew each other through family connections but were largely strangers to each other. Piecing together their recollections, a handsome young man in his twenties, recently arrived from Australia via Palestine, was in search of a wife. My mother, younger by nine years, beautiful and hopeful, accepted the request for her hand in marriage.

'My father asked me and I was silent,' Mum explains. 'This meant I accepted him.'

I don't know how well my parents clicked. What they talked about. Mum tells me she cornered Dad one day and said, 'Teach me English.' I don't think it was a romantic courtship in the modern-day sense. But I look at old photos and they're bursting with youth and vibrancy.

Is that perhaps what sustains us? The anticipation of the journey, no matter how difficult and challenging it might become?

As life did become more challenging in Australia, my mother grew in resilience and resourcefulness. And over the course of many Fridays, I see how well she sustains herself through humour. Even if Dad wanted to feel sorry for himself, it would be difficult with Mum calling him on it.

She complains to me about Dad's flat mood. 'He's like a groom at an Arab wedding, just sitting there like a statue.'

I roar with laughter at the image she's created in my mind. The cheesy Arab wedding set-up – a bride and groom on a grand sweetheart chair, the bride beaming on her special day, the man frozen to his seat, happy, but wishing he was some-where else.

Another time, Dad complains about how slow people are. He is a quick thinker, fast-paced; he was never the type to sit still, though he does take a moment now and then these days. Mum tells him that they're not slow. 'You're just in a hurry.'

But I think my favourite is when my parents go into a café, only for Dad to turn on his heel. 'They're all old here,' he declares.

Mum delivers the blow of a reality check: 'What do you think you are? A spring chicken?'

Then, one day, this: Mum tells me she's nicknamed Dad 'the silent man'.

Actually, I think humour sustains us all. Sometimes in small ways. The feelings can be large, the solution doesn't have to be.

One afternoon, my friend Catherine calls me for a chat. We don't see each other often, but we're in each other's lives; have been for thirty-five years. It's a special kind of friend who doesn't expect to see you to know you are there. We joke about our respective Dad-health issues. Her father's at the same hospital my father goes to. We quip that we should just meet there. It's strange how you can laugh at it, when a month before it threatened to undo you.

Another significant development comes out of Friday breaks with Mum. I find myself reading more often about Palestinian food, a cuisine inextricably linked to my childhood. Recipes like points on a timeline. Spices that sit in the kitchen cupboards. Hearty casseroles. Flavour bursts. Memories. And though I'm not a great cook, the idea of no record of my mother's recipes shakes me a little. It's always troubled me that I don't hold this knowledge, but now, as I become a companion to my parents on Fridays, and now a record-keeper, I want to write down Mum's recipes for posterity. She makes them sound so simple.

I have finally found a use for a beautiful red notebook my best friend, Jo, gave me a couple of years ago. A bright red cover, gold-lined pages, the words 'Paint the town red'.

Recipes from my mother's kitchen. Page one: Vine leaves (wara eneb). Traditionally a social dish. It requires a lot of time and effort, so it's best made with friends and family.

5.

FIGHTING THE NURSING HOME FATE

What invisible things *are we fighting?*

Nothing garners such a strong reaction as the mention of a nursing home. It's completely understandable. Nobody wants to anticipate a future that looks cold and lonely, bereft of purpose. People want to age in place, surrounded by their possessions collected over the years; where memories have been made; close to their family and friends. Nobody wants their end to be in an institution. People visibly recoil at the thought of it. And they speak of plans to safeguard themselves. One woman, standing in her kitchen, swept open her fridge door to reveal a row of medicine boxes. 'See these?' she told me without wavering. 'Two doses could kill a horse. I'm *not* going into a nursing home.'

More specifically, she didn't want to go into a nursing home because of the care she saw her mother receive, other people's mothers. 'I've seen poor care. What they do, and they do it in hospitals as well. They don't let any attachments form . . . It's so cruel. They change the staff around all the time, so that you never can attach or they can never get to know you.'

She wasn't alone in that sentiment, often expressed by someone elderly who lived alone and didn't have children, or considered any reliance on family an unseemly burden. 'I wouldn't want to do that to them' was a familiar refrain. One daughter told me that her mother has instructed her to help her exit before the indignity of old age afflicts her. 'My mum has told me in no uncertain terms that she does not wish to be a burden, and she would like to end her life should she become incontinent or should she not be able to look after herself; she does not wish to be here.

'I understand it. It's a value that I personally echo. I believe that my mum is a very dignified woman and I feel like she yearns to leave in a dignified way.'

Another woman documented a family history of dementia that trickled down the maternal line. She shared similar feelings, but didn't want to involve her children. 'Anyone who's in that situation, it's in the back of your mind when you start getting older, and you forget something, or you stuff something up, whereas that's just normal. But you start to think, gosh is this the end?' She adds that she is doing her utmost to stave off dementia. 'I just keep up to date on the things they've shown reduce the chances of developing it. So I eat lots of turmeric. I exercise frequently. I have a busy social life. I do things like puzzles.'

But she had already planned her exit should she become afflicted by dementia in her declining years. 'Quite frankly, I would commit suicide rather than go through that whole dementia thing. So I've got my technique worked out. And you just have to hope that you come to a stage where you can still do that.'

The government's Australian Institute of Health and Welfare (AIHW) reports Australian Bureau of Statistics (ABS) figures in its 2017 web report 'Older Australia at a Glance'. In 2016, 3.7 million Australians (15 per cent of the population) were aged sixty-five and over; that is, more than one in seven. By 2056, it's estimated there will be 8.7 million older Australians (22 per cent of the population).

'With those demographic changes, you're going to get more and more people aged eighty-plus,' says aged care psychiatrist Dr Robert Llewellyn-Jones. 'And, of course, they are the group that are most likely to end up in care, because the older you get, the greater the likelihood that you'll get chronic conditions, particularly dementia. Dementia's one of the primary reasons why people end up having to go into care, because they can't look after themselves.'

'It's like they've died and you've lost them, but they haven't'

Pam, eighty-one, keeps busy. She frequently attends classical music concerts (matinees for the 'grey hair' lot), she swims every day, a pastime she once enjoyed with her husband, who now suffers dementia and resides in a nursing home.

Pam has been married to John for more than sixty years. They have five children together, one of whom has passed on, and thirteen grandchildren. With a big family, Pam admits that she's never lonely, and it helps having a newborn great-grandchild.

Beside the bathroom in her apartment is a wall of personal history. Ageing photos that, not surprisingly, offer a romantic glimpse of her past. Photos of weddings and children in sepia and black and white. On another wall are the modern ones, full of colour, the beaming faces of generations, modernity enshrined.

Pam is softly spoken, thoughtful, perhaps even a little distant. I don't find her evasive; rather, uncertain. As her story unfolds, however, it's clear that she's a lover of life, of beautiful things; someone who never just dips her toes in the water – she dives.

'Music keeps me alive, I have to say.' She likes the usual classical pieces: 'the old ones'. The Beethovens and Mozarts. 'I do love Elgar in particular. Especially "Nimrod".'

As we speak on her balcony, the dulcet tones of a classical piece filter through the door. 'I go to the theatre matinees. I don't like going out at night much anymore. But I like the afternoons. And I've got a group of friends I do it with, which is really, really good.'

When her kids left school, Pam joined a friend in an antique business. 'We used to sell at markets, and then we got into a little co-op shop, which I did for quite a few years. I bought most of my own furniture through all of that in the good old days.'

John was a businessman who travelled a lot. 'We did most things together, family was very important. But when he retired he did things like golf and bowls and that sort of stuff, and I've never been very good at any of those things.'

They have different interests, but they did swim together. 'He loved swimming. And I can still continue my swimming.'

John semi-retired. He did consulting work for a few years. He and Pam travelled together. He was in his early seventies when he retired. Then, when he turned about eighty, a few years ago, there were signs of decline. Little things. Nothing dramatic.

'Probably took close to three years where it just deterio-rated somewhat. And in the end we were home for the last year. I had to get carers in through my doctor, who said she felt I couldn't really cope. I couldn't leave much,' explains Pam. 'So, I was very lucky. I got a couple of women who came twice a week. There was only three hours, but at least I could go out and go to the shops or go and have a coffee.'

It was fine, Pam says. John was quite happy, and the carers were very good with him, and he liked them. It worked well. 'But then it got to the point where he was not sleeping terribly well, which meant that I wasn't. I was constantly, you know, one eye open during the night; and he'd get up and go to the toilet, and . . . I was aware that he'd fall or something.'

They went to see a neurologist about a year after the symptoms began. A friend of John's urged them to.

'He said to me, "I think you should go and see this guy, because I think John might be losing it a bit." He was showing signs of that in golf . . . or bowls. He knew the rules but he didn't always follow them . . . Most of them were very nice and they often picked him up, took him, and that gave me a break, but then there were a few – old men, old women – who complained.'

And John was getting a bit agitated about that too, Pam thinks. The tension of trying to live a normal life when the mind and body aren't working. But the big blow came when his doctor declared him unfit for driving. He was still driving okay, says Pam. But his navigation skills had deteriorated. He didn't always know where he was going, or whom he was driving to see. John's doctor said she couldn't any longer, in all good conscience, approve him driving.

'So that was a bad day. It was a bad day for all of us.'

John burst into tears. '*I* burst into tears,' says Pam. 'Even the doctor did, because . . . she said, "I hate doing it, but there comes a time." A hard day. Then, the car sitting here. His car. If I went out I'm thinking, "Oh my god, I hope he doesn't try to [drive it]."'

The loss of their driver's licence is a major marker in many people's stories. It's symbolic: the stripping away of independence. It's proof that things are different; a big moment. It gives me some relief that it was a slow burn with Dad rather than a sudden striking loss. In fact, one day, he expressed his relief that he no longer takes the wheel. 'I'm used to not driving now,' he told me.

He loves taking the bus – people-watching; taking his time. Journeys, that's what Dad likes.

Ultimately, Pam and John traded in their two cars – getting rid of John's and changing Pam's small one to something a bit larger, comfortable for John to get in and out of. 'He still to this day recognises that car,' says Pam. Mainly because John gave her number plates with her name on them on her thirtieth birthday.

'If I'm taking him out and I'm picking him up, he'll walk out and he'll go, "Oh, the Pam car."'

John 'sort of' knows Pam. 'He doesn't necessarily call me by my name, but he says to other people, "Where's Pam?"'

She visits him just about every day. Sometimes she takes him out – down to the park for a coffee, or just for a walk to get him out for a while.

'I don't bring him home. They recommended not to do that. But occasionally on a weekend I might drive him down to Balmoral where we swim . . . I'll say, "Remember we used to swim from those steps?" And he goes, "Yeah." It's unlikely he remembers. 'He likes the people walking by, kids, dogs . . . All of that.'

I begin to ask Pam how she deals with the loss of, well, all of him, but before I can finish, she simply acknowledges, 'It is a loss.'

'It's like they've died and you've lost them, but they haven't. It's like a death but it's not – you know what I mean?'

+

Still, Pam counts her blessings. She remains in her home, where she's comfortable and has neighbours who look out for her. 'Depends on how long John lives for and how much it'll all cost, but at this point in time I can stay here. That gives me a lot of security, because I'm fortunate that everything is at my fingertips. If I can't drive I can walk to the ferry, I can get a bus.'

Meanwhile, Pam knows John is well taken care of; it's not glamorous, but she thinks the care is particularly good. 'By the same token, I walk in there and I think, oh god, I wish he wasn't here, because . . . he is in high care, you see. So it's not just like being in a nursing home, where you've got people with varying problems. It's always dementia, and a lot of them, a lot . . . Particularly women . . . can be very aggressive.'

As many people have told me, dementia sufferers may get aggressive, may experience paranoia. How many stories have I heard about patients who thought the staff were stealing from them? How often did people sadly recall a parent's brutal mood shifts, as though they were encased in a prison of the mind? Or in prison, period.

It's not something Pam has to worry about. 'They're treated very well. They're mainly Nepalese, the nurses, and they're just lovely girls. They all call him by his name. One of them, she's a sweet girl, and she always calls him "Daddy". She said to me one day, "Do you mind me saying that?" I said, "No, I don't. You're always so lovely to him." And she said, "Well, I lost my grandfather when I was quite young, and to me he's like my grandfather."' Pam was pleased; she felt John would like that.

She has posted up photos on John's wall. She'll go a step further and show him photos on her phone. 'It does trigger a bit. He really can't comprehend to read anymore, or write. And verbally he's lost a lot. He'll come out sometimes with totally coherent stuff, and other times he's talking about something, I'll have no idea what he's talking about. It must relate back to business, I think, which was obviously an important part of his life.'

✦

Both Pam and John were seeing an aged-care psychiatrist for a time, following a recommendation through their GP, who thought it would be worthwhile during the early stages of John's decline.

'Did you see that helping your husband?'

'I did. Funnily enough he would open up – this was before he lost a lot of his verbal skills. He would say things to our psychiatrist that I was surprised he said.'

'So you were always there with him?'

'Always.'

'Do you feel the sessions helped him to deal with what he was going through?'

'I think so. He didn't say an awful lot. He didn't not want to go, though. I think he always felt quite comfortable. I'd say, afterwards, "Well, that was good, wasn't it? You got a lot out today." And he'd say, "Yeah, I did."'

Later, when John was communicating less, Pam did more of the talking.

'What was it giving you, to do those sessions with your husband? Was it helpful to you as well?'

'It was, because it helped me, if he could get something out that I wasn't aware of. That was helpful.'

Upsetting and sad at times, but by and large helpful.

Now Pam sees her psychologist every five months or so.

'What do you feel you get out of that now that your husband is in care?'

'My psychiatrist is very concerned about me. He's worried that I have to take care of myself. He reiterates that all the time.'

He also encourages Pam to do things, to go away every now and then, advice she took when she went on a group tour of China with good friends, younger than her. Keen travellers who promised Pam they'd look after her.

'That was amazing. Culture shock.'

It took some convincing. 'They said, "If you decide, get a single apartment, don't share a room, and we'll be there the whole time. It's only two weeks, and John would be okay for two weeks. You go and see your sister for a couple of weeks."'

Pam did the necessary calculations to ensure she could afford it, but also sought her psychiatrist's advice. He told her to go, as did her children.

'They did lift their game quite a lot,' says Pam, adding that even some of her grandkids stepped up to fill the gap. A small time difference helped keep Pam's mind at ease.

Pam has successfully moved her own boundaries. China helped her surrender to possibilities – she'd taken a step, she was far away and there was nothing she could do for John. 'It took away a bit of the guilt, I think. You know? I mean, I felt a bit guilty going, but once I got on the plane, I thought, well, there's nothing I can do about it now. That was quite good in a way.'

When Pam returned and paid John a visit, she was greeted by the nurses, who showered her with questions about her vacation. 'And John looked on, and then I said, "Did you miss me, darling?" And he said, you know . . .' Pam trails off. 'They said they'd felt that he knew something was different, but time is immaterial.'

It eased her mind. No accusations flung her way for leaving him.

'Do you miss him?'

'Oh yeah, I do. The hard thing is . . . I mean, I've still got the queen-sized bed. The first few months – that was terrible;

going to bed, that he wasn't there. I mean, I slept next to him for a hundred years.'

They had a good marriage.

Time made it easier. Just time. Just getting on with it.

'I've always been one of those people: well, there's nothing you can do about certain things. Providing in your own conscience you feel that you've done the right thing by him. I'd ideally love to still have him at home, but it just was not going to be possible.'

Pam says their children have always been very close to John. They feel guilty, too – for not visiting him enough, or not helping Pam out more. 'They're busy. They're all working. They've all got kids. You know what life is like at this stage,' Pam says. 'I tell them not to worry about that, because I'm close, and I don't have their commitments anymore. I've only got myself to worry about.'

Pam says she's not lonely; she keeps herself busy. She makes a point of cooking for herself (her sister's advice is to eat properly, maintain normalcy). She'll enjoy a couple of glasses of wine in the evening. 'I still have that. We always had that. We'd always sit down and have a drink before dinner and a glass of wine with dinner. I still do that, but I mean you've got to tell yourself not to overdo it, obviously.'

Pam doesn't have major life plans in place. It's a day-by-day proposition for now. Friends from the beach she swims at, including people who knew John, are a part of her life. They are aware of his situation; they'd always kept a bit of an eye out for him. When he could no longer swim, fellow swimmers would sit with him to allow Pam a swim. Now they invite her for a quick coffee some mornings. They're younger than Pam, but they encourage her to socialise with them. They're good company.

'When you're looking at this man who you've loved for sixty-plus years – do you see the same man? Is that a comfort for you, seeing him every day?'

'I do. Yeah. Every day. It is. I'll say, "Hey, I haven't had a kiss today . . . There's no one looking." You know, we have a bit of a joke. And he'll laugh and he'll give me a kiss. And occasionally he'll look at me and say, "I love you very much." And that comes straight out.'

She adds, 'Other times I'll say, "Do you love me?" and he goes, "Mm." I'm obviously having a bad hair day.

'But yesterday I was at the park and one of my sons rang, and I put it on loudspeaker, and I said, "Oh, John, Tim's on the phone." Often he just looks at the phone and it doesn't register. Tim said, "Dad, Timbo here, how are you?" And John replied, "Oh, good, Timbo, how are you? Lovely to hear your voice." That breaks Tim up a bit, of course.

'I mean, he's still there, but . . . [My psychiatrist] explained to me that they have these little windows of being quite coherent. Plenty of clarity comes out. And then, as soon as it's got out, it's gone.'

'It ends quickly,' I say.

'Gone.'

'Are you there for those?'

'Yeah. Yeah . . . and he'll say something quite coherent and I'll carry on and say, "Yeah, well, you know, if we did this or that," and you can see he's thinking, what's she talking about?'

'You've got to keep going'

One of the first things I notice about Ellen* is how her house and possessions seem frozen in time. Like so many of the older people I met with, she still uses a landline, which she takes off the hook as a courtesy before we begin.

She is unfailingly polite, almost formal. 'My name is Ellen,' she begins, speaking into the recorder, 'and I'm here to talk to Amal on the effects of dementia on being a carer, on me.'

Ellen is eighty-one. She is in recovery following spinal surgery last year. She was told that if she didn't address the problem she'd be in a wheelchair by Christmas. 'I could hardly walk. So I went ahead and had it done, which was a very big thing for me to do. I had a very good surgeon.'

She was in a state of distress, she got counselling. 'But I'm the type of person who . . . if I know I've got to do something, I'll go do it. Just go.'

But when she returned home, Ellen believes she suffered post-traumatic stress. The rush of adrenaline had dissipated. 'I thought, here I am, I can't do anything.'

Ellen had help from her family, and she feels this was a primary lesson from the operation – 'I have to have help. And I know I can't do everything. I've had to accept that this operation has slowed me down, and it's been really good because I've had to stop and think and accept what I can't change. Because the thing is I couldn't garden; I couldn't do any damn thing.'

Six months later she is doing very well. Golf might have to wait, but she remains social. 'I make myself go over and see the girls twice a week. But I just find I've had to stop and look at my life.'

She has become more spiritual, grateful that a doctor enabled her to continue walking, perhaps added years to her life.

'I found my life was just . . . I had to be busy. I kept thinking I had to be here, I had to be there. It was crazy. But now I'm happy in this world.'

Ellen says that now she can just lie down on an idle afternoon and shut her eyes and listen to music. It's been an important lesson, given the responsibilities she carries in life. Grace*, in her eighties, is Ellen's sister-in-law. She suffers from dementia, but remains at home despite her short-term memory being shot. Ellen looks after Grace with love and care, but she makes a point of declaring that she's changing how she deals with people. 'I'm not worried about anyone else . . . I used to be the one who was checking on everyone. I'm not doing that anymore. I've just sort of thought, no. So I don't know whether that's good or bad.'

I venture that it's good.

'Because I'm peaceful, I'm at peace. I'd say I'm at peace with myself.'

Ellen does exhibit acceptance. She says uplifting things. 'You've got to keep going. You don't give in.' Then she declares, 'I said I've got nine years of living, so I'm going like a train now. I'm going to live.'

And, Ellen says, she's happy. Her children are all getting on with their lives. They have nice chats together, they don't whinge to her about anything. She busies herself with gardening and cooking; both are tasks she can manage, even if she has to cap off the gardening at half an hour. 'But I could stand there and cook all day. I just can't do what I used to do. And I've got to admit that I'm nearly eighty-two. I say to myself "You've got to, you know," but then I think, should I be saying that or should I just be pushing on?'

One way she just 'pushes on' is in her capacity as a 'sort of' carer to Grace.

'It started about four years ago when she started to forget things and was having a few accidents in the car and denied them – was denying everything. I had my eightieth birthday two years ago and she didn't know anyone there. She was introducing my family to my family. It was just awful.' It was heartbreaking for her kids and grandchildren, Ellen says.

'Grace never married. This lady travelled, very intelligent, the most beautiful, sweetest lady you could ever wish to meet, would never complain. She does get a bit crabby with me, but not too often. She was taking my grandchildren to their brother or sister and introducing them, and it broke one's heart. It was awful . . . There was about fifty people and I think that she was overwhelmed. She didn't know who was what.'

It's Grace's contrast to her former self that Ellen seems to grapple with most. Forgetting or missing appointments, making appointments on top of appointments, doing silly things. 'This lady is beautiful, as I say well-travelled, had a big job, never married, very religious but she . . . got progressively worse and she was denying everything. She sideswiped a car and nobody knew about it [because] she just went home.'

Ellen describes how the accident took place and the disparity in accounts – Grace saying it happened at night, the insurance company and witnesses declaring it had occurred in the morning. She says Grace would never have been travelling that way at nine o'clock in the morning. 'She will stand by that till she dies. I didn't argue with the insurance company, but how can you when they have written statements?'

That was the start of it. Then Grace drove through a parking barrier at a shopping centre, after trying to get out using a Medicare card. She knows who Ellen is; she even asks about her back, post-surgery. But she gets Ellen's kids muddled up if she's speaking to them on the phone (her recall is better if they're face to face). If Ellen asks Grace to take out the garbage, she'll bring in the mail.

'The problem is she tells little lies to save herself. She does quite bizarre things. I'll go up there sometimes and I can't find her . . . and she'll be down in the garden, right down the corner sitting on the ground.' Grace will tell Ellen that she's talking to the cat.

So Grace isn't entirely engaged, not entirely able to go about day-to-day activities. But she's sweet and loveable, and knows how to mask her decline. She's wily, and has no intention of going into a home. Ellen visits her about three times a week, and Grace has a carer on three days for three hours.

Grace forgets to eat, says Ellen. Instead, she discovered, Grace has a liking for red wine, which she consumes while watching the news.

'Then somebody said to me, "Does it matter?" See, she wants to stay in that house, that's the end of the story, and a couple of my children have said, "She's happy, Mum. She's in her world where she is. She has a cat. She has a garden. She doesn't venture very much past the side gate." How she hasn't fallen and killed herself, I don't know.'

Grace sends off random cheques to the taxation department. She doesn't shower, and she wears the same clothes all the time. 'She looks like a bag lady, and she's got a lot of money,' Ellen says.

The carers adore Grace. It's self-flagellation that besets Ellen – she finds it difficult to visit Grace and leave her, seeing her not comprehending things. 'I come home and I'm so . . . blah.' Ellen looks pained. She can't be a full-time carer to Grace; she knows that Grace needs more care, but is powerless to deliver it without Grace's permission.

Ellen has experienced heartbreak and loss. She reflects on how her parents' health and decline affected her, the way life seemed to get worse before it got better. Trips back and forth to help them as they dealt with poor health. But Ellen was married to a supportive, loving man, who himself later fell ill with cancer. 'It's awful. But, anyhow, everyone has their pain. Nobody gets out of here without some suffering. We have to work to get here, and we're going to have to work to get out. I do believe that, don't you?'

Ellen's expression tells me it's not a rhetorical question. 'I don't know what brings us here, to be honest,' I say. 'I don't know what I think about that, but I definitely feel that nobody is immune to pain. I think that if you think you are, then you are drinking something that you shouldn't be drinking.'

We share a laugh.

Ellen visits an aged-care psychiatrist. He has told her, 'You've got to get more care, end of story.' He is witness to her sorrow and grief, and sees that self-care is paramount if Ellen is to avoid spiralling downwards.

Years after her husband's death, Ellen says her psychiatrist helped her through the turbulence of loss. She tried to run away from it, but it caught up with her: her husband passed away from cancer twenty years ago, but the pain of losing him took a physical toll years later, and eventually her doctor recommended she see a psychiatrist.

'I've got a big family and I've got very caring kids, grand-kids, sisters, brothers, so I really kept busy in that first period of about six, seven years. Then I went crashing down. That's when I went to [my psychiatrist], so he's been very good,' says Ellen.

She is clear on why having that counselling helps: she suffers anxiety. She didn't marry again, or form any long-term romantic partnerships following her husband's death. 'I know my husband said – which, by the way, is a terrible thing for him to say before he died – "I want you to find somebody else and make them happy." There's no way I could sit with another man in this house. I've got friends. I play golf with men. I go out, but I don't go out separately with men. We go, groups of us.'

Ellen still frets about Grace, despite her determination to care less about others' problems and focus on herself. 'My problem is, I know the carers, and some of them have said,

"You've got to be hard. You're not hard enough." I can't . . . I don't want to take her independence away, you know what I mean?'

She doesn't want to order Grace about, calling her out on bathing, or changing her clothes. 'I cannot bring myself to do that because to me that's just taking her everything away . . . It's a very tricky situation for me.'

Ellen worked as an aged-care nurse for thirty years, which included nursing dementia patients. 'When I was nursing, I was giving those patients love and attention. Course, today it's probably different . . . today maybe [nurses] hardly talk to anyone and they're all doing paperwork. That's when I got out. With Grace, it's too close, and it's hard for me to see her. I could help the others but I can't help myself with her.'

Grace doesn't admit to having a poor memory, but an outing with Ellen's son recently saw Grace confess to him, 'You know, I can't remember things now.' It was emotional for Ellen's son, who adores Grace.

There is a sad aspect to this story that relates to Grace's past. Her mother was a milliner in the 1920s, making hats for department stores. Grace still has some of those hats, in their original boxes. She offered them to Ellen for her daughters, retrieving them from storage where they'd been for a long time. Grace wanted to dust them off, put them in the sun. 'She said, "I don't want to throw them out." Oh, that breaks your heart,' says Ellen. Then Ellen's daughter paid Grace a visit, helped her stock-take all her jewellery and decide who Grace wanted to receive it. Grace revealed a wardrobe with clothes from 'way back'.

'[My daughter] said she pulled them out and they're all moth-eaten. Grace was livid. [My daughter] said, "Mum, I've never seen Grace angry. She got them out and she threw them all on the bed."'

Ellen wonders aloud about this: how to deal with this decline? There is something to her expression that suggests it's an expansive issue, that a sense of helplessness permeates us all when we witness the effects of cognitive decline. It seems, I realise, that she is asking, *what can you do when it seems like nothing can be done?*

'Things change as you get older'

There is currently no cure for dementia. It's something Dr Naganathan doesn't believe he will see in his lifetime. 'I could be wrong on that, but that's my personal view. So the big question is, can you do things in your mid-life that will reduce your chances, delay the onset of dementia?'

And other problems – your body collapsing under the weight of ageing. Because many things can go wrong with your body. I ask Dr Naganathan about prevention – of conditions such as heart disease, for example. People checking in with their GPs and monitoring these things. For young people, is there hope for them; is there something they can do? Is healthy ageing just luck?

'It's a bit of luck,' concedes Dr Naganathan. 'But it's all probability . . . So, you can decrease your probability by small amounts . . . If the individual adopted in their middle age a healthy lifestyle, and watched the medical things, which are blood pressure, cholesterol, they would decrease their probability by a small amount . . . If the whole country did that . . . it probably would have an impact, right? And it must, because there are so many studies to show the influence of socio-economic status on health. So lifestyles must influence health, even in a wealthy country like Australia.'

He breaks it down to Sydney. You can see the differences in heart-attack rates, he says. He gained insight when working in hospitals in the western suburbs. 'We see the same diseases, but they were happening to younger people as you went out west.'

In essence, for individuals, adopting a healthy lifestyle and addressing risks factors such as blood pressure and cholesterol lifestyle changes are going to make a small difference to the chances of getting a heart attack, but if the whole country made these changes it would have a big impact on the health of the community. 'That's public health for you.'

Dr Naganathan says that believing something won't make a difference can lead to cynicism. 'But it's why general practice is so important, because that's where you can do these things that can have a public health impact.'

He offers another example – weight loss. 'They say that for middle-aged people, obesity is a risk factor for heart disease. There comes a point where, for all the frail people, being a bit overweight or even obese is actually better for you. Statistically any weight loss above a certain age is actually harmful. So you see, it's really tricky. You've had a lifetime of being told you need to lose weight and you need to worry about your cholesterol. You get older and frailer and then actually you're better off . . .'

Because how many of us have experienced a parent losing their appetite, as my dad has, and their clothes getting too big for them, and conversations become entreaties? 'Please eat.' But, they say, 'I'm not hungry.' In that situation the weight loss is more harmful.

'[And] we talk about this all the time: you can end up on too much medication. Even the evidence that above a certain age blood pressure is a risk factor becomes a bit weaker. That cholesterol is a risk factor. Things change as you get older.'

Dr Naganathan jokes with medical students that one of the most satisfying things is to tell a woman aged, say, eighty-five, who's been denying herself chocolate cake for years because when she was sixty her doctor warned her about cholesterol, 'Now that you're eighty-five, you can eat that chocolate cake. I want you to put on weight and I don't care how. Eat all the things you enjoy.'

He warns that wording the advice correctly is essential. 'I've made the mistake of saying it jokingly, and it's been misinterpreted as "I'm eighty-five, so you don't care." Or, "I'm eighty-five and you think I've lived long enough, that's why you're saying to eat the chocolate." I go, "No, no – scientifically, the evidence is that once you're eighty-five, low cholesterol could actually be more harmful. Having nutrition is more important than worrying about your cholesterol. So I'm saying it to you for two reasons. One, scientifically, maintaining your weight's important, and it doesn't matter how you do it. And two, I think you should eat chocolate cake because it's quality of life, then." So, that's complicated to explain to people.'

'We're grieving because we're losing the person'

Dr Llewellyn-Jones says that with increased life expectancy it's beholden on health services to prevent, as much as possible, degenerative diseases of the brain.

'For instance, the risk factors for developing vascular dementia, such as high blood pressure, high cholesterol, diabetes and heart rhythm problems, can begin in peoples' forties and fifties. So if you're going to have an impact on the vascular health of a person's brain, they need to adopt a healthy lifestyle well before they actually get into their sixties,' he says.

As an aged care psychiatrist, he observes that people fear the loss of their physical and mental functions, and they fear death. Taking a preventative approach in your thirties and forties offers no guarantees, but it increases your chances of a healthier old age. Things like reducing alcohol (a potential carcinogen), not smoking and exercising regularly reduce the risk of chronic medical conditions in older age. 'Because if we were able to choose, I would imagine everyone would like to live as long as possible with pretty good, robust health, and then when it got to the end of their life, they would have a brief period of illness, not suffer too much pain, and die peacefully. Whereas what happens at the moment is that people can spend many years lingering with multiple chronic medical conditions, multiple impairments and handicaps, which in itself becomes something of a living death.'

So we're not getting that part right. 'By controlling people's blood pressure, their cholesterol, getting them to eat a healthy diet, doing regular exercises – not rocket science – keeping to a reasonable weight, et cetera, you're going to have a substantial impact on the likelihood of people developing vascular dementia later in life. The bottom line is that what's good for the heart is good for the brain.'

Alzheimer's is a lot more complicated because it's related to abnormal amyloid protein being deposited in the brain. At the moment we don't understand why that occurs, and we can't prevent it. None of the doctors I spoke with expressed much hope of a cure, or even significant advancements, any time soon, though news stories offer the promise of advancements. In 2018, *TIME* reported that a new anti-amyloid drug tested by Japanese company Eisai and US-based Biogen showed promise. But the same report noted that other experimental treatments had ended in failure.

Alzheimer's is the main type of dementia, but vascular dementia is not far behind. Recent statistics from Dementia Australia report dementia as the second leading cause of death of Australians. More specifically, 5.4 per cent of male deaths, 10.6 per cent of female deaths, making dementia the leading cause of death among Australian women, eclipsing heart disease, the number one killer of both men and women for decades. In 2018, Dementia Australia said that more than 425,000 Australians have dementia.

'The brain's a bit like a sponge,' says Dr Llewellyn-Jones. 'It's full of literally millions of blood vessels. If all these blood vessels were laid end to end they would be over 600 kilometres in length. These tiny blood vessels are called microcirculation. And to keep the brain cells healthy they need to remain open and . . . to pass blood from one to the other. If, due to high blood pressure or high cholesterol, they start breaking down or getting blocked, you get what's called "small vessel disease". So it's not like you have had a stroke due to blockage of one of your brain's major blood vessels, and a whole segment of the brain has died, and you can't move an arm, or a leg or speak. With small vessel disease you get damage scattered through-out the brain, which means although you can still move and talk, its overall functioning is impaired.'

Dementia mainly affects older people, but is related to the diet and lifestyle risk factors Dr Llewellyn-Jones outlines, as well as to genetic factors, high blood pressure, hypertension and high cholesterol. He has patients with different types of dementia, generally signified by a loss of cognitive function-ing and short-term memory, including people in their fifties who are suffering young-onset dementia. These people face a sudden shift in their timeline – what they projected for them-selves upended. As Dr Llewellyn-Jones explains, 'Many of us talk about, "I'll do that when I retire," expecting that life will go on limitlessly in front of us, and we'll have the health to do whatever we want to do. So you can imagine the loss that you'd feel if you found out in your early fifties you've got dementia. Particularly if you have the insight to know what that means, and know you might not be compos mentis in seven years' time. You'd look at all the life ahead you've suddenly lost. So it's a huge adjustment.'

Making matters more difficult is that most dementia services are designed for people in their seventies and beyond.

It's common for Dr Llewellyn-Jones to see people with depression, young and old. People who are experiencing grief, especially older people dealing with the loss of a spouse or an adult child, which may develop into a clinical depression. Anxiety disorders are reasonably common in older people, he adds. 'And sometimes very difficult to fix, because often people have been anxious their whole lives, but towards the end of their life they sort of lose their resilience and coping strategies.'

When they were younger, they were anxious, but coping. But if they experience a 'cascade' of losses, such as that of a partner, their physical health, the death of a friend or a pet, to name a few examples, 'This cascade of different stresses or traumas erodes their resilience, and their anxiety disorder, which was once manageable, becomes overwhelming. I find that's a heartbreaking thing.'

He says that people who don't want to talk about their troubles will never end up in his office, scared off as many are by the stigmas attached to mental illness. But, he points out, one in two people experience a mental health problem at some time in their life; and one in five people suffer depression at some point. 'These aren't uncommon problems. So, generally speaking, when people come to see me they're willing to be here.'

Dr Llewellyn-Jones cuts a sympathetic figure. For all of his knowledge, he's also willing to share his own experiences of tragedy or hardship. On why he was drawn to this work, he circles back to discuss an opinion piece he wrote for the *Australian* in September 2017 headlined 'Child abuse royal commission's work must continue', in which he wrote about the cruel effects of abuse suffered by the victims. He is an abuse survivor, and he treats many like him. His personal experience of knowing what it's like to live, powerless, in an institution 'means that I have a real sense of what it's like for some of my older patients living in an institution, where their human rights may be limited or taken away from them'.

He doesn't want to generalise, but he reiterates the importance of treating people as individuals. 'A basic human right is that our dignity should be respected. But often my patients in care, and their families, tell me they're not being treated compassionately, and that carers can lose sight of the person who's been imprisoned by the disease that put them into an institution.'

Dr Llewellyn-Jones is deeply empathetic, but also pragmatic and solutions-focused. You can address situations, but not everything can be solved. 'We live in a world where we expect that everything can be fixed . . . Maybe we have to be more accepting that there are certain things that just *can't* be fixed.'

In his own life, this has played out personally. He has an adult son who has autism and he recalls how deeply he questioned his son's condition. 'I can well remember being in my early thirties, questioning, why me? Why should this happen to me? Why should it happen to my son? Because he has very severe autism and was and remains severely intellectually handicapped.'

His son would be up most of the night for years, leading to countless sleepless nights for Dr Llewellyn-Jones and his wife. After one such night, he says, a voice came into his head. 'Being a psychiatrist, I knew I wasn't crazy. [It said], "You're asking the wrong question, Rob. The question is not why Damian, but why all the other kids? Why Daniel? Why Peter? Why Charles? Why have they got it? That's the question you need to ask, because without asking those questions, you won't be able to help them. And by helping them you might achieve some sort of meaning out of this tragedy."'

Dr Llewellyn-Jones went on to establish Giant Steps Australia, a charity for autistic kids, which now has schools in Melbourne and Sydney, helping hundreds of children.

'In my own life when I've dealt with tragedy, I've tried to get some meaning out of it. And, for me, the meaning is trying to help other people who are maybe going through similar things. Because if through me going through this I helped somebody else, at least it's not in vain.'

Each individual has to determine their own way of achieving meaning, he says. 'But I personally would find it very hard to live in a universe that's completely random and all these bad things happen to people, and there's absolutely no meaning in it.'

It's here that Dr Llewellyn-Jones encourages younger people to put themselves in the shoes of older people. We should all care very deeply about how people cope with old age, as one day it will be our turn. If the right services for older people aren't here now, they won't be when we need them. Older people tell Dr Llewellyn-Jones that they feel invisible in our youth-oriented society swept up in massive technological change. 'You don't see a lot of older people in movies or the media.' It's improving, but the media is focused on youthful figures. In order to improve the care given to older people, working-age adults who are carers need to understand what it's like to be an older person. 'Because you have to sort of walk a mile in that person's shoes, or put yourself in their shoes, to understand what it would be like. And I think that's something that, unless you've either been through it yourself, or you work with older people, you probably don't necessarily have a natural understanding of what it's like to be old.

'When society was structured differently, you grew up with granny and grandpa living in the same house, you would automatically have understood what it was like to get old, and maybe you would've seen your parents looking after their parents, and that would've been a role model for you to look after your parents. Whereas now, so many frail older people are no longer in their homes or in their family's homes, they're in institutions.'

And a group that he feels is particularly invisible is older carers. 'It may be you're looking after your husband who has dementia in your family home, and, you know, you're up all night because he's up all night, and he can get very upset and agitated about having a shower or shave in the morning, or he gets up in the middle of the night and pees in the fridge, or whatever. All of that sort of stuff does happen. But when you go down to the shops, people don't know what you're going through. The burden that you carry is a silent burden.'

He says that most of his patients and the families he cares for are stoic about it. They don't complain. 'So what of the mental state of carers? Don't they need help, too? Of course they do. I think that's very under-recognised, how traumatic it is to be looking after a loved one who has a serious illness, whether that be cancer or whether it's kidney disease, or dementia, or any number of illnesses. It's traumatic to see the person change so that they're no longer the person they once were. That's very confronting.

'In a way, we're grieving because we're losing the person,' he adds. 'We're losing the person we married, or the person who cuddled us when we were a child, or who was always there for us. And they're grieving, too, because they're losing the person they used to be.'

He recommends counselling, for both the person afflicted by age and illness, and family members struggling with the changes. 'Because as human beings it's very hard to deal with helplessness and powerlessness. You love that person so deeply, you want to help them. You want things to be better.

And sometimes they can't be because the person doesn't want to take the help that's available. Or sometimes they can't be, because the illness and the condition can't be fixed.'

Even psychiatrists need a tune-up. Dr Llewellyn-Jones says he meets regularly with colleagues to talk about difficult cases and to provide support to one another. 'I do a lot of physical exercise as a way of coping with the stress of my role.' Though of course, as he points out, for some older people exercise may not be possible.

The purpose of counselling is to try to help the person to a more balanced place. 'So that there's a lot more of what the person can still do, and less of the cancer or kidney failure or whatever chronic illness they're dealing with.'

Father's Day

We're at my brother Alex's house on a sunny afternoon, having a family lunch, shaded by a sprawling umbrella as we debate who among us is Mum's favourite child. Mum pretends that such a thing is impossible. But we all believe it's true, and we can joke about it. Some things, though, we don't make light of: experiences, relationships, memories better forgotten. We all have our hidden depths. We all have our singular perspective on how we were raised, how we were taught to see the world, and how we treated each other.

We're a tight family. But things are different now. Weightier. More significant even though the bones are exposed. Sometimes everything we didn't talk about, so compressed, threatens to come to the surface.

Isn't childhood difficult for everyone?

It becomes increasingly evident that how we age is not simply a matter of frailty and failing bodies, wandering minds. It's about who is by our side as we age, and what rises to the surface in each of us. I think about this frequently. The significance of having support, company and a reliable network of family and friends. I think about it as friends from Dad's past hove into view. Dad and Mum aren't as social now. I have tried in vain many times to take them to visit old friends, the ones who marked their early memories in Sydney, as has my brother Hossam, who frequently spends time with my parents. Sometimes they seem keen, other times Dad evades the suggestion. He's locked into the present and the past is haunting, I think.

Still, daughters of Dad's friends increasingly reach out to me on Facebook. And one day, a friend of my father, Abu Jamal*, calls me on my mobile. 'Do you know who I am?' he says in Arabic, his kind voice immediately familiar.

'Yes,' I tell him.

Abu Jamal has tried to reach my father and, having no luck, has called me instead.

'Just tell me, is he okay?' His need to confirm that my father is well, and something in his tone, send a ripple of deep emotion through me. The concern, the love – it's all there, and my heart breaks open in gratitude.

'He's okay,' I tell him.

Dad's the guy people who work in cafés know. 'We haven't seen you in a while,' I've heard people say, looking genuinely surprised, hurt almost.

I tell Dad about the call, and it seems to trigger something. He finally agrees to an outing to visit these family friends, people my parents have known for decades. Abu Jamal has cancer. His doctors have told him treatment is pointless at this stage.

It's a bit of a drive, and we make a day of it. Dad's mood is practically ebullient. A familiar journey, one he used to take so easily in the past. It seems to boost his mood. And when he meets with his friend, the relationship dynamics haven't shifted. My mother sits with Im Jamal*, and my father retreats to the backyard with Abu Jamal to inspect his garden. Everyone gardens in old age. I listen as my mother and her friend converse, the 'old days' the recurrent theme. They lament never learning how to drive (Mum tried, but with kids and no one to look after them, finishing her lessons proved impossible). Memories. Im Jamal lifts hers into the present, lighting up simple acts and feelings into something richer and more meaningful.

The good old days.

We tip our cups upside down, but we fail to glean much insight – the coffee was too watery. There's hardly any residue.

Later, I take Mum and Dad to an Arabic grocery store, the kind that's more warehouse than shop, stuffed to the gills with products from any number of homelands. Scents of home.

As we pack our groceries into the car, a realisation dawns. 'Dad, remember how you used to take me out to the western suburbs all the time when I was younger? Now I take you.' I laugh, because it's not a sad moment. It's a calm, nostalgic, happy one.

6.

SAYING GOODBYE

My parents have their complex stories. How long have I diminished their pathways as being less complex than mine? They often speak to me in Arabic. I reply in English. How long have we spoken two different languages and how does that make them feel?

Stepping into a carer role will vary in its levels of responsibility. Some caregivers look after one or both parents, or a sibling with special needs. For some, it's a profoundly life-changing endeavour, which will reshape both lives. Certainly, all the people I sat with and spoke to reported a shift, often seismic, not only in them and their assessment of their own mortality, but also in their relationship with the person they were caring for – especially when it was a parent.

Getting old or dying. Either one, where children are involved, is a process of reconciliation – of past and present situations, and of a new way of looking forward.

'You understand where they've come from'
When we meet, at his expansive property in a seaside suburb of Sydney, James* is all smiles. But the grin hides the lingering pain of his father's recent death. His mother passed on several years before.

'It's still quite recent and raw for me,' he says, his body tensing up, his eyes a little moist. We're sitting at his dining table, floor-to-ceiling windows allowing in bright light on a sunny day while music fills the space. James presses a button on his phone and the music stops. It's that kind of house.

James launches into a detailed explanation of what happened to his mother, speaking like someone who understands the human body and medicine. He sounds like a medical professional, not a business owner.

'My mum was diagnosed with terminal cancer near the end of 2010, and it was stage four at the time, but it was pretty much stage five. Straightaway she had a gastroesophageal junction cancer, which was inoperable and untreatable. So she deteriorated very rapidly. She went through treatment, radiation therapy and chemotherapy.' He takes a moment.

His mother died in April 2011. In his words, her death was 'quite a horrific and painful deterioration'.

'Yeah, it was torture watching my dad go through being there for her. He could do nothing for her. Dad was very mindful of it. The last five years of his life he's actually been quite different.'

James's parents had been together for more than sixty years, a couple who rarely spent time apart – sleeping in the same bed every night, waking up together. James's father had mesothelioma, a tumour in the tissue that lines the lungs. His initial diagnosis of lung cancer seemed odd to James. He asked his best friend, an accomplished surgeon, to study the results, and she similarly frowned at them. Something wasn't right. James told his father to get a second opinion.

'They had said that he had a lung cancer and had ruled out mesothelioma. And I'm looking at it thinking, this has all the hallmarks of mesothelioma . . . The nature of it and the type of tumour just screamed mesothelioma. I thought, fuck. And this is the kind of thing that needs to be treated immediately or else it's lethal – it's going to kill you. And as it turns out it was too far gone anyway.'

The mesothelioma was the result of his father's days as an apprentice electrician working in a mill where he was exposed to asbestos fibres and tape – dust in the air. 'At the end of the day you'd hit your overalls, dust it all off, hang them up, come into work the next morning, put them back on, at the end of every week you'd go home, wash them and bring them back for the next week.

'So he's breathing this asbestos fibre continually all day, every day.'

The average time from exposure to development of meso-thelioma is about thirty-five years; some might develop it ten to fifteen years later, others not for fifty years. Though some people exposed to it their entire life may never develop meso-thelioma, it's rare that they don't.

James's father developed it aged eighty, sixty years after the exposure. 'So you could argue that he got a really, really good life out of it, but I'd argue that if he wasn't exposed to it he would have lived to be ninety or a hundred.'

+

Of his relationship with his father, James says, 'We were really close. I've always been closer to my dad. Dad and I have always "got" each other. We talked a lot. We shared a lot of commonality. He's stayed in his outlook, and we had a good relationship. We could talk and talk and talk for hours.'

'Did anything shift for you?'

'You understand where they've come from,' he says, almost as a question. 'Like you filled in all the little blanks . . . Why they've become the person, or how they've become the person that they are. But when you understand how they got to where they got to, it makes a difference.'

James says what he misses the most is his regular call to his parents. 'Every single Sunday, no matter where I was on Planet Earth, sometime between three pm and six pm Melbourne time I'd call, and almost always Mum would answer the phone, and I'd talk with her, or if Dad answered the phone I'd talk with him briefly, and then talk to Mum for twenty minutes, half an hour, whatever.'

They might talk throughout the week but there was this Sunday appointment. After his mother died, his father would answer the phone. 'And I had to bite my lip because a few times I went to say, "Oh, is Mum there?" And now after Dad died there's no one to call on a Sunday anymore, and I've been doing that for thirty years. Every single Sunday for thirty years.'

✦

James's life has been deeply shaped by the loss of a brother when he was young.

'I shouldn't say we lost him; we know where he is. He died.'

James's younger brother, Daniel*, collapsed with a brain tumour at the age of eleven. The event meant that the next ten years of his brother's life completely changed the dynamic of the family. 'He had four major brain surgeries, and if the same kind of thing happened now he would have had one surgery and he'd be fine for a long lustrous life but . . . that kind of treatment, that kind of surgery wasn't developed back then. So he had a lot of issues.'

We are here to talk about ageing and illness, and all that comes from it, but James's story about his brother taps into a similar vein: mortality. The good life and who is lucky enough to have one.

Daniel transformed from a 'ridiculously cute, just crazy kid', James's best mate, into an entirely different person. The damage from the tumour and the treatment created all kinds of psychological problems. Daniel withdrew and was placed in psychiatric care.

'He basically just wanted to die,' recalls James. 'He had brain injury, injury to his vision, he was an entirely different person after the fall.'

It would be fair to say that not only did Daniel suffer, but so did everybody around him. 'It changed our family.' His family was Mum and Dad, and three kids, James in the middle. They went from being 'the community family' – involved in the football club, sports players, et cetera – to a completely changed family, one struck by the severity of an unexpected condition. 'We weren't prepared for it and we never ever recovered from it. Not that it's something you recover from but . . .'

The counselling services the family were told would arrive never did. 'We just sort of struggled through.'

At the age of fourteen, James was changed for life. Years later he is still dealing with it in counselling, 'just to try and make a considerate effort to be a better man'. But despite his youth James also clicked into a practical gear, making conscious decisions about what his actions and thought processes would be just to get through it all.

'I was always a bit of a perfectionist before that . . . I was the A-grade student, the genius . . . over-achiever. I skipped grades in school and was going through accelerated learning classes, all that kind of stuff. But I made a decision there and then that I was going to be perfect at everything I did and not be a problem for Mum and Dad because they had enough on their plate.'

He indicates his home. 'From then on you can see what I've done with my life. That's where it comes from.'

But James concedes that prospering professionally and financially don't equate to emotional success. He inhabits what he describes as the biggest house in the suburb, 'and I'm on my own'. He has a tight-knit group of friends, whom he loves dearly, but he doesn't have a partner or kids.

'Do you wish you could have done things differently along the way?' I ask. 'Do you feel like this single-minded focus has stopped you from having those things?'

'Not stopped me. I've made decisions that at the time seemed like the right decisions but I don't regret those decisions. Had I been in a different space psychologically I may have done things differently. There were people in my life that I turned from and walked away.'

This includes partners with some major issues – alcohol dependency or a particular mindset. 'I would have done things slightly differently, but not massively. The decisions I made were based upon the person I was and the situation I was in at the time.'

I get the impression that James, being a manager of people in business, manages his own life well. Or perhaps curates it. A moment later he explains, 'I've always been the go-to guy, the guy that solves the problems, the guy at the top of the food chain. There isn't anyone I report to; [in] any job I've ever done, I've been the lead consultant, the manager, the head of whatever. For me the penny drops in any situation. Very rarely do I not see an issue and know the answer straightaway – and that's not conceited, it's just a developed observation. Because my brain works differently to most.'

He admits to some awkwardness in how he deals with others. But with me he says he is comfortable sharing these stories with emotion attached rather than the copy-paste version you give some people. He vividly recalls formative events, including how, as a kid, he'd get a clip across the ear, or a spank. 'And my father grew up that way, my mum grew up that way. I wouldn't do it with my kids. I'd be tempted to but I wouldn't. I'd let them know I grew up differently, but I'm going to do things differently . . . But I remember the power shift, like I grew up and was a fairly big, strong boy, and there was a time that my father rose his hand to me when I was sixteen or seventeen, and I stood my ground and I fronted up to him, chest out to him. And it was a change, an immediate change. All of a sudden I was a peer. Like I was still his son but I was not going to stand for it anymore.

'I feel incredibly emotional about it because I carry around this veiled guilt that I emasculated my dad; and I know it not to be true, but I look back on it and I think, oh fuck, I wish I could undo that, I wish I could.'

It was a big thing for James; it still makes him emotional. It makes me think of all of the emotional wrestling that comes with becoming a carer. How so many troublesome, painful memories must be put aside or dealt with in order to allow the relationship gears to change. What James is talking about is how his emotional, and physical, freedom came at the cost of his father's; it is entirely universal. But there's another memory that holds power for him. When his brother asked him if he wanted to say anything at their father's funeral, his father's comforting strength came to mind in the form of a resonant memory. 'If I think about my dad, it's the thing I think about first and foremost every time. It's really, really important.'

Drives home on the weekend, from a barbecue or a short break, James always sat on the left-hand side because it was the safest seat should there be a car accident. He'd fall asleep, and when the family arrived home he'd be somewhere between sleep and awake. 'And Dad would come round the back of the car and, in his big strong hands, he'd scoop us up one at a time out of the back seat of the car and carry us in and put us straight into bed. And that's the thing I carry around for my entire life. I never felt more safe, more secure, more loved. Dad was pretty much a gentle kind of guy but the strength . . . That was when the capacity to love was most on show with my dad, when it was one on one. He was not a flashy guy, he was just very intelligent, but not flashy at all.'

'It's absolutely God's waiting room'

A couple of years ago, Delma, who is sixty, and her partner, participated in a motorcycle ride around Australia. Her riding group of five people – all in their mid-fifties to mid-sixties – felt spritely and young in comparison to some of the other motorcyclists. Out there, she says, 'the grey power' was every-where. 'There's people in their seventies going into their eighties out there; they're travelling.'

She reflects on this because of what she knows to be true: that the moment you develop a health problem, the moment you suddenly find yourself needing to go to doctors, your whole world changes.

'We can all be out there doing amazing things into our eighties, and truly up until eighty-four Mum was doing amazing things.'

We're here to talk about her mother, Margaret, whom Delma was forced to place in a nursing home when Marga-ret's dementia worsened and she required greater care.

'Mum had always said in her healthy self that if she got dementia she just wanted someone to hit her over the head, just get rid of her, don't let her go through that. And so to have to see her go through that, to have to see her wear the incontinence nappies and things like that – this was my mother, who was very proud of her appearance for a long,

long time. This was so against everything that she believed in. But of course, that's it. We don't have those choices,' Delma says.

She acknowledges her mother's feelings; you'd like to have a choice, she says. 'No one wants to die painfully . . . and in the end for Mum it was quite painful. She's a fighter and she really did fight until the end. She'd broken a hip in a fall, she had heart problems. You know she was in quite a bit of pain . . . no one wants to see anyone like that. I don't want to go out like that. But I think the other thing I've realised is that very few people get to just close their eyes and go peacefully in the night.'

Delma, like James, is still in a state of mourning when we connect, following the recent death of Margaret. Not that she's lost her sense of humour: when I ask her to introduce herself – name, age, profession, and so on – she tells me she's a 'domestic goddess'.

Delma's father, Ron, has been gone twenty-nine years and she still mourns him. 'I miss him. Every day I think about my father. So that was really difficult. Mum, we had a very different relationship. Obviously I'm still thinking about her now; it is still quite fresh.'

She says she was her father's little girl. She and her mother 'were never the closest'. 'But we respected each other and we got on and I was the carer from the time my father left – you know how it is: daughters always are.'

Daughters – yes, a regular presence. Atul Gawande notes that the chances of avoiding nursing homes increase with having kids, especially a daughter. Most people I speak to believe this to be the case. In fact, they argue that cultural differences melt away. They argue that, in terms of being a carer, culture differences aren't as important as gender; that gender defines how children cope with their ageing parents.

Visiting a retirement village, this was further affirmed when the owner, Chiou See Anderson, told me that in the two instances when a resident left, 'Both times they left willingly, and both times assisted by their daughters. I think in this conversation daughters are still probably more involved.'

In my search for stories, not only were the carers more often women than men, but many were acting as carers in addition to other responsibilities. The sandwich generation comprises many such women, who also have to deal with the emotional aspects of their role.

'I didn't dislike my mother, but if my mother hadn't been my mother we probably wouldn't have been [great friends]: politically poles apart, different views, different opinions,' Delma continues. 'But we had a relationship. We were able to discuss things, talk with each other, disagree on things . . . She was always a very strong person, a really strong person, and that's where it's really difficult to watch the decline there. They just turn into something completely alien from this person that you knew.'

But, as Delma points out, it's not just the emotional aspect that is difficult in a parent's decline. 'We all have busy lives, and it's hard enough looking after your own stuff and family and whatever, without taking on someone else's.' Delma has an intellectually disabled brother, Owen, for whom both she and her brother, Peter, are guardians. 'Even though he's in independent housing we're responsible for him; we're responsible for his medical and financial needs.' It places pressure on families, and brews feelings of guilt.

When Margaret went into the nursing home in Canberra, Delma was in Melbourne. 'I was there once a month and it doesn't matter how good the care is, you feel guilty you're not there. They need someone they know – on and on and on it goes.'

Still, Delma says that even if she lived close to her mother, she required the services of a nursing home. It was the only place that was right for her.

'We all face it, we all go through that. We're children and then we bring up our children, and then we look after our parents. It comes to most of us at some stage, it really does. It's a difficult thing . . . because no matter how much you don't want it to happen, you always end up behaving like the parent to your parent. And it's not right. It isn't right . . . they are individuals, they should still be treated as individuals.'

Delma's experience as a carer is an interesting and long-ranging one. Dealing with ageing parents for her really began when her father passed away in 1988.

'My mother was just sixty then, so a year younger than I am now, and a very different time, I guess.'

Her mother was guardian of Owen. Delma took on the everyday responsibilities of a helpful daughter: she was living close to her mother, so she helped with grocery shopping, getting anything Margaret needed for the house, or garden supplies. Delma eventually moved away, as her mother was capable at the time. 'She didn't drive . . . and she never really did her own grocery shopping, Dad had always done the grocery shopping. But Mum was perfectly capable.'

Owen had a bicycle accident that left him bedridden for quite some time with a broken ball joint in his hip. Delma moved in with her mother to help take care of him. A few years later her mother had to have a hip replacement so Delma moved in again. All of this happened within five years of her father's death.

Owen was in assisted housing, but following the death of Delma's father, her mother worked hard to get Owen back into her house, which she did. 'So it became a matter of trying to manage looking after her when she needed it, but also being there for Owen.'

Her mother, Delma says, coped well until she was in her mid-seventies. 'She really was quite independent, and cognitively all there. She was diagnosed with a bowel tumour in 2006. She was seventy-eight. And probably a really lucky thing for both my brothers and I because it turns out we had that horrible gene. So we all have our fabulous colonoscopies.'

Family (medical) inheritance. Delma's not the only one to have unearthed one. Louise*, a woman in her late thirties who had stage four uterine cancer, similarly discovered troublesome genes, which led to revelations for her own sister.

'But,' Delma continues, 'as the doctor said, he's never had a patient who's had some regular colonoscopies develop bowel cancer, so, yeah, gotta go with that. Had Mum not been diagnosed, we may have gone further and had a polyp removed.'

Some believe that there is always something good to be found in the darkness of life. Wasn't it Leonard Cohen who penned the lyric about a crack in everything being how the light gets in?

Despite the late-age diagnosis, Delma's mother surprised doctors with how quickly she 'came back', two years shy of eighty. 'She was again still independent, but . . . she never really got back to being quite as energetic as she was before. But, again, cognitively all fine and it was really just a matter of taking care of the things she couldn't do on her own. Read, being able to drive and things like that.'

Delma, living in another city, spent school holidays visiting her mother with her daughter, Tessa, or bringing her mother and Owen on holidays with them. But then her mother needed the second hip done. She was nearly eighty-four. 'I see that as being the beginning of the decline, the real decline. After yet another general anaesthetic for the hip operation, she had problems with her circulation, would get abscesses. So she was literally on antibiotics all of four years. And that's when all the changes really started happening. This person who was completely capable, she forgot how to cook, she forgot how to do things, and obviously still had her intellectually disabled son living with her; and the very thought of removing him from her home would cause such pain.'

Delma's mother desperately didn't want to go into a nursing home. 'And we really tried to keep her at home. We got home care eventually, when she did get the diagnosis with Alzheimer's dementia, which was only last year. And it wasn't too bad. You know, it really wasn't too bad. But six months later you couldn't recognise her.'

They knew there was dementia, but by the time they met with a geriatrician and went through the procedures, twelve months had passed since they had recognised the need for an assessment. Six months after that there was very little of Margaret left. 'It really was quite rampant.'

The father of Delma's partner, Andrew, was diagnosed with dementia in 2011, but Andrew's father experienced a steady decline. In about six months Delma's mother went through everything Andrew's father had experienced over several years.

'That was really hard. So obviously then we had to do something with Owen. So we got him into assisted housing, which isn't a good thing, it's a great thing. He's independent and having a bit of social life. He was, after all, living the life of an elderly man – he's sixty-four now, but he was living the life of an eighty-odd-year-old. So that's been good for him.'

In the nursing home, Delma's mother changed further. In the last six months of her life, Delma recalls a very angry person, someone who wasn't pleasant to be around. But the one thing her mother clung to was her memory of Owen. She would ask anyone she recognised about him. 'And if he walked into the room, beaming smile, always recognised him, never ever failed to recognise Owen.'

'That's kind of beautiful, isn't it?'

'Yeah, it was . . . She'd be in the middle of screaming at the staff that they were stealing from her and doing horrible things, and Owen would walk in and there would be this big beaming smile and, "How are you?" Then she'd go back to screaming at the staff. So it was quite funny [but] it was awful to watch. It was really difficult because you couldn't communicate with the person that she was because she just wasn't there anymore. She knew she hated being in the nursing home. She literally locked herself in her room, she wouldn't go out and communicate. Whereas Mum had been this really social person who loved having a chat and a cup of coffee. But she just would not leave her room.'

The nursing home was, for Delma, 'a horrible choice to make', but a necessary one. They had tried home care and it wasn't enough; it was becoming dangerous. 'My mum would get up at night and wander. The last night in the house she almost burned the house down. She, for some reason or other, decided to put a pan of hot water on the stove and that boiled dry. Luckily Owen was there and he turned it off. So that was it – she could not stay in the house any longer. She was having falls and it just became impossible.'

What Delma describes is common among people who live with someone who has dementia and requires high-level care. One woman, Stephanie*, deals with two parents who have serious health conditions requiring 24/7 care – a father with dementia, his mind and memories lost; a mother with a physical ailment that sometimes requires oxygen. Her father adores her mother, she told me. But his state of dementia means that he doesn't understand or can't remember that his wife is unwell, that she can't simply get up and do things as she used to.

Stephanie's father is not in a home; he's still able to function, but only in the short-term bursts so notable in dementia patients. A matinee at the theatre invites excitement, but it's forgotten a few hours later.

The same day I spoke to Delma, I met with Dr Llewellyn-Jones, who says simple adjustments can make a monumental difference to a dementia patient. 'I always recommend that the family get photos [of the patient] when they were well, and put them around their room,' he told me. 'I want to show that this is still a person, even though they might be almost non-communicative now; they were once a mum or a dad and they had a job and they loved horse riding or . . . sailing. They're not a thing.'

'I absolutely agree with that,' says Delma. 'Mum's room was full of photos. And I'll be honest, most of the photos were of a younger her . . . my father when he was younger. Because you know with dementia they're far more likely to remember when they were young.' They remember snatches of the past, of who they were.

'It is that one-size-fits-all problem, where everyone with dementia is treated like a child and not as an individual. And I can make no complaints about the staff where Mum was. They were terrific. But they were very limited in what they could do.'

Delma taps into another force at play with nursing homes: no matter how well-intentioned the workers are, 'it's a one-size-fits-all'. 'They're all infantilised. And it's really hard. I don't know how you fix that problem. Obviously the wages for the carers are low. Certainly with the home care the problem was . . . it wasn't that they didn't try, but they were on very, very strict time limits. They had to do everything and be out and off to the next place. So nothing was ever done properly. No matter how much they cared they just didn't have the time.'

Dr Llewellyn-Jones has worked with older people for more than thirty years. He decided to take up the career after seeing first-hand the appalling conditions in some nursing homes while he was at medical school. He described the problem in a similar way – that for all the best intentions of staff at a nursing home, often they are not properly trained, they are not paid well, and the residents in these homes are not treated like individuals. '[The nursing homes I worked in while I was at medical school were] highly institutional. People were often treated as things rather than people. And I thought there must be a better way to provide care for our older people.'

There are still problems, he says, but the buildings are mostly a lot nicer, and certain standards have improved – things like having your own room and an ensuite. 'When I started working in aged care, it was like these big wards where you might have twenty, sometimes thirty people in a hospital-style ward with no privacy and no outdoor areas.'

But what constitutes a good quality of life?

'You can go into one nursing home, where the care is very basic and the people with dementia are given very little stimulation, provided very institutional care. Their basic needs are met – they're bathed and they're dressed and they're provided with nourishment, but that's kind of it,' Dr Llewellyn-Jones notes. 'And they'll be pretty depressed and miserable people. You can go into another nursing home, where there's a very high level of dementia literacy, and people are doing everything they can to provide those individuals with the best quality of life. And, you know, those people have a far better quality of life than the other group.'

It's an example he gives to illustrate how we, as a society, approach these degenerative illnesses of late life. 'If we feel that it's important to value and care for the most vulnerable in our society, and put resources towards that, then those people, or even people with pretty severe cognitive problems, can still have a good quality of life. If, however, that's not one of our core values, and you don't put those resources in, well then, those vulnerable people won't have a good quality of life.'

Problems with nursing home models are increasingly well-documented. In *Dear Life* Karen Hitchcock speaks of the loss of a person's liveliness when confined to a small life and few pleasures; Atul Gawande in *Being Mortal* extensively documents the highs and lows of aged care options, show-casing how people thrive under the right conditions. He speaks movingly of the loss of autonomy:

> The terror of sickness and old age is not merely the terror of the losses one is forced to endure but also the terror of the isolation. As people become aware of the finitude of their life, they do not ask for much. They do not seek more riches. They do not seek more power. They ask only to be permitted, insofar as possible, to keep shaping the story of their life in the world – to make choices and sustain connections to others according to their own priorities.

In essence, being treated as a human being, with complexity, emotion, purpose and life, should not be negotiable. Our bodies can fail us, our minds may quickly follow, and prevent-ing a downslide of both is essential to living well, or simply better than you think your old age might allow. Gawande and Hitchcock both consider the impact of giving elderly people a cause beyond themselves, such as having a pet.

However, while Hitchcock talks about people not wishing to go into nursing homes, a geriatrician I spoke to attempted to temper the criticism of such places a little. Professor Lindley believes a poor reputation precedes aged care facilities. Of all the things he says, his cautionary words around nursing homes stand out: 'The one thing I really think you should avoid is, "I will never put you in a nursing home, Mum." That's a really bad thing to do because a lot of people will need nursing care at the end of their life, and if you've made that promise to your parents it causes all sorts of difficulties.'

As a geriatrician, he's seen lots of examples where aged care has been 'a fantastic solution for a difficult problem'. People are comfortable when they're getting the care they require, he says. 'So if you do require twenty-four-hour nursing care, you could be quite uncomfortable in the care of your family, who are not doing it very well, and you can be quite comfortable in a nursing home. And therefore that quality time with your family when they visit is not dominated by the caring role, whereas it would be if they were struggling to be looked after at home.'

I put forward the common concerns I have read or heard about. That nursing homes and aged care facilities do not cater to the individual. That there is a lack of connection – between residents themselves, and residents and overworked, under-trained staff. That there is little to keep the residents engaged, entertained, vital. 'God's waiting room' and all that.

'We can do things better, I'm sure. I've read in the lay press, not in the scientific press, about these fantastic trials in other countries,' says Professor Lindley. He cites a recent example in the Netherlands, where student accommodation and aged care are co-located; as rent, students do some work in the facility. 'One of the things that predicts healthy ageing is community connectiveness. And I think having cross-generational friends and carers is fantastically good because it means that when your own cohorts are dying off you're not losing all your friends. If you've got friends in the generation beneath you and beneath them, they're going to be around, they're still around when you go yourself.'

Diverging from his professional to his personal feelings, Professor Lindley airs his dislike of retirement villages, 'where everyone's old and frail and complaining about their next medical appointment', because he doesn't believe they're as connected with the community as they could be.

'I think the students in the aged care facility is a fantastic idea. I think having childcare facilities and aged care facilities side by side is a fantastic idea, although it might not be so good in flu season, but . . . I think we need to be far more imaginative about how we look after older people and keep them in a more community style.'

+

There was humour in the nursing home experience, though, says Delma. 'Every time I walked into Mum's nursing home I would look at [the residents] sitting there, all lined up looking out the windows into the garden in their recliners that were lined up there. And I would always think of Spike Milligan and his description of Woy Woy, where his mother lived for many years in New South Wales. He described it as the only above-ground cemetery in the world. So every time I walked in there I would have a little chuckle because Spike Milligan would have just died laughing, I can assure you.'

Another woman I met recently divulged her own perspective on dementia when she discovered I was writing a book about ageing and illness.

'Is there humour in it?' she said, her expression thoughtful. For Mary*, there was. Her father had dementia and resided in a nursing home until his death. She says he was the brutish type when he was unwell – aggressive and mean. One day her brother-in-law arrived to pick him up for an outing. He arrived to a chaotic scene: Mary's father standing over another old man, hitting him with his walker and yelling accusations.

When Mary's brother-in-law intervened with a hello, the change was instant. Suddenly her irate father was bubbly and charming. She found this hilarious – indeed, her story shows the importance of seeing the humour in the potentially traumatic.

Sophie*, the nurse, had her first introduction to a dementia ward during an aged care practical allocation when she was studying. 'The word "hopeless" is probably a bit too extreme, but these patients . . . you had to have a sense of humour to work there,' she told me. 'It's the only way because these patients – you're telling them something and they're coming back twenty seconds later and they've already forgotten . . . I think you need a sense of humour in nursing. Definitely in aged care and the dementia wards. That's hard work. That is really hard work.'

But again, what to do with these ailing patients who can't look after themselves, says Delma. 'So you wheel them out, you put them in front of this big window to look at a garden and you leave them there for hours and hours and hours.'

Dr Llewellyn-Jones also recalls scenes like this. 'In the bad old days when I was a medical student, we were told to get people up, and they'd be wheeled out to the so-called garden area, which was just concrete, and no plants or flowers, and they'd be tied into their chairs, set there for a regulation hour or so, and then taken back somewhere else,' he explains. 'I think things have changed a lot for the better in that way.'

He accepts there may have been nursing homes with better facilities. 'Nevertheless, you can still miss out on the care you need even if you're staying in a five-star luxury nursing home, because it's not just the environment, the built environment, that's important. It's [that] older people need lots of time and human contact, and if the places aren't staffed well enough then the residents aren't going to get the time they need.'

It's not that he's against nursing homes. 'There are some very good ones where the care is excellent. But they don't suit everyone. There should be a greater number of smaller facilities providing personalised, home-like accommodation.'

It does seem that as a society we don't know how to deal with our ageing population. Older people often talk about feeling invisible. They're made to feel invisible. We don't esteem the elderly, and we certainly don't, as young people, want to think about getting old. 'Believe me, when you're in there and you're caring for them, it brings your mortality into you, it's staring you in the face,' says Delma. 'You realise, this could very easily be me in the not-too-distant future. It's confronting. But, like I said, there is humour in it, too. I think a lot more humour could go places.'

'The other thing is animals. They all respond to animals. One of the nurses brought in a little puppy dog and it was kept around the nurses' station and she used to walk around with it now and again, and they all loved that puppy. Which is crazy because it was a smelly, horrible thing. But they all loved it. And children. You know, you want to see their eyes light up around a young child. A toddler walks in and every one of those women literally . . . you see them transform before your eyes.'

I'm reminded that Sophie said the same thing about babies and geriatric patients in hospitals. 'So actually just giving them opportunities to engage?'

'It's absolutely God's waiting room . . . These people are not going to get better, so we'll just make them comfortable and we'll wait.'

'And that's something we can change. We absolutely can change it,' I add.

'They do need to be made more than just comfortable. They need to be made to feel as though they belong. And with Mum that was not easy.'

Delma's mother didn't experience theft or verbal abuse, but she had delusions in which people were coming into her room and stealing things. 'So I don't know how you improve that. But again there's got to be a way. A puppy dog. Children coming to visit now and again.'

Delma's story finishes in a swell of pathos. She laments not seeing her mother in the final few days of her life: she was moving house, her brother had the flu. 'We weren't there for those final couple of days. I hate that. I just hate that.'

'You don't know what's going to happen to you'

Carolyn, fifty-four, has a good relationship with her two grown daughters. But she didn't enjoy a similar connection with her parents. Her father, Lester, died in 2010; Carolyn's mother, Valerie, died in 2017, in a progression of events she described as 'very fast', following a diagnosis of Lewy body dementia.

'Robin Williams [the actor] had it,' Carolyn tells me. 'It has a lot of the attributes of Parkinson's that are hard to diagnose. Often they can only diagnose it when somebody has died.'

Carolyn's mother didn't really have any symptoms, but one of the neurological tests doctors do is to ask patients: can you draw a clock? Valerie couldn't draw a clock. 'She couldn't figure out where the numbers went.'

Valerie had worked as a bookkeeper. 'She was very with it and very particular about things,' Carolyn says. 'That was a great frustration to her. I had noticed that she'd stopped reading books. She mainly watched television. She didn't have any capacity for reading anymore.'

Valerie had resided in a retirement village for around ten years before her death. She lived alone. And as her former husband had done (Carolyn's parents divorced when she was fourteen), Valerie transitioned from the retirement village to a nursing home.

'She had a fall and she fractured her pelvis. When she went into hospital, they were saying she'd have to go into long-term rehab in order to be able to get walking again. Everything was fine. She just went into a deluded state where she thought the nurses were trying to kill her. She'd always watched and read a lot of British murder mysteries. That was really her thing. I think that fed into a lot of it because . . . I would go in and she'd say the nurses pushed someone downstairs last night. I thought that it might have been a urinary tract infection because that can make you go quite crazy when you're older.'

Carolyn said she kept waiting for her mother to 'get back to normal'. She never did. Valerie subsequently had another fall and broke her hip, which led to a replacement. She refused to cooperate with anybody who tried to get her up and walking. Consequently she couldn't walk and Carolyn had to put her into a nursing home.

'They had said to me Lewy body is very fast.' In Valerie's assessment for aged care, her condition sent her to the top of the list – straight into a nursing home. 'Mum hadn't even really believed it then. That she had it. She kept saying, "I don't have anything wrong with me. I think they're wrong."'

The neurologist told her she would no longer be able to drive.

'She was really horrified by that. She'd always been independent.'

At the time, Carolyn talked to her mother every day and saw her often. But she had a complex relationship with Valerie.

'She was very self-centred always,' reflects Carolyn. 'All my life.'

Carolyn has a sister, Heather, who has lived overseas since 1987. Carolyn says her mother would hit them when they were young; she linked it to her mother's own experiences of abuse.

'Her mother used to really beat her. [Our mum] wasn't as bad with us. Thank god our father never, ever hit us. We were genuinely frightened of her. It could be a tiny thing. I can remember being hit on certain occasions but I can't even remember what I did.

'When we were teenagers, we went to every concert that was on, and my sister and I used to go to *Countdown* when it was on in Sydney, and stuff like that. We never did anything wrong. Never, ever, ever. Because we knew she would kill us.'

Carolyn turned to her husband, Darren, for advice; and, despite the physical distance between Carolyn and Heather, who felt guilty for not being here to help Carolyn, they made decisions together regarding their mother.

'My sister just said to me, "Whatever decision you need to make, you make that decision." Because she works in the health industry, whenever I would tell my sister the professionals were saying this, she would go and find a geriatrician in her hospital and ask them. She would also give me things to ask.'

'Do you think the advice you generally received was pretty sound?' I ask. Were the staff helpful?

'I think that they were pretty good. The hospital that she was in, they had a nurse who just dealt with older patients. [The nurse] also gave me a lot of really good advice on where were the good nursing homes ... for Mum's particular condition, and who would be good. She would ring them and rustle up a bed and that sort of thing. She also advocated on Mum's behalf and made sure that the hospital kept her in there until she could get into a good spot. They would have a meeting with me and her and the geriatricians and the physios to basically say, "This is what's happening and this is what we think will happen." Where I would just cry and embarrass the young physiotherapist.'

Tears flowed due to the swiftness of Valerie's deterioration. 'It was really quick.' It was very different from the experience Carolyn had had with Lester, whose decline was a longer, slower process.

Valerie fell in March; she had passed on by May. Carolyn was shell-shocked. 'About how quick it was . . . And Mum had said to me there's a part of her that knew she was not normal at this point. She would say to me, "Don't let anyone know and don't let anybody come and see me."'

Carolyn describes Valerie as being 'very, very proud and horrified by the indignity of it all'. She was mortified when friends would pay her a visit in those months, barely speaking out of embarrassment. She couldn't be reasoned with – she was genuinely seeing things.

'She would say, "Can't you see them?" She was hallucinating. She would see her father, which was good because that was quite soothing because she loved her father. That she knew wasn't real. It was interesting that she thought the nurses were trying to kill people and lining up for funerals; that she had to get away from them. That's why she fell a bit. But she knew that seeing her father wasn't a real thing. She found it very comforting to see him.'

Valerie, a Christian, was in a Brethren nursing home. Carolyn made a point of posting up family photos in Valerie's room. She also placed one of her wooden carvings of hands in prayer above her bed. 'It was almost like I was declaring she's a Christian. Giving her her best shot.'

'Do you think that helped her at all?'

'I don't think it gave her any solace in the end. At all.'

Valerie was upset about her circumstances, about being in a nursing home and confined to an oversized chair or bed. She couldn't do anything for herself. She couldn't even feed herself.

'I would always make sure that I told the minister at the hospital, "Go and see her, whether or not you think she's [receptive]," Carolyn recalls. 'I did that with my dad, too.'

The chaplains at the hospital were responsive to her request for her father, pleased to be asked, surprised even. 'Especially because my dad had advanced dementia. He was in the hospital a couple of times. I said that just because he's not responding much . . . these are all familiar things to him. Please go and pray with him.'

'And did they?'

'Yes. They did. I would know because they'd always leave the card on the bedside table.'

Carolyn did the same for her mother, telling the religious visitors, 'Whether or not you think she's connecting with you, this ritual is very important to her.'

'In the end it wasn't,' says Carolyn simply. 'In the end there was nothing.'

+

Lester, Carolyn's father, was living alone in a flat when he experienced an acute episode. 'He had an episode where he thought it was the 1970s,' says Carolyn.

'My uncle rang me and said, "I just tried to ring Lester and he keeps asking where you all are." It was nine-thirty at night and we were a long way away. We sent around a doctor, but my father wouldn't let him in. The doctor said to me, "We won't send the police. He's safe. He's indoors. Don't [call the police] because you'll scare him." We went around first thing the next morning. Darren came too, and my dad thought Darren was my cousin John, who's lived overseas since he was nineteen. Mum came too because I said, "Maybe if he thinks it's the 1970s he thinks you're still married." He didn't recognise her, of course.'

Lester had been misdiagnosed with depression and was taking too many antidepressants. A two-week stay at Concord Hospital brought up contraindications between the meds; then it turned out that Lester wasn't suffering from depression. He had dementia.

'It's the same face,' Carolyn explains. 'Apparently the dementia face, that blankness, is very similar to the depression face. He had a series of tiny strokes and he'd had an operation. That's what caused his vascular dementia. [His doctor] didn't even think to explore that.'

Lester was also the type of person who did what his doctor told him. He would never have said, 'Do I really need all those?' He would just take the tablets. 'My dad was very old-fashioned. His mother was from Yorkshire and very superstitious. He was very, very reserved. I didn't even know him that well because he wouldn't dream of ever opening up or anything like that. He just wasn't that type.'

Carolyn feels the lack of emotional connection to her father made it easier. 'Because when he was in the hospital there was a woman opposite and she was with her father. You could tell that they were incredibly close. She was caring for him in her own home. I'm thinking, "That's madness. I would never do that – be his nurse." For me it was a lot easier because we did have that distance so that I could make the decisions. In consultation with him, because he got a lot better, and he ended up living in a retirement village. It was attached to a nursing home.'

Every day Lester would walk from his little unit at a thousand-acre Anglican retirement village to the neighbouring nursing home for lunch. Carolyn says they kept an eye on him there. 'They rang me one day and said, "It's time for your father to move into the nursing home because he's not looking after himself well enough now."'

It was a difficult move – Lester didn't want to relinquish his little unit. But within two weeks of moving, his dementia had taken a further hold on him and he had forgotten what he'd left behind.

'What has it taught you as a person? What does it make you feel in relation to the ageing process?'

'That it's all a bit of a gamble. You don't know what's going to happen to you. He was perfectly happy. He was really happy.'

In fact, while Valerie's form of dementia plunged her into darkness, Lester was 'a lot nicer than he was before', Carolyn says, no longer the belligerent father he had been to them their whole lives. In its place came gratitude.

At one stage he went missing for two days. He had a UTI (men get them, too). But he hadn't gone far – he was in the school next door, lying outdoors for two nights. This led to a hospital visit for Lester, then eighty, and more decisions for Carolyn. The emergency room doctor asked her, 'You don't want us to take any heroic measures, do you?'

'I'm going, holy –. I'm ringing my sister in London . . . In her mind, she's thinking about booking flights. I go home that night and that's running through my head – this could be it. The next morning I walked in. He's sitting up in the ward having breakfast. He said, "Fancy seeing you here." He's saying to everybody, "This is my daughter." I said, "Dad, do you realise what you've put us all through?" He was physically unharmed. Just dehydrated.'

When he was younger, Lester was a fit man who jogged and was mindful of his weight. 'I think he had a period where he smoked and that probably led to him getting the vascular dementia.'

+

One thing I find particularly touching is how well Carolyn's parents were cared for in their respective nursing homes.

'He was looked after well, I must say. When my mother was in the nursing home, they made sure that all of her clothes went together. There were complete outfits. They brought in a hairdresser. Even when she was dying . . . They rang me and they said, "Your Mum's having difficulty swallowing." That was just them being oblique on the phone. I went in and I said, "She's dying." They said, "Yes." I said, "You can send her to hospital."'

But the nursing home was very good with care. It took a couple of days for Valerie to die. In that time, the staff washed her and changed her nightie. They played hymns at her bedside the entire time. Drugs and oxygen ensured she didn't suffer in any way. 'The minister came and prayed beside her, I think at least three times within those couple of days,' says Carolyn.

She wasn't there when her mother slipped away, but Carolyn takes some satisfaction in knowing she 'sent her off in the right way'.

She bursts into tears, her measured tone changing in an instant. 'I had a really complex relationship with my mother. She was, in a lot of ways, a very cruel woman. But I was making booties for a friend's daughter the other day and I thought, I can't remember how much ribbon I've got to buy for booties. I can't ring Mum and ask her. It's all of those little things.'

You don't have that person anymore. But for Carolyn and her sister, they no longer have to suffer their mother's disapproval over their life choices. 'Which is very freeing, because I don't have to think about her. I've always had to think about her.'

Neither of her parents ever said 'I love you,' Carolyn tells me. 'Mum would do it with my children because they would say it and so she would say it back.'

'Grandkids are different,' I say.

'Yes, very different.'

'I felt a lot of guilt about my mother's death. For a long time. Because of the series of decisions from the outset; was I making the right decision? Then I felt relieved. Having to tell people, like having to tell her friends at the village. Because she's now in a nursing home. For them to be quite incredulous because she had been perfectly fine. Then they went to see her. All these Christians, they said that they all had a prayer to give. They got to give a prayer and they said, "We hope that she doesn't live long because she wouldn't like living like this" . . . That's the tactlessness sometimes of older people.'

'You can't really prepare yourself'

Sadia* was living overseas when her father, Hassan*, became ill and required emergency surgery. He was diagnosed with cancer, but she had no conception of the severity of his condition. Taking leave to travel home to Australia, she intended to be back at her desk at the not-for-profit organisation she worked for within a couple of weeks.

'And then he had surgery, and it was successful . . . the tumour that they took out was benign,' she recalls. But the surgery revealed trouble in another area in his liver. It was cancerous. They waited a month for the assigned oncologist to return from leave; she would be able to provide them with treatment options.

'Then when we met with the oncologist, she was like, "I can help you wrap up things at work and you know you've probably got about eight months . . . to a year." Sadia smiles wryly at the memory. 'We went into that appointment thinking, okay, we're looking at options, to hearing, "Yep, you've got about a year left; I can help you with organising super." So that was a shock.'

We're seated opposite each other on the pavement surrounding Lake Burley Griffin in Canberra. In the distance, the large water spout periodically shoots through the air in a refreshing splash. It pierces the occasional moment of quiet reflection, as Sadia unpacks the death of her father four years before to that aggressive cancer in his liver.

A revelatory moment occurred in her father's reaction. Her very strict father, who had never showed much emotion, cried. He was 'totally changed', says Sadia. 'I remember he was talking to my uncle and my grandfather who live overseas. He used to regularly talk to them on the phone. I think that appointment was on a Friday, maybe? And he was speaking to them on Saturday. And he just totally broke down, and I think the last time I'd seen him cry was when his mum passed away about twenty years ago.'

It felt more real then, she says. 'It felt like, okay, so this is happening. Because my dad was someone who had – if something went wrong in my life, he had a solution for me. If it wasn't A, B or C, he'd find another option to make it happen and to fix things.'

Hassan's brief emotional breakdown signalled to Sadia a loss of hope: perhaps there weren't any options. Still, she recalls how her father was clear-headed enough to tell the family to keep his prognosis hidden from Sadia's younger brother, who was undertaking university exams at the time.

Sadia says nothing specifically offered comfort. Raised in a Muslim family, her life already consisted of daily prayers, fasting during Ramadan and a fairly conservative lifestyle. But she recalls family friends visiting and urging her to start wearing hijab and pray more. 'I thought, no, I don't want to do that. I want to do it my way . . . And these are smart, educated people, so it was really surprising.'

Their suggestion was laced in the notion that prayer would magically fix the situation. 'But you've got to look at it in a practical way as well. My dad was looking at it in a practical way.' He wasn't getting chemo or any sort of treatment, only medication to manage his pain.

Sadia did ask of the unseen why this was happening to her family. She even blamed herself for going away from her family. Was the cancer a punishment? 'Knowing very well it wasn't my doing. But still questioning that, thinking maybe is it stress that causes liver cancer? Which is not true. Obviously it's your lifestyle choices over many, many years.

'I also felt a lot of anger towards not just the situation but towards my dad because it was almost like, you did this to yourself and you did this to us.'

'How did he do it to himself?'

'Just his lifestyle choices. He never drank. But . . . it was fatty liver cancer, which is caused by not eating properly for ten, fifteen years; not exercising. He had Type-2 diabetes. So stuff like that leads to chronic diseases.'

Her father didn't smoke, either, but, 'He loved his food,' she laughs, 'which is fine. And I remember I spoke to my parents when I was in my early twenties, saying "You need to eat healthy; this is not going to end well." And it didn't.

So I went through a stage where I was really angry about that.'

The tumour didn't allow for surgery or a liver transplant. Chemotherapy was a possibility but an appointment with another specialist offered a dim prognosis; they were told, 'You can do it and you'll probably have another six months to live at this stage, and you can spend six months either getting chemo and your quality of life would drastically reduce, or you can just spend the six months how you are now.

'In the end, they called us back and they said, "Actually, on second thoughts, we don't think you should get chemo, so there is no other option."'

It was a tough year. 'I was living at home at the time [of his diagnosis].' She had three months before returning to work, so she spent that time going to appointments with her father; her mother was still working, but was taking leave. 'I would hang with my dad during the day and take him to appointments, make his lunch and all that kind of stuff.'

Sadia didn't share her feelings about her father's lifestyle choices with him. Hassan's mellowing after his diagnosis led to a reformation in his relationships with his family. Sadia in particular saw a notable shift in her relationship with her father in the last ten months he was alive.

'He was a totally different person. He was calmer. He was more present. He was more accepting . . . it was almost like he was the dad I would have liked to have had my whole life, which is nice in a way because I saw a different side to him. Don't get me wrong, my dad was a really great dad growing up, but he was very strict and not emotionally there.'

'Did that make it harder, in a way, getting a glimpse of what was possible?'

'Yeah, yeah, absolutely.'

Sadia never spoke to her father of this glimpse and the effect it had on her. A friend suggested she should, but to Sadia it would have seemed a cruel exercise. 'What good would that do? That would probably make him more upset, knowing that he's going to die.'

'Did you learn anything about your father that surprised you?'

'He spoke a lot about his childhood. One of his brothers, one of my uncles from overseas, came and visited towards the end, so we would have lots of fun family chats. And . . . I just found out about . . . their childhood.'

Sadia says her father did struggle with the 'why' of his diagnosis, but he eventually came to terms with his situation: 'This has happened to me, and this is what's happening, and it's all in God's hands.' Though he did question it sometimes, she concedes: was it a punishment for something he'd done? Had he done something to someone who now wished him ill?

✦

So much gets lost in the process of illness. We all change. How we see ourselves, whether we are the ones dealing with illness, or are witness to it, we grapple with the loss of everything that is familiar. The snow globe effect: everything gets shaken up. You lose the ordinary things. You search for and find normal moments and experiences, only for a phone call or development to torpedo the normality again.

It felt like too much for Sadia, all the time. She didn't resume her overseas position after her father's death. So she sacrificed the new life she was enjoying, and her options thinned out – she stayed in Australia because she couldn't leave her mother alone.

Now Sadia feels limited, restricted by circumstances. She doesn't share a home with her mother but she's in touch with her daily – Sadia's only other sibling lives in another city. She'd feel guilty neglecting her mother, who lives in a large house by herself. Looking out for her is not a hassle, but it eats away at her social life.

As Sadia ponders the possibility that she may one day, depending on her circumstances, play a more substantive carer role for her mother, she reflects on the descent of someone in poor health, observing as the helpless bystander. She told a friend, 'I don't know what would have been worse – knowing that he had a year left, or just him passing away without us knowing how long he has.

'And when he did pass away I don't know if it was easier to deal with it knowing that it was going to happen, because you can't really prepare yourself. You know this person's sick and I guess they're in a better place but . . . I don't know, you just can't prepare yourself for that.'

'Do you believe he's in a better place?'

'Yeah, absolutely.'

Friday

It's October and Sydney is flooded with the bright purple of bountiful jacaranda trees. I'm reflective, flattened and subdued by the accumulation of stories I've collected. But also invigorated, to not be wasteful or take anything for granted.

Fridays with my folks continue, a solid appointment that even colleagues are now aware of; often, they'll preface a call with, 'Sorry, I know it's Friday but . . .' People understand, but life trots on. It's been more than a year of Fridays.

There is a difference now. Dad doesn't take so long to warm up. Like that new pair of shoes, his changed reality has become more comfortable with time, with greater acceptance. He is quieter but he finds pleasure and excitement in the things he's always enjoyed. He has changed and admits this himself. Still, while the volume is lower, perhaps, the music is playing.

Mum and Dad also seem to have settled peacefully into their memories. They're not fighting them or reinterpreting every image and thought. Now these moments are allowed to exist as they were at the time, unblemished, whole, the burden of experience not so scalding.

Their quirks have become familiar. The odd turns of phrase, common for people for whom English is their second language. Dad's playfulness, when he's not 'the silent man', the way he puts on a funny voice to demonstrate a good mood, the way he calls people 'baby' – even my brothers, relatives, my mum. 'Maybe,' will come his response. 'Maybe, baby.'

Other things, too. Mum's conspiracy theories, usually related to cafés and restaurants, which explain poor service – food comes late because the staff want the café to look full; something is delicious and carefully assembled on the first couple of visits, but once you're a regular they don't try so hard to impress you with good food. 'Not conspiracy theories,' she tells me, 'True!' And how sugar is responsible for all ailments, something that nowadays a dietician, or nurse, or even the podiatrist we visit might affirm.

Mum continues to study her coffee cup for symbols, a strange comfort she takes in the possibilities of life. It indicates that even in the toughest times, hope lingers. Stretched out. Elastic. Mum, my father's constant companion, the mother bear.

Dad frequently observes, 'It's your mum's fault.' He throws blame to her for just about anything. Mum is his full-time protector, monitoring his diet and activity, his mood. She's pushy and watches him, militant, a bird guarding her nest. Maybe that's why he's learned to deflect stuff. If he eats something that doesn't agree with him, it's Mum's fault.

I call him on it. 'You blame Mum for everything,' I say. 'If there was a tornado tearing up the road you'd blame her.'

Even Dad finds this amusing.

+

With Dad not driving, I'm constantly reminded how he sees the world differently as a passenger. He points out buildings like they're monuments. Sometimes there's a history tied into them. The old building that sits at a large intersection near Central Station – he applied for a job there. The GPO building at Martin Place – he had his first job there, at the postmaster-general's department (PMG; what would become Telecom). Places he and my mother have lived in, the first house they bought – in Bondi in 1971. He declares Bondi Beach beautiful more than once. Its fame had reached him all those years ago when he first arrived, and he wasted no time in setting out to explore it. The building formerly known as Crown Street Hospital near Darlinghurst. 'Lots of memories,' says Dad, because four of his five children entered the world there.

He knows the inner workings of the city, its unseen passageways. He's walked every street. He still gives me directions when I'm driving him somewhere, and he's taken to public transport with a passion. My father relishes noise, he likes spaces teeming with people. And, for a traditional man, he admires progress. His favourite word is 'results'. He seems constantly to marvel at the reconstruction of Sydney. Repetitively so – it's clear he doesn't ever find it boring. Each new building, each site of destruction, holds promise and positivity. It's progress. It's results. Sydney is booming. 'Beautiful,' he says as we pass a new development.

When we go shopping, Dad browses the fruit and vegetable aisles like a tourist. He studies the names of obscure fruits.

He and my mother argue over how much to buy – his fruit intake is of course limited.

He notices things – the birds, trees. I notice them, too. Whenever Dad walks past a tree or flowers, he stops to touch them, then places a hand to his nose to take in its scent.

I walk slower with Dad, too.

In noticeable ways, Dad's condition has changed him. But I also see that his health affects my mother on a deep level – on multiple levels. She's with him 24/7. Questions fill her mind: why did it happen so soon?

Still, at least the two of them can come and go, Mum acknowledges. You lose other things in the process, but it occurs to me how unafraid my parents are. Mum tells me she's grateful that her kids are around, helping, being there. It's support for Dad, she says, but in my mind I feel we're also offering her support. Carer fatigue is a slow burn.

Dad agrees that he enjoys his outings with his kids. His birthday is coming up. He's never much cared for it. He's tetchy about it now, still. He doesn't care about celebrating birthdays, never has; but he embraces living.

There is a change in me, too. It's not a rebirth or newfound sense of joy. It's a simplifying – of things, of unnecessary situations, of negative people. A clearing. I don't know if it's age, or a weathering of my being. But I don't feel attached to things. I don't want to accumulate. I don't seek permanence. Life is fleeting, ephemeral. You don't take anything with you. So I don't want a life burdened by need, or belongings.

One day, would that I just float away, free, no possessions, a life well-lived.

7.

THE NATURAL
CYCLES OF LIFE

*I want to demystify death and **its power over
people.***

Friday

My parents inform me that a relative overseas has died from
cancer. The daughter of my mother's cousin. A woman barely
in mid-life. The father is in deep mourning for his daughter,
who, unmarried, was still living with him.

We talk about it, and about death more generally. How
flimsy it seems from a distance when it hasn't happened to
someone close to you, or when the passage of time has lessened
the weight of loss. We reflect on how we've all been visited
in our sleep, the ghosts of those who have left us appear-
ing, normal, healthy, free of disease and suffering, there to
reassure us, or foreshadow something.

At times we can talk about this easily. Dad can be flippant
about the cycles of life, acknowledging that 'nothing stays
the same, baby'. Mum, too, lends humour to the heavy topic.
When I wonder aloud if whatever follows life, as we experience it, can really be any worse than what we deal with here,
Mum comes back with, 'The afterlife is probably boring.'

But we've all been up close with death.

My father has lost both parents, and with that loss
the intense desire to be back in his home town, though a

homesickness lingers, and always will. My mother lost siblings from a young age: three brothers who have passed on, and her sister, gone three years ago now. My maternal grandparents passed away within weeks of each other. My mother was in Australia when her father was involved in a road accident. She managed to get to Kuwait in time to see him before he died. As Mum recalls, she saw him twice before he passed away. 'It was the shock of my life.' She needed to be medicated. Mum returned to Australia but a couple of weeks later her mother died. She offers up prayers for them all every day, reciting Quranic verses.

My mother lost her brother Waleed when he was thirteen years old. Afflicted by a condition that couldn't be treated in Jenin, he was taken by their father to Kuwait, where he died on the operating table.

'We didn't know he died. My father didn't tell us.' Mum was on her way to Kuwait with her family to meet them when it happened. She knew Waleed was gone from the expression on her sister's face when Mum arrived at the hospital.

This tragedy had a deep impact on my mother, who was fifteen at the time. 'You should have seen how my mother wailed,' Mum recalls. 'And she was good at it, too.' A note of pride almost creeps into her tone, but it's overwhelming sadness that seeps through her words. 'He was a beautiful kid, eyes so big.'

Losing her brother Samir when he was in his fifties was different – she had spent more of her life being his sister, knowing him. Losing her sister, Rusmeah, in her sixties – not having seen her enough, but a firm attachment in place nonetheless – was devastating in its unforgiving suddenness.

Uncle Samir was dear to me. When I was a child, he graced us with yearly visits every January. A captain of the stewards on Kuwait Airways, he was handsome, fun and full of life.

I watched his body's descent from cancer. He was given a timeline by the doctors.

Then, three years ago, Aunt Rasmea. A phone call from Mum that chilled me to the core – there had been a road accident. My aunt was hit by a truck. I sent love from a distance to this kind relative, whom I'd met several times but who loved me as though I were an everyday presence in her life. Her death shook all of us to our core. An introduction to a new form of grief. It empties you of trust – the unexpectedness of it, the unfairness of it.

Does it make it easier at all, I still wonder, to know that your time is limited? For the body to fade, violently or softly, an inevitable decline in old age, or to be given a sentence? There is a difference between losing someone in old age, when you're older and have decades of memories between you. My mother tells me it's hard to lose someone at any age, but that you feel it more when you're older. She was deeply troubled by her sister's death: the sudden trauma has left her not quite the same. She hadn't seen her enough. At the time, I threw something out there, unsure of where exactly the advice came from, knowing only that it must be given. 'When you pray today, Mum, light a candle and speak to her, and tell her what you want to say.'

Mum later told me she lit a candle and spoke to her sister. Tears streamed down her face, hot and unrelenting, as she honoured her, thanking her for being a good sister. But the tears, she told me, didn't feel like hers.

'From the moment life begins, it's ending'

Halloween is coming up when I meet with Stacey Demarco, the self-titled 'modern witch'. The northern hemisphere is headed into the darker winter months; however, their Halloween is our spring (litha). Stacey's a self-proclaimed 'nature luster' and a pagan, and therefore believes she is a natural part of the earth, not better or worse than other living things. 'I'm going to have a cycle like anyone else. A birth, death . . . I am no more special than anyone else or anything else.'

In most cultural mythos, Stacey explains, death is the start of life. 'Pagan peoples have always had death very much as part of life, and the cycles of sickness and health and birth and so on.' The 'death' card in the tarot major arcana is symbolic not of an ending but a new beginning – a rebirth. 'It's the void,' Stacey continues. 'In the Norse [mythology], it was a void, it was a place of infinite possibility, of nothingness. It wasn't a place to be feared.' Norse mythology depicts a potentially jolly afterlife, depending on where you go, based on your deeds in this life. Though there is a hell, in the form of a death goddess, Hel.

In the past, in some traditions, with that concept of death being a part of life there was great celebration around a death. 'People would come from far and wide to bury somebody. And if you think about it, people didn't live very long. We didn't have antibiotics, we didn't have all those sorts of things. So you would definitely see a death.'

Even now, Mexicans honour those who have passed on, with *Día de los Muertos* (Day of the Dead). It's a healthy practice; one that celebrates the natural tides of life, rather than dreads them.

Stacey goes on to make an interesting observation about how humans struggle with death – they have a difficult time even farewelling pets. She recommends that people with a pet that has been euthanased bring it home. 'You wash its paws, you prepare the body, you give it flowers, you get your kids to cut some fur off it to keep. You see, especially for kids . . . it's not horrible, he's just not here anymore. He's gone to the next [place], whatever your belief system is.'

Stacey has done this for friends, as a friend not as a paid service. 'I've done it for my own pets and I found it incredibly helpful because to actually make the decision to take the life of an animal that's been with you for fifteen years as a friend is horrendous for most people. They can't handle it. So shouldn't we honour that creature in some way?'

The pet should be wrapped up, it may be cremated. This takes away the charge of death – it's not as frightening.

Stacey tears up as she talks about her own pets who have passed. 'Generally, I've been holding them . . . and I've sung them out.' But the tears aren't of sadness, just 'the beauty of it'.

Pagans also sing when ushering in new life. Stacey has been present at many births, where they sing songs of welcome and joy and a beautiful earth as the baby enters the world. 'And look what you've got to look forward to. You're coming and we all love you . . . Come on, let's go. And that's before the baby even breaches, we're singing it in so that it's tempted to come out. And it's the same with death. We have rites of passage.'

It's all about cycles. 'Because I've always been very nature-orientated, I've seen there's a cycle out there. And to be frightened of it or to ignore it never made a lot of sense to me.'

For some people, such easy communion with life cycles beyond our control is far from achievable. My best friend, Jo, is one such person. She has difficulty coming to terms with the finality of life. She feels overcome at the idea of death – the reality of never being able to see someone again, to hug them, to speak to them. To Jo, ageing equals dying. 'I've always been that way,' she tells me one day. 'From the moment life begins, it's ending. It's a countdown. I'm so aware of being here, but is when you go predetermined?'

I think of Gawande's similar, stirring observation in *Being Mortal*: 'There's no escaping the tragedy of life, which is that we are all ageing from the day we are born. One may even come to understand and accept this fact.'

I only discover, in the process of drawing out Jo's thoughts and fears on ageing and all it entails, that her realism about life, her sense of endings, is a pervasive worry.

'My favourite song is "Forever Young". I cry when I hear that song,' she tells me mournfully. 'Do you know the one?'

We've always been silly together so she freely begins to belt out the chorus. I join in: *for-ever young.*

As it turns out, Jo does want to be forever young. The morning sunrise brings with it possibility and enthusiasm for the day ahead. Sunset extinguishes her positive mood. Another day gone, fading away. She is emphatic in her response to whether she's afraid of getting old. 'One hundred per cent.'

I talk to Dr Naganathan about people's fears around death. I tell him how the vast majority express little direct fear around their demise; that their anxieties float in a sea of worrying possibilities: a life of dependence on others, a low-quality life, a life that isn't the one they have come to know and cherish.

Dr Naganathan smiles at this. He has some insight on how old people who have disease view death. 'When people are asked, "How do you want to die?" everyone says, "I just want to drop dead in my sleep." But you know . . . statistically . . . it happens to less people. Actually, people end up with lots of diseases at the last stage of their life.'

He also wants to address the question. 'I suppose I'm prepared for that at some point in my life. If I live long enough, that probably will happen.'

'Does it scare you? Seeing it every day?'

'No, no, I don't think so. No, I don't think it scares me. And I don't think for many people it scares them . . . how it influences people is that they probably know the importance, when they reach a certain age, of setting their advance care directives and planning and talking to people around them . . . people in health probably are more aware of the importance of doing that, I think.'

I did speak to one woman who described what could arguably be termed a 'good death'. Ginger, a social justice journalist, who faced her own mortality when she had cancer in her thirties (and nearly died due to a hospital error), was there in her father's final moments. She says she has done a lot of reporting on death and dying. 'Why do we deal with it so badly?' she queries, before reflecting on how some cultures view death, perhaps more positively. 'Like, if you think about the way the Irish deal with death, historically when they're keening they've got the body there for days and everybody comes, and they tell stories about the dead person and it's very much a part of life.'

Ginger points to 'the real deep, the kind of entrenched discomfort' humans feel about death.

For an award-winning radio project in 2003, she gazed at death from different angles. She prepared a body with a mortician, she visited a hospice and interviewed a dying woman, she spoke to the volunteers, and she watched a body being burned at a crematorium.

'Just fun stuff, right?' I say lightly.

But Ginger says there were a lot of funny moments in the radio project. 'I interviewed this amazing gravedigger who was probably one of the funniest people I've ever met. The thing was about it, it was so full of life, it was so beautiful.'

'I love that. A story about death was so full of life.'

'It was just so human, and it taught me so much about being alive. The people who worked with dead people every day, or dying people, they had an indescribable humanity about them, and so looking through that lens it's hard to understand why we're scared, and why we're awkward around people who are incredibly ill or dying.'

Ginger says that her father's death was actually 'the most beautiful experience'. 'We stayed with his body for a couple of days, and that again was so much medical kindness.'

He was in a small regional hospital, but he wanted to be at home when he died, on his property, which featured a native garden he had spent years cultivating. The hospital called for an ambulance, but Ginger says they expected he would die in the hospital. 'It was the most beautiful hospital because on the ground floor there was all wind blowing through it, so it was really full of air, and he was rasping and rasping and we thought he was going to die here in the hospital and we wanted to get him home.'

When the ambulance turned up, Ginger's mother apologised to the paramedics and told them to go back – she felt it was too late. 'Those ambos said, "No, we're going to wait for you, we're going to wait."'

Another kindness followed when the head nurse came in and, placing a hand on the shoulder of Ginger's mum, said, 'I'm so sorry for what you're going through.'

'And it seems like a really small thing, right? But because I've been in big hospitals – and I nearly died in a big hospital because of mistakes that were made there – that moment of compassion is so rare . . . and important, and I thought, she probably sees this every day, but she's taken this time to say this.'

Ginger's father picked up the tiniest amount, prompting the paramedic to say, 'Okay, let's go. We'll get him home for you.'

I think of how many people wish for a quiet death, a peaceful exit in their own bed, and how rare it is.

'They put him in the ambulance and they gave him quite a lot of oxygen, and that was amazing too because I thought it serves no other purpose than getting him home to die.'

They delivered her father home, and put the hospital bed beside his window. 'He was in front of his amazing garden and we said to him, "You know Dad, it's okay, you're here, you're home, you're in front of your banksias, you can see them all, you can die now."'

He died on the day of the Melbourne Cup, while the race was on. 'It was kind of amazing because he loved the Melbourne Cup. We just all sat around with him . . . in this very beautiful way, telling stories about him, talking to him, holding his hand. My daughter had been taken out of the room, because she was two and a half, but she came and gave him a cuddle. We explained that he was dead, and that his body was broken and he wasn't going to get better again. It wasn't scary, it wasn't morbid. It was actually the most wonderful goodbye.'

Ginger's father loved wine, so the family retrieved a bottle out of his cellar. We both tear up as she recounts the story. 'It lasted a long time, so it was sad, but it was happy, you know? It's incredible that we got him home, and we only got him home because of that medical kindness.'

8.

RETIREMENT LIVING

Brian Eno's Oblique Strategies advises: 'Fill every beat with something'. It's a cure for writer's block, but sometimes it feels like a guide to life.

Friday

In my parents' yard, Dad's plants thrive. The large lemon tree of my youth is long gone, but the row of hydrangeas down the side of the house blooms each year. A small rosemary bush remains, as do a variety of pretty flowers and the lattice of vine leaves my dad occasionally picks for Mum. There are new additions: a herb garden, corn stalks and pot plants.

My dad tends his garden in his going-out clothes. He doesn't dress appropriately for the earth work of a gardener. He eschews the need for gloves and is puzzled when he suffers a cut. And he gardens in snatches – on his way out the door; on a quiet afternoon after he's done exploring his city. Some-times I'll be in the driver's seat, warming up the car, watching as Dad bends down to snatch out weeds from the ground, ripping out the old to make way for the new.

Dad was a gardener and landscape designer in the early days of his life in Australia. He speaks of those days often – the beautiful gardens he tended around Sydney; the people he met, not always friendly to him when they discovered his heritage. The way he managed to travel to jobs on a Vespa, transporting a minimal amount of equipment on the back of it. Ten dollars a day for gardening work, riding from the eastern suburbs over the bridge to the north shore.

I try to imagine Dad zipping around on a white Vespa, Mum in her trendy short dresses and heels sitting behind him, clutching on for dear life. My parents were once young and cool?

They had the Vespa for five years, until a thief relived them of it. (Just as well – Mum was pregnant.)

My father isn't a man of hobbies. He's a man of hard work. But he loves his garden, so it blooms, and I document it. Every summer I look forward to the majesty of the fig tree that stands in the yard outside my former bedroom window. Every year I monitor its progress. Every year I try to pluck the figs before the birds peck at them. Every year I fail. Last year we tried hoisting a giant net over the tree. The birds still managed to swoop in and feast on the fruit. Mum doesn't mind. She used to feed the pigeons so well, they grew too fat to fly. Eventually she stopped.

This year, I buy Dad citrus trees for the garden – mandarin and lemon. Alex buys him a portable shed, and Mum rolls her eyes to the heavens. Where to put it? Dad won't use it. Et cetera, et cetera. How does anyone do Christmas?

Mum as curator has lost the battle over the greenhouse, but she draws the line at the fishing rods also purchased by Alex and his family. Dad has been known to buy things that never get used. We chuckle about the rods ending up with the violin he acquired years ago, now gathering dust. Alex finally persuades Dad to buy a nice camera, because he likes to take snaps on his phone. It's sitting there, still unused.

Dr Naganathan, the geriatrician, warned me that older people don't change in the essentials, and that the hope of a parent taking on fulfilling hobbies might be more detrimental than helpful if they've never been the sort to do this. A 'conflict of expectations', he called it. 'Dad wants this; daughter wants this.' It's partly about guilt. He runs through a common scenario. Father and daughter come in. Father has medical problems. He's a widower. The daughter beseeches Dr Naganathan to have a word with her father – urge him to go out more and go to men's clubs, though her father isn't interested.

'I have a chat with him, and ask, "Did you go out to clubs and to the pub [in years before now]?" and he'll say, "You know what? My wife liked doing all of this. I never particularly liked it, and I'd only do things with her anyway. And I did it to please her, and . . . I didn't mind going with her. But I'm not the kind of guy who ever went and hung out with my mates and did that. I really like my own company."

'So I then take the daughter aside and go, "You know what? People reach a certain age. You don't suddenly change your personality. Is part of this that you're feeling bad that your father's alone, and you're feeling guilty? You realistically can't be expected to go and be there the whole time for him. Mum's died and so part of it is your own [guilt]." And it's daughters who generally want to be more helpful to Dad. There's a real strong bond between daughters and fathers. I've observed that. Daughters want to help their dads. I think that's a very natural thing. But [sometimes] it causes conflict. So I would like to think I'm being helpful when I point that out.'

The other common issue is when kids believe that their parents going out and using their brain will help stave off dementia. A classic example: the daughter shoving crosswords on to her father who is forgetting things but has no interest, and never had any interest, in crosswords. A desperate daughter looking to unverified solutions.

'What I say to people is the evidence that doing crosswords will somehow prevent dementia from getting worse is [scientifically] weak. But more importantly, I'd hate to think that [the] father–daughter relationship has degenerated to this,' Dr Naganathan says. Sure enough, upon further enquiry he almost always discovers that this insistence is leading to fights. Dr Naganathan tells the pair that as these activities aren't going to make a difference, why not just enjoy each other's company?

It's not difficult to travel mentally, in conversations like this, to my experiences of similar challenges. My relationship with my father grew more peaceful when I accepted that he's not a person who values hobbies. It wasn't fair of me to expect him to be anyone but who he is. I could not take it personally when he didn't blossom anew based on my advice.

I think back to a conversation with Mum one Friday. 'Ask your father what his personality should be like in your book,' she tells me. She clearly has her own ideas about this but we both know what will tumble out of Dad's mouth, and he doesn't disappoint.

'Hard working,' he says, and nothing more.

Dad's currency has always been work. And when he could no longer work, he felt emptied out, lost. He never longed for retirement. He has always been a hard worker, and without that as a purpose he feels frustrated and aimless. So many people say their fathers were the same. So many stories echoing each other, bumping up against invisible, nameless forces.

A lot of things begin to lose their shape and structure with age. Health and vigour diminish; perhaps people feel less needed, no longer a valued employee in a workplace; families grow but often apart. Older people may view themselves through a lens of decline rather than growth and achievement. They have peaked and now it's a downhill slide.

You may come to understand what fuelled a person, where they held their self-worth, by how they age.

Everyone has their stories; rarely will they merely travel through life as an observer, or professional, a fixer. This is evident with every interview I do, including those with medical professionals. They all willingly share personal stories – their parents' ageing process. Their family relationships. A doctor and I compare notes on having fathers who love work.

'He had to have a trial-run retirement, because it didn't work for him and he had to go back to work,' he tells me.

'What does a trial-run retirement look like?'

'Oh, he retired and he was so stressed that . . . he found he was looking at job ads, and then he just decided to go back to work.'

'Was he too young to retire? Was that it?'

'He probably was, and he probably couldn't set aside his own expectations, or I think he just – like you're suggesting – he identified too strongly with the person who worked, and he couldn't really see himself as the person who didn't work.'

Dr Naganathan makes another important point. Sometimes fathers, or older people in general, just want their kids to hang out with them. 'The funny thing is, certainly with the men . . . they don't particularly want to talk. They've never been particularly chatty with their children. They want their children around, they want to know that they're all right, because that's still the father instinct. Sometimes more with their daughters. But the children don't particularly want to just sit there, and so they are coming with the expectation that this is going to be good, quality time . . .'

But quality time is a concept of this generation, not necessarily of the previous generation, says Dr Naganathan. This strikes me as a reasonable observation. I'm reminded of Dad telling me he wished I could have breakfast with him and Mum every day. Of how relationships become more important as we age.

'It's about being needed, not needing'

Chiou See Anderson calls me 'little one' and acts like a big sister. Despite the affection in the nickname, she's the tough-love kind, who will give you a kick up the arse rather than sympathy if she senses a deluge of self-pity is imminent. She's the kind of manager who cooks lunch for her staff to ensure that everyone is eating well. And her philosophies on life trickle into the management of her retirement village in Queensland, Elements Retirement Living, where she wants people to live big, and in their truth. 'We have big apartments because we don't want people to live small,' she tells me, as we tour a model apartment. It's spacious, new and beautifully furnished. Chiou See happily decorated it herself.

Despite the resistance many demonstrate to the changes our ageing bodies impose, at some point difficult decisions must be made. Moving house is never easy, particularly for people wedded to the hope of ageing in place, in a home they may have occupied for decades. But a day at a friend's retirement village reveals to me that adaptation and an open mind can yield positive results in the right hands.

At Chiou See's village inclusiveness and community spirit are important. She fosters an environment of respect for differences – and she lectures her residents on that. 'One time I had two ladies come into my village and they go, "Oh, do you have Muslims in this village?" I said, "You know what, I grew up in Singapore and I have a lot of Muslim friends, I have Hindu friends, I have all sorts of friends. If that's your attitude, then this isn't the village for you."'

Chiou See interviews all her applicants. 'If you open your mouth and say, "I hate Muslims" or "I hate Chinese", then it's game over. You cannot come in . . . because you'll just create trouble all the time. Why are Muslims any better or any worse than the Baptist people?'

I've known Chiou See for several years. We met at a retirement living and aged care conference back when I was an editor on a property industry publication. We were in a room packed with property people, mainly men, and she stood out – a brassy Asian-Australian woman with a sense of humour and a no-nonsense approach to business. We immediately hit it off.

It was around 2012 and the property players were peering into the collective future of Australia's ageing population, assessing where the value propositions lay from an industry perspective. A distillation of sorts was occurring, as was a seeding of new possibilities when it came to getting old and being taken care of. How to pay for our ageing population to live well? To be cared for in facilities when needed? How to create profitable industries that served community needs? What role, if any, could industry superannuation funds play in the establishment of facilities for the ageing?

For many, it's only in recent years that a clear differentiation has been made between the varying needs of ageing people. Aged care is a vastly different prospect to retirement living, and the two should not be conflated. Within aged care, there are tiers – the patients who require high-level care, who may be suffering from dementia; know themselves only through the photos of their younger self. Then there are your lower-care nursing homes: they're not appealing options, even less so when you consider that often their residents may deteriorate further because they don't require full-time care but are constantly bored and unstimulated.

Chiou See is focused on creating a pre-emptive solution to a nursing home, and an older person's declining lifestyle within one, rather than bandaging over a problem: her retirement living is centred on community, social life, activity and hope. A prevention rather than a cure for the isolation and physical deterioration old age threatens.

'I have not had one case of dementia in my village,' she tells me, explaining that this is why she emphasises the need for social interactions, for 'playing' in the village.

This isn't to say no resident has ever had dementia. Chiou See is pointing out that no one has developed it under her care. 'When you live in a community, you actually have to do things. It's about being needed, not needing.'

Because one partner in a couple is usually a carer, Chiou See watches out for carer-fatigue syndrome. 'I never worry about the one with dementia; I worry about the one who's caring for the one who has dementia.'

Chiou See will ask that carer questions like: how are you? Are you looking after yourself? Are you eating? Are your children rotating in and out with you? Are you getting out? Are you getting your hair done? And she'll offer to sit with one partner while the other is getting her hair done. You need to get out or you'll get sick.

'People age differently. So there'll always be one more dominant or a healthier partner who ends up carrying the burden. It's unfortunate.'

In one unique case, the couple is co-caring. Recent arrivals Adrian, sixty-three, and Cynthia, a year younger, both have schizophrenia. They have been married for nearly three decades, and monitor each other's symptoms. Adrian is a poet – he hands me self-published books. He likes to keep to himself. Cynthia is enjoying some peace, finally, after years of struggle, keen to socialise with Elements residents, fretting about not burning the roast when her son comes over on the weekend with his new girlfriend.

They offer only kind words about each other; they have weathered many storms together, including suicidal periods suffered by Cynthia. In fact, it's how they met – after an attempt, she reached out to Adrian and another, who led a community group for people with schizophrenia. Adrian sat with Cynthia. 'I thought she was a very worthwhile person.'

Adrian reads aloud a poem he wrote about Cynthia, a whimsical take on the joy of ordinary life – Cynthia cooking, smiling. 'She's so brave,' he says. 'Her smile is just so brave. Even when things are bad and terrible, she's brave.' Cynthia's response is shyness. 'Well, you're my hero, too, darl. You are indeed.'

Chiou See is motivated to help people steer their lives towards a fulfilling end of life. 'I would consider that my people should not have to go into nursing homes. I would consider that I can create that care environment and bring enough care into my village not to let them go into a nursing home.'

I ask her how she can achieve this: sometimes bodies just fail us. No number of pools, community centres and Japanese Zen gardens (the village has all three) will necessarily change that.

'I don't believe in a nursing home concept. I already have partnerships with nurses who come in to provide care to my residents. So my job will be to facilitate, bringing care into their home and not putting them in a nursing home. And that means I will have to be more hands-on in watching and coordinating,' she says.

'And I say to all of my residents, "My wish is that you die with me. That is my ultimate wish. I do not wish for you to leave me to die somewhere else. You should die in this village."'

✦

For years Chiou See has encouraged me to visit her burgeoning community, which is nestled in the Queensland bush of Springwood. It's a short drive from Brisbane Airport, where

Chiou See picks me up and immediately launches into her plans for the day. Not surprisingly, she's taken my brief – to gather a variety of perspectives and experiences of ageing (and please, I need more men!) – and delivered.

In her village, Chiou See zips around in a buggy, greeting anyone she passes, including construction workers who continue diligently in the rain building a new home. As a witness to these casual interactions, it's evident just how embedded Chiou See is here. And it becomes abundantly clear within a day how much her ownership and manage-ment of Elements factor into people's decisions to retire here. Some people, I discover, were on her radar for years. She has brought in residents with whom she's established a rapport – widows, couples with one reluctant but the other not. She wonders at how she ever managed to get her first few buyers when Elements was nothing more than an off-the-plan project that would take a few years to build (literally) and then a few more years to grow (people-wise). She has achieved financial success; now she is people-focused. The goals have changed from financial imperatives to altruistic purposes.

'It's almost like the Maslow hierarchy of needs, where you've got the food, shelter sorted, and now you're looking for a more altruistic reason. So I can go and volunteer in some not-for-profit, or I can turn back inwards and look after my own people, people who have actually trusted me enough to buy into my product even though they knew I didn't belong to one of those big listed companies; that any day I could have gone bankrupt and what they bought into could have been drastically changed. But they came along for the ride and I'm so close to all of them.'

Chiou See knows everyone's medical problems. 'Do you know that when they press their medical emergency at night,

I get the phone call? I get a phone call before their children get a phone call. And they know that I'm watching, and I'm forever watching.'

Hearing this confirms my belief that it's her authenticity that draws people to Chiou See. 'I do not patronise residents. I'll say, "Get off your arse – if you want something done, get off your arse and move those blinking chairs,"' she tells me. 'And I see that as a form of enablement. I can say, "Poor [such-and-such]. Stay there, I'll get the chairs for you." I go "No, there's nothing wrong with you. You might take a bit longer. Can you get off your arse and start putting the chairs away?" And they all do it. I say, "If you have the energy to have a party, you can vacuum the floor."'

More than keeping the residents active, it's about engaging them on equal terms. And this is what she tells them: there's nothing wrong with you. 'You have all day to do it. But you have to be responsible.'

She takes a similar approach to the loss of a loved one. She doesn't indulge in pity. She never cries with residents. She encourages them to see where new life and opportunity lie.

Chiou See talks about death a lot – how she deals with it, and how she's trying to combat a tendency to believe that a person's departure from this earthly realm must be a 'bad' one.

It's isolation, helplessness and illness that degrades life, and at Elements there's a focus on living a 'normal' life. The point isn't that you're old; it's that you can still function as you would, with more support and activities aimed at the things you're capable of with an ageing body.

Gawande's *Being Mortal* is like her bible; his insightful exploration of what it means to prolong life when suffering may be involved. He asks at what cost, and why, if the purpose isn't to prolong a *good* quality of life. It's a tricky area, full of shades of grey. Dying with dignity, euthanasia, palliative care – who decides how a person leaves this earth, and how do we make sure it's the person on their way out who has control of it?

'*Being Mortal* taught me how to look at dying from the dying person's perspective,' Chiou See says. She notes how all of the deaths in the book were horrible, 'which was nobody's fault. It's just so strange that he was surrounded by people who did not die well.'

Gawande documents his own father's decline due to unexpected illness. A heartbreaking, personal reckoning that has shaped his perspectives. 'And his father also suffered the same kind of old people's disease that is inflicted on people who are less educated,' Chiou See muses.

'But doesn't that just show that nobody's superhuman? That even though he was a doctor, there was nothing he could do about it?' I suggest.

Here, Chiou See wrestles with an inconsistency: why bother looking after yourself, exercising well, getting educated and fit in the hopes of ageing well if the fates are going to get you? I realise that this all ties in with her mission statement – to provide a safe, joyful space for people to grow old in, together, and surrounded by a solid, functioning community. In her ideal world people age gracefully and well. They do not become afflicted with dementia. They don't die of crippling illness.

'I thought that was a bit depressing [in the book]. Here I am telling people to exercise, to eat well, to live well, and . . . then it all comes to nought because if cancer can strike you so randomly and all those things, what incentive do we have when we cannot even prevent cancer?' She searched for answers in the genealogy of Gawande's patients – they all had cancer, or they were from his wife's side. 'They all got premature diseases. Not just general wear and tear.'

But she feels strongly that death is not designed to torment you. Very casually, and more than once, she riffs on the idea that she could die at any moment and it wouldn't bother her. 'I'm quite happy to die today. Because I don't think of life as a joy. I enjoy my life but I don't think life is a joy, I think life is a task and you've got to get work done. So if I have to wake up the next day, that means I've got to do more work. If I die tonight, that's good – it means I don't have to work tomorrow.'

She believes that how a person goes through the process of dying influences how others deal with their death. She offers up recent cases – four men, village residents, who have passed away – and her observations about the people these men left behind – more specifically, their wives. Chiou See says those who are left behind don't generally require special care or support. She indicates that what follows is a liberation of sorts: sadness at loss, yes, but perhaps also a sense of relief at the end of suffering.

I think of some Red Hat Society women I once observed: white-haired dames in bright red hats, congregating over lunch in Brisbane, catching up on laughter and fun. Like it had all been bottled up and could finally burst free. We do that, don't we? Wait for some magically 'right' time for life to begin, to feel free, to be happy.

Chiou See doesn't try to offer the ones left behind a lot of sympathy. 'I'm trying to teach them that this is good. It's good for the person going, and it's good for you. Because now you can look after yourself. Don't be silly. You've already spent so much time with him or her . . .'

Of course, people do get lonely. Chiou See says the stages of loneliness aren't avoidable. 'But the more important thing is when they're ready to play, and when they want to play, it's all here for you to play with. I've never cried with them,

I've never felt sad with them. I just think it's a great opportunity for the ones left behind to get on with their lives.'

+

Chiou See takes me to the community centre, a spacious room with a library and kitchen in which a fridge is stocked with bottles of alcohol (operating on an honour system). The centre brims with social activities – everything from exercise classes to arts and crafts. She proudly points out the impressive works of her residents. Nearby is a hair salon (priced reasonably for the retirees), and a pool with a ramp. Up the road is a workshop, mainly used and taken care of by the men (though it's open to all).

The day I visit, the village is set up for Christmas, with tinsel and animals fashioned out of ropes of light, lights decorating every home ready for a Christmas event the next day. It's missing the snow, but it looks like Santa's village. However, it's the Japanese Zen garden that I find most impressive. It's not imitation Zen – Chiou See paid gardeners and designers from Japan to construct a genuine Zen space, complete with a *Kamigake* (God's Gate) to ward off evil and maintain purity and warmth; a tall weeping willow near the entrance; a pond and waterfalls; and a tea house (though residents tend to drink wine there, not tea, Chiou See grumbles).

Placards explain the meanings behind every plant, tree and waterfall. 'Streams', one reads. 'The streams of both waterfalls are purposefully different. The first male stream is winding and represents exploration and caution . . .'

It's not just couples Chiou See accommodates. Sometimes friends move in together – widows, for example. She recently had one such pair purchase an apartment. Chiou See worked tirelessly with her lawyers to create a fair contract that would protect the younger, healthier one, who was 'assuming a huge responsibility'.

In fact, it's her prediction for retirement living: widows moving in together, a new life.

'I like silence, to tell you the truth'

It's only been ten days, and Charles, who's seventy-five, is struggling a little with the move to his new place at Elements, about half an hour from his previous home of eight years.

'Still hard to get my head around it,' he says, with the hint of a chuckle. He admires his view – towering trees, bush as far as the eye can see; but it's not the scene he once enjoyed, a panoramic view of the bay. It's little things like this he is trying to adapt to and appreciate. It's nice in the bush, but it's different.

He mentions more than once the challenge of downsizing, because it's not simply a smaller space to inhabit – despite Chiou See's aim to provide large apartments – it's still, in a way, a smaller life for some people.

His wife, Cath, has Parkinson's disease, and two years ago suffered a stroke during a surgery. The move, Charles says, was only decided on six weeks earlier.

'Things were getting a bit hard and I thought Cath might get a little bit more attached to other people and things to do . . .'

'Have community?'

'Have community, yeah.'

Charles speaks thoughtfully, often pausing, but by his own admission he's not much of a talker. He seems almost pained at times, but I'm not sure if it's the downsizing or that he's being asked to speak to this stranger with a recorder and a notepad.

'It's a big life change for me from two years ago . . .'

Part of the struggle seems to lie in the suddenness of it all.

The loss of his familiar life – the shock of the new. 'I had no time to think about it . . . This happened quick.'

Retired and a father of two, Charles, a Vietnam veteran, was a truck driver for close to thirty-five years. He loves driving. Even now, he'll take long drives, enjoying the empty stretches of road ahead.

'I like silence, to tell you the truth. I'll live in my own little space, watch the countryside go by . . . It was a hard life but we did all right. I can't complain.'

Charles's day begins with caring for Cath – helping her shower and dress. 'Because she's very confused. Some days she doesn't even know which clothes to put on, where to find her undies or things like that. She just can't comprehend what's going on. And the next day, good as gold,' he says, with a laugh.

Cath's deteriorated condition is the result of deep brain stimulation to treat her Parkinson's, which led to a bleed and the stroke two years ago, Charles explains. It was a difficult experience that hasn't got easier. Charles's life was, in reality, downsized from that time. Hobbies, like golf, are no longer viable pursuits. He doesn't feel comfortable leaving Cath alone for more than a couple of hours. They sold their caravan but plan to travel – a couple of cruises in the next year or two. 'She says no, no, no, but if we go, she'll like it, I'm sure,' Charles says. 'But at the moment I'm just mucking around here, trying to get rid of some more stuff.' He chuckles, like he's laughing uncomfortably at the ludicrousness of circumstance. Later, he reflects on the challenge of reducing the props of your life – it's hard, he tells me, to get rid of things that hold value.

'Being here, in a way I feel a bit . . . closed in. But it's only been nearly two weeks, you've got to get used to it. There are lots of nice people here I've talked to and met. I'm sure I'll get used to it.'

'Do you think that being here will help in terms of having a bit more time for yourself?'

'I hope so. We haven't got involved here yet because we're still organising ourselves, but there seems to be plenty to do . . . and we just have to . . . fit in and see what we like to do.'

His own interests are simple: going off in his fishing boat; playing a round of golf (easier when he lived two minutes away from a golf course); and reading. He just likes fiddling about, if attending to home duties allows him the time to do so. But even simple hobbies are affected by the lifestyle changes his wife's condition has introduced. In an hour life irreversibly changed. 'I never thought this would happen to us . . .'

Charles describes the stage pre-operation where his wife was dealing with Parkinson's as 'not too bad'. It was after the surgery that everything became more difficult. Cath still functions, Charles says, but she gets confused at times. She used to crochet. Her day would begin with the radio. Now she doesn't listen to it at all. Crosswords puzzles, once a regular pleasure, no longer figure in her life. She struggles to find words: 'She keeps saying, "You know what I mean, you know what I mean." But that's the way it is.' Charles laughs. 'I've got a lot more patient than I used to be. You can't live the way you used to.' And he draws support from his wife's family and his own. 'I don't feel alone. If I called one of her sisters, she'd be here in half an hour.'

Their children and grandchildren are also involved in their lives, though distance can affect how regularly they see each other.

Charles hopes that Cath will create attachments at the village, people she can talk to. 'But not run their doors down. That's what I'm hoping for. Maybe it's asking a lot, but at least she gets to do things at the community centre.'

He has a chuckle at how his situation varies from the norm – wives looking after their husbands. Indeed, he's one of the few men I speak to who is older, able-bodied and a carer. He's healthy at seventy-five, active, able to take walks in the bush.

We're ready to wrap up when he apologises for not being more effusive and open. But talking about the past isn't easy for him. In fact, he refused to discuss Vietnam until 1991, nearly thirty years after he completed his tour of duty. An ex-army mate contacted him about a gathering in Townsville. After that, Charles got involved. 'It's released me, put it that way.'

Every month Vietnam veterans get together, thirty to forty people. 'It's really a stronger bond than your brothers and sisters. They watched your back for twelve months and you watched their back for twelve months. It's hard to describe, and nobody can say, "I know how you feel." It's just not possible. You haven't got a clue,' he says, more passionately than I've seen in our conversation. 'That is a real outlet for us.' His wife loves to go, too, he adds. The women look after Cath. 'Let's put it this way, I don't have to look after her for four or five hours. She gets looked after. She's always loved that.'

Charles gets up and disappears into another room, returning a minute later with several black and white photos from his childhood (he's one of nine children); one of Cath when she was young, pretty and blonde; and a few snaps from Vietnam. In one, a handsome young man stands, bare-chested, in army pants and boots, dog tags around his neck, a cigarette in his hand, as he poses with an expression that suggests neither happiness nor displeasure. He looks as though he's about to say something. In another, he sits on grass beside a mate in front of an army truck, both smiling into the camera, their breakfast kit in front of them.

'You were a handsome fella,' I remark.

Charles shrugs, modest. 'Some people say I was,' he replies. 'Do you still have the dog tags?'

'I have. I still have my pay book,' he says, breaking out into full, throaty laughter. 'You find a lot of these things when you're moving.' His brother has scanned the photos and saved them onto a USB, he tells me, and he looks at them on the television.

Charles shows me a more recent photo of Cath. She's aged gracefully – you can see the same woman in both the old and newer photos, the same smile.

'How did you meet your wife?'

'Well, there were two girls walking down the road one day, and I had a little car and I turned and did a U-ey!' He laughs again.

He tells me he commissioned a painting of the black-and-white photo of Cath in her youth and retrieves a large frame in which the full-colour picture sits. Married six months before he went to Vietnam, Charles paid an artist in Vietnam to paint Cath's image. 'Because that photo went with me . . . [The painting] cost me $15.'

Once again, I'm taken aback by the energy of the photos. Proof of experiences that slip into mythology as we age. I thank Charles for sharing them with me. He's quiet for a moment, looking a bit sad. 'I get emotional, but that's the way it is.'

'There's a lot of co-dependency'

Geoff has no qualms admitting that he came to Elements 'kicking and screaming'.

'I used every excuse known to man not to come here.'

He's seventy-four, retired, and has been living at Elements for three years, with his wife, Julie, who is ten years his junior. They are unique for the forward planning that shaped their decision to move in to a retirement village. I would venture to argue that, in some ways, they are taking the 'ideal' approach to graceful retirement.

We're in the staff room at Elements, eating a lunch cooked by Chiou See. Julie and Geoff sit opposite each other at the large table, ready to share their experiences. They are funny, not always intentionally, exhibiting a kind of lovable tension – Geoff brims with sardonic observations, while Julie displays a stoic thoughtfulness. They frequently finish each other's sentences, one half-sentence flowing into the next. Julie is quieter; she gives the sense of someone who has experienced her share of challenges, and for whom a pleasant retirement is her gift to herself. And, as both Julie and Geoff like to point out, they expect her to outlive him.

Between us sits Chiou See, and the teasing runs merciless and thick. When I ask Geoff what attracted him to Julie, he responds, 'I haven't the slightest idea. I'm still working on that.'

Married for thirty-four years, for both it's their second marriage. They have no children together (a conscious decision), but Julie has two from her first marriage.

I commend them on their number of years as a couple. 'That's not bad,' I say.

'Not *now*,' says Julie.

'Not recently,' affirms Geoff.

They have no secret recipe to happiness, both being on their second marriages. They admit to not having a conventional relationship. When asked if they consider their marriage a good one, Julie says it's 'different'.

'We're not like an ordinary run-of-a-mill couple that live in a retirement village. I know that. That's good,' says Julie.

'What are you seeing in others that you're not seeing in yourselves?'

'We're not normal,' replies Julie.

'What's normal?' I ask.

'Well, to me it's like a couple who, I don't know . . . the bloke does stuff and the woman does stuff.'

'Let's put it another way,' says Geoff. 'These people that we've met here and we know, you can guarantee are a certain type. It's five pm, "Oh, I can't ring them now. They'll be having tea," or such and such, so and so. Then they're walking at a certain time. We don't do any of that.'

They are also friends, adds Geoff.

'I think probably a good way to describe it is they are not co-dependent,' says Chiou See. 'I think that comes up a lot in relationships. There's a lot of co-dependency.'

Julie says she's not the type for Valentine's Day affectations, despite being moved by it in those around her. 'I don't want to be like that, but I know people who are. If something happens to Geoff first, I'll be shattered. I'll be absolutely shattered, but I will know that the things we did together were enough. That was great. A lifetime of stuff.'

'You can look back on the bad, or you can look back on the good,' says Geoff. 'It's up to you which one you want to choose.'

Julie reflects on how, upon meeting Geoff, she could imagine them growing old together. 'When I got married the first time, I was seventeen and the person I married was fifteen years older than me. Then I got pregnant, and on and on and on. My life was on a roller-coaster, didn't stop . . . And when I met Geoff, I could imagine . . . looking into the future; I could imagine getting older with Geoff. My only fear was he wouldn't live long enough because of the way he was abusing himself. There were many times when I thought I would have to get out of it because I couldn't stand to see it anymore. The only time that I was really serious, and Geoff knew, we ended up at a psychologist.'

'Got in with a couple of them.'

'Thankfully it was somebody that Geoff could actually listen to. That's when he decided he'd do something about it.'

'I made a choice. I went to AA. I've done the whole bit. Now I don't. I could easily slip back, but here it's good.'

'It just made me sad. I know the person underneath all that. That's not him,' says Julie.

✦

It was a story in Brisbane's *Sunday Mail*, written by Chiou See, in which she spoke of her vision for her retirement village, that first caught Julie's attention. The idea of it sat in her. When she paid a visit the village was incomplete, but she loved the setting. However, at the time the village didn't allow pets. 'We had two dogs, so I sort of discounted it. Then Chiou See came in here . . . and she was in a big hurry to get down the coast to . . .'

'Pick up the kids,' chimes in Geoff.

'Pick up her children, but she still made enough time to actually speak to us.'

Julie's dog now lives with them at Elements. Chiou See realised her residents tended to be pet-lovers. She commissioned a new report to work on the pet problem – previously there were restrictions due to the local fauna. 'It was a long-winded process . . . There was this big war about "Oh my God, we've got to protect all the koalas." It was a blanket protection policy, not an informed protection policy.'

It took three years to convice Geoff to move to Elements. He puts it down to male ego, rather than fear of losing himself. He had built the home he lived in for thirty-odd years. But, he admits, their social life wasn't as functional as their house. They had friends, but not a huge cross-section of them.

'Did you have an idea in your mind of what you wanted your life to look like or did it just sneak up on you?' I ask.

'No. Logic dictates that I would probably, because I'm older . . . go first,' says Geoff. 'Me being who I am, I thought if we moved in now, I'd get the benefit of being here while I'm still young and handsome and . . . Half of that's right.'

As a couple, Julie and Geoff would visit Elements, but they weren't residents. Eventually Chiou See delivered an ultimatum of sorts to Geoff – no more attending functions in the village until he got his cheque book out. In Geoff's defence, he says, the place was still being built. 'There was nowhere for me to live, and I wasn't going to camp out. I didn't like it that much.'

'He kept changing his mind whether he wanted to live here, and he would've lived as far away into the forest as possible because it was the last building built,' explains Julie. 'He did not want to come at all.'

But one well-constructed home and an appealing community later, they are settled in.

Is it generally the woman who's driving the move to the village, I wonder. 'Generally,' says Chiou See. 'Occasionally we have a few males who want to come and then the women don't come, but probably 80/20. Eighty per cent of the time it will be the husbands resisting, which is normal.'

There's quite a bit involved in moving in, says Geoff. He wasn't going to compromise on his garden shed, but he's pleased to report he has twice as much as room in the garage.

It was easy to physically make the change, Julie says. Although, she doesn't think she's a good people person – she doesn't do well in groups. 'It seems funny, strange moving into a community, but I moved because of lifestyle as well. I wanted a change. I didn't want to spend my life in the one place looking at the one street and the same people.'

So she had no fears coming to Elements, and the major drawcard was lifestyle. 'I didn't want to come here and wait to die or wait to go on to the next step in aged care. I wanted to come here and actually live and enjoy what we had to enjoy.'

And Geoff has discovered that what he could do in the outside world he can do in his new home. 'There's been no difference for me because I've always repaired things. People break things. I fix them. That's always been the same. Even here, hasn't it? When something goes wrong here, quite often Chiou See will call me.'

'Because I have to,' says Chiou See. 'I'm trying to give you a purpose in life.'

9.

ON COUNTRY

*Who is your kin? **We aren't always connected by blood.***

My explorations have led me to the heart of Australia, where issues of illness and ageing take on a new significance.

In Alice Springs, the heat soaks into your skin. A sleepy town by day, Alice is blanketed in punishing desert heat, seemingly stuck somewhere in the past. On the drive in, I pass a section of an Old Ghan train, rusted and disregarded by the side of the road. There's an Old Timers museum. Billboards for fast-food joints and an Indian restaurant jar against the town's earthy, humbling landscapes. The sky is a bright blue and even the withered tree trunks are hauntingly picturesque.

I wonder what Mum would think about it. She has expressed a desire to visit Alice in the past. And for a moment I contemplated a trip here with my parents, so my mum could live out her earlier desire to visit the town. But I'm here to work. The reality is, while my parents have experienced many of Australia's various landscapes, I suspect it would be harder now for them to deal with the heat here.

Alice is a place full of people who are far from home. And some are here because they have been diagnosed with renal failure and must undergo dialysis treatment. In central

Australia kidney failure rates are fifteen to thirty times the national average. Out of the coastal centres the survival rates of people on dialysis are improving, but the age they start dialysis is much younger. In the general Australian community most sufferers of kidney failure begin dialysis anywhere between their sixties and eighties. In central Australia, the age range is thirties to fifties.

Alice Springs is a town that tells a story of displacement. The nightmare of being tied to a dialysis machine for life is different, heavier, here. It comes loaded with social and economic factors that aren't shared by all Australians. Remote Indigenous communities have some of the highest rates of chronic disease and preventable illnesses in the world.

It's a focal point for the Honourable Ken Wyatt, the Commonwealth's first Indigenous minister, sworn in as Minister for Indigenous Health and Aged Care under Malcolm Turnbull's government in January 2017. Wyatt wants to reduce the prevalence of otitis media (middle ear infection) in Aboriginal children – according to the World Health Organization, they have the highest rates of otitis media in the world – as well as look at eye health and renal disease. 'We're losing too many people,' he tells me in a phone interview.

The Indigenous health portfolio holds special significance for the minister, a Noongar and Yamatji man from Bunbury in Western Australia, who has worked in Aboriginal health in two states and has always focused on education and health. In October 2017, then prime minister Malcolm Turnbull acknowledged problems with the government's near-decade-long Closing the Gap initiative, a strategy to improve outcomes in health, education and employment for Indigenous people in Australia, all of which consistently fail to meet targets and progress.

President of the Australian Indigenous Doctors Association Dr Kali Hayward has told media, 'It is very important for Aboriginal and Torres Strait Islander doctors to know that there is someone [such as Ken Wyatt] in a position that can effect change and affect decisions being made about Aboriginal and Torres Strait Islander health.'

In May 2018 the Federal Government announced its intention to spend $57.8 million to support Indigenous dialysis patients, which would see a greater number of mobile dialysis units in Indigenous communities. The Purple House, where I'm headed, was allocated $25 million, an amount the CEO, Sarah Brown, told media was 'staggering'. The funding, she said, was a 'game-changer'.

As the minister takes time out of a busy day to speak to me by phone, Wyatt focuses on several key areas: training more Indigenous doctors and nurses; maternal child health, which he says will always remain a priority; and men's health (Wyatt recently lost his cousin, Jason Bartlett, a singer–songwriter who succumbed to end-stage kidney disease aged thirty-six). The minister doesn't discount treatment for renal failure, but he encourages prevention, visits to the GP. 'Because what you want to know is what's happening inside of you, if your kidney's starting to fail . . . You may not be able to turn it around, but how can you slow it down?'

Wyatt recognises the challenges in this, bound by the reality that 'all of us grow up thinking we're immortal'.

'In the past, if I think back say forty thousand years ago, it would've been based around the family – building an understanding of how to care for your body, how to look after yourself, and how to live much longer, and be well and fit. We've gone away from that. Culture is still extremely strong, it'll never diminish. Our country is our country, our community, and the families we're a part of, will always remain that, but our challenge is: how do we take what we have as a strength and use that to build our health to be better?'

A challenge that expands, given there are so many other confronting issues for Indigenous people to deal with. 'We've got gaps in so many parts of our lives [but] if we could just all stop and think: do I want to end up on dialysis? Or is there something I can do at my age that will prevent me becoming attached to a dialysis machine, which I can take responsibility for, and I can change [even if] I will need my GP at times when I'm sick? If we do that, I think we can turn around some of our health challenges.'

Wyatt is refreshingly candid about the lack of money allocated to Aboriginal health. In the months to come, the Federal Government will announce the funding for Indigenous health, but it becomes clear how deep the issues and imbalances run when we speak.

Take a large circle, he says. Draw a very thin line from the edge of the circle to the middle, and you have the total amount of money for Aboriginal health in the big bucket for health. 'But I will continue to fight to increase the amount of funding going into the health of our people in all fronts. And I just want to see our culture, and our knowledge, and our history living much longer because every time we lose an elder, or a senior person, or any individual, we lose incredible knowledge out of our communities.'

Wyatt has visitors from Indigenous communities wanting solutions or advice. 'I enjoy the good conversations. Sometimes I'll get jarred, but that's part of the job that I have. That's also part of me being from our community because people do have expectations of us.'

An example of being jarred is when an elder from Wyatt's own country chastised him for not making sure that the needs of older Noongar people are addressed. 'Then, when she finished telling me off, or jarring me, then we had a conversation about the challenges, what we need to do, this strategic way that they've got to engage others as well, and what I can do.'

Wyatt asked for numbers – how many Noongars are now needing aged care so they can help them. 'And part of the challenge is our people, when you don't know what you don't know, then you don't ask the right questions . . .'

'Are you finding that people are generally responsive to that? They'll say that they'll help you?'

'Yeah, they do. One thing about our people, it doesn't matter where you are, and you would have seen that at the Purple House, people pitch in and help. And if we need something badly, then we work together and by doing what we can to achieve some of the outcomes. And certainly the Noongar women and the elders who came to see me have said that they will continue to work on this issue and get me that information so that I can start to work on their needs. I've got a sense of, luckily, the age range in Perth metropolitan area, but I also need to know people who live outside of Perth in Noongar country who aren't accessing any services so we can help them as well.'

He says there's a whole range of different programs that the health system runs, and Indigenous populations need to access them. 'I've got some work being done on plotting where all the GPs are, plotting where all the community-controlled health services are, where all the hospitals are, and then where the Aboriginal populations are. Because what I want to do is look at the points of access near that community that we should see them dovetailing to, and getting support from, and that's the important element about making sure people know what services are around, and what they're offering.'

'Keeping our spirit alive and strong'

In central Australia, people say that the spirit is held by the kidney. 'So if you've got sick kidneys, you've got a sick spirit,' says Sarah Brown, the CEO of the Purple House, or the Western Desert Nganampa Walytja Palyantjaku Tjutaku Aboriginal Corporation. 'It's Pintupi,' she explains of the language, which is from west of Alice Springs, out near the Western Australian border.

The Purple House is an Aboriginal community-run organisation. Twelve directors sit on the board, all Pintup/Luritja people from remote communities of the Western Desert, some dialysis patients themselves.

'Our name means "keeping" or "making all their families well", so it was in recognition that if people are away from their country and their family, and their sacred sites, then they're sick and homesick, and life has lost a lot of its meaning,' explains Sarah. 'But also they're not there in the community to pass on their cultural knowledge to their kids and their grandkids.' The whole community is lessened because of it.

The Purple House is an organisation dedicated to supporting patients in Alice Springs, helping as many of them as possible to get home and be 'on country'. Their mission is to improve the lives of people suffering renal failure, reuniting them with their families; and more broadly to reduce the impact of kidney disease on Aboriginal communities. It is set out clearly through three strategic goals, depicted in a circle: in the centre is 'on country' (*ngurra*) – 'help people to be on or return to country'; surroundings that constitute 'a good life' (*kurrunpa wanka*) – 'help patients and their families to live the best life possible'; and on the outer is 'right way' (*tjukarurru wangkantjaku*) – 'the organisation will work hard to do the best we can for the patients, families and stakeholders'. Sarah emphasises that this also means the 'right way culturally'.

In December 2017 an article on the ABC website, 'Proving the link between living on country and improved Indigenous health', reported that 'First Nations people who spend time on country have better health outcomes', with a significant study, 'Mayi Kuwayu' (National Study of Aboriginal and Torres Strait Islander Wellbeing) underway at the Australian National University Centre for Epidemiology and Population Health.

There is a strong idea among desert communities about holding on close to people, being present for ceremony, passing on stories of country, and looking after your family well. An undercurrent is this concept of doing things the right way culturally. All of this is threatened when people leave their communities to receive dialysis three times a week in a town new to them, for the rest of their lives.

'When they are leaving their bit of land, their sacred sites, their family connections, they're often leaving their houses and their jobs and everything that is significant to them,' Sarah says. 'And having to live on someone else's country – because Alice Springs is Arunta country, and these are Pintupi people – causes people great practical hardship, but also people said they were living in shame on someone else's country, waiting for their next dialysis day, and waiting to die.'

In 2000, in a bid to address the growing number of Aboriginal people migrating to Alice to receive treatment for end-stage renal failure, Sarah was part of a group knocking on the doors of politicians to point out that the lack of dialysis services out bush was the reason for Alice's growing population. They appealed to the practical mindset – that people were using public housing, hospital beds, and social workers because of this migration. At the time dialysis was only available in Alice Springs and Darwin. The aim was to have a dialysis machine in Kintore, a remote Northern Territory community a little more than 500 kilometres west of Alice Springs, but the politicians weren't interested.

I first met Sarah at the Art Gallery of New South Wales when she was on a flying visit to Sydney. The gallery is a place that holds significance for her and the Purple House, because it was there that large, collaborative paintings were sold at a fundraiser – work from people from Kintore and Kiwirrkurra auctioned off with the help of the Papunya Tula Artists (a community-driven arts centre) and Sotheby's. They raised over one million dollars.

It was a 'disruptor', says Sarah. 'Here were these people who suddenly had their own money that no one else could tell them how to spend, and they were determined to find a way to do dialysis out bush. And they weren't going to take no for an answer.'

The Purple House was established in 2004, and works hard to get the sickest, most unstable patients safely home on country. The organisation placed a machine in the back of the primary health-care clinic in Kintore. 'And so we just really gently, quietly started,' Sarah says. 'We dialysed an old lady in Alice Springs. We got her really well, cooked her up her favourite food, which was rabbit and ox tongue,' Sarah laughs, 'and then we got her back to Kintore, and she was the first person to go home to a remote community in central Australia.'

The Purple House grew organically from that. Nowadays the organisation is providing dialysis as far as Warburton, past Uluru, and in Kiwirrkurra, 850 kilometres west of Alice Springs. The roads to both are mainly dirt ones.

The system is flexible. Everyone has a dialysis centre in their regional community, whether that's Darwin or Katherine, Kalgoorlie or Perth. Next year Adelaide and Port Augusta will also have dialysis chairs. The directors will consider a person's situation. If someone is very important to a community and doesn't do well in Alice Springs, he or she may be given a permanent spot for treatment; the younger ones will take turns. 'It's the difference between being community-controlled and government-run,' says Sarah. But the system varies depending on the area. And always, there's a push for greater funding. Years ago the Rudd–Gillard government commissioned the Central Australian Renal Study, which looked at the issues for dialysis patients in Central Australia. Warren Snowdon, then the Minister for Indigenous Health, presented it to Parliament in 2010, with dollars attached for the Northern Territory government, which the Purple House has been chasing for the last seven years. The Purple House has now funded dialysis in Papunya, Mount Liebig and the remote Indigenous community of Kaltukatjara.

Nonetheless the organisation needs more money than the funding allows, for running costs and paying for nurses, so it occasionally sells paintings and runs GoFundMe campaigns.

The presence of the Purple House in those communities means there is now either a separate building or a room at the back of the clinic, 'or a something', explains Sarah. 'And we have dialysis machines running six days a week, fifty-two weeks a year. We have nurses living and working in those communities. And then we've got the Purple Truck, which has been on the road for seven years now.'

The Purple Truck is a two-chair mobile dialysis unit that can go anywhere. It is designed for the places that are culturally and spiritually significant, with small populations, where the likelihood of having permanent dialysis is quite low. The truck had an immediate positive effect on people who had no prospect of ever getting home, except for their own funeral. A hopeful twist to a dialysis story of living in a strange town, in a hostel, lonely, bumping up against the hospital system three times a week, far from home.

✦

The day I arrive at the Purple House in Alice Springs, it's also the day of the first dialysis at Mount Liebig, where the Purple House has recently taken over an aged care facility. 'Our directors agreed to take it on,' says Raewyn Kavanagh, the Purple House's Quality Manager, a.k.a. 'the Happiness Facilitator' (Sarah's unofficial title for Raewyn).

They've been out at Mount Liebig since July 2017, but their funding agreement only came through in October. They spent six months setting up the centre and it's passed the quality audit, Raewyn says. It's a home-care service, with laundry and kitchen blocks, and uses a house reclaimed from another service. The Purple House set it up as it used to be: a place ladies remember as one of respite, where they could sit inside in air conditioning when it was hot, watch TV, have lunch and hang out. 'It's a place where the kids can't come in and out. It's a bit of peace and quiet for the old people,' explains Raewyn.

Mount Liebig is around four hours from Alice Springs, up past Papunya. 'It's a rough road, it's not an easy trip to make out there. It'd have to count as one of the most isolated parts of Australia,' says Raewyn, who has lived in Alice Springs for twelve years. Her husband drives the Ghan. 'We came up when they put the rail line through from Alice to Darwin.'

Her role centres on Continuous Quality Improvement (CQI) – taking something and making it a bit better, and meeting quality audits and international standards.

Raewyn has been in community roles most of her working life. She has an interest in Aboriginal issues, and she praises the Purple House's clear vision. 'When we were taking on aged

care, we had to question . . . this is not our core business –
we do dialysis on country. But what's become obvious now is
when you're having patients go home for dialysis, if they have
an aged care service that will work in with that, they will get
better care. So this is the only example that exists of aged care
and dialysis side by side.'

Raewyn reflects on the impact of having to leave home,
family, and wider community for dialysis. 'Imagine if you
had to go on to dialysis, but you had to go to Germany to
have it, assuming you don't speak the language. And it would
be really hard and expensive for you to get home, and that
would only happen through a lot of organised arrangement,
so it's probably not going to happen that they're going to send
you home to see your family.

'So that's how it is for people when they come to Alice
Springs. They're in a whole different world, different language,
they have to navigate things like Centrelink, banking; they're
living in a hostel – so never a home, it's always a hostel, which
[has] really rubbish food and [they're] not treated well in a
hostel, always as if you're in a motel, passing through, when
actually, for a lot of people, that's where you're going to live
for several years.'

Anyone aged fifty or over can access the service, Raewyn
says, as Aboriginal people can access aged care younger than
the general population. 'A person fifty-plus has usually got
some fairly significant health issues. We've got someone with
terminal cancer; I think every single one of them has got renal
issues. We've got one who's got major heart problems and has
had a heart attack previously.'

It's an important service for community ties and wellbeing.
Women tend to be more involved, Raewyn says. 'The men
tend to be more self-sufficient as far as organising activities,
going with the men.'

The aged care service now has client assessments and care plans in place, and bush trips are helpful in learning about women's conditions. 'All those sorts of things come out with just spending time with them, hearing how they're going: that is the best way to inform your assessments and understand. You can find out if maybe one of them has just lost a grandson to suicide; or maybe someone's husband's been diagnosed with something so they're worrying about that, and that person might have been their carer.'

Culturally, direct questioning doesn't work, Raewyn says. 'If you say, "How are you?" they'll say "Good." And you can dig deep, and even if you know someone – certainly if you don't know someone – they're not going to tell you anything. If you know someone well, they might tell you a little bit. But if you go on a bush trip, they'll tell you everything.'

This is affirmed in conversation with Deb Lillis, director of clinical services, who has been with the Purple House for just over twelve years. Currently she oversees all the clinical practices and staff within the organisation, as well as the more crucial elements of patient health. 'I think the real value in being here for so long is getting to know very well the people I look after, and to some extent also the staff,' she says. 'That's very important with Indigenous culture because you form relationships and the barriers come down. And it's amazing what you find out when the barriers come down, and how you can help more when you understand what's happening in people's lives.'

Deb says the regulars at the Purple House are very allowing. 'You're taught general rules when you first come into this culture, and you're quite fearful of breaking those rules . . . and they're the core ones, like not mentioning the name of someone who's recently deceased.' But they're keen to teach, she says. 'They don't get angry with you when you make mistakes. At the end of the day they're very willing to form relationships when they realise that's where you're coming from too. The barriers come down very quickly.'

Language barriers are not an issue. While the interpreter service in Alice Springs can be difficult to access, Sarah tells me there are a number of workers at the Purple House with language skills, as well as Aboriginal staff. In the Top End, more than in Alice, they've employed 'patient preceptors'. 'People who are on dialysis or have had a transplant, and were really good at working their way through the system, who come and help other dialysis patients.'

In the last twelve months, the Purple House has done 6000 dialysis treatments for 157 people across all their centres. 'So 157 people got at least some time back on country,' says Sarah.

It's not enough: in most places the organisation only has enough money to do one shift a day. And working against them are the beliefs that it's up to government to fund the dialysis, and that people who have end-stage renal failure are going to die anyway, so why spend all this money on old people? Early intervention and prevention are where the money should be directed. 'And we go, well, we've got to do this,' Sarah says, patting her head and rubbing her tummy at the same time. 'In what society do you choose between treating sick people and prevention? You've got to do both. We shouldn't have to choose. We are a sophisticated society that can do both. And some of the things that communities are working on to try to reduce the incidence of kidney disease are going to take some time.'

People are living longer on dialysis now, and people are living long enough to end up on dialysis. Ten to fifteen years ago, heart disease was on everyone's radar because Indigenous people were dying of heart attacks in their thirties and forties.

'There's been a big push on heart health and managing blood pressure, and people aren't dying so young of heart attacks, so they're living long enough to be on dialysis. And we'll get on top of kidney disease, and the likelihood is you'll see that the rates of cancer in remote communities will increase. So people are just kind of tracking behind whitefella society. We'll have cancer and dementia being bigger issues.'

✦

A couple of years ago, the Purple House surveyed dialysis patients, asking them two questions: 'Why do people end up on dialysis?' and 'Why are you on dialysis?'

In response to the first question people pointed to fast food and soft drinks, as well as high blood pressure, being overweight, not enough exercise, not enough greens, smoking, childhood infections, premature births. 'They knew,' Sarah tells me. 'They had quite sophisticated whitefella knowledge about chronic disease. And they also said that you get it from your family.'

However, in response to the second question, 100 per cent of the responses – across ages, language groups and sexes – blamed sorcery. Punishment for missing 'sorry' business, or perhaps a brother did something wrong in men's business and wasn't around to receive punishment, so the person with kidney failure is getting punished instead. 'You will have heard about pointing the bone?' asks Sarah. 'Someone will point a bone at someone, it's like a hex. So one hundred per cent of people, despite the fact that they knew about this whitefella story of why kidneys get sick, believe that, for them, it was because of this other world, this spiritual world.'

Management sat down with the Purple House directors and asked, are these stories so far apart, or is there a way to put them together? This led to the creation of a new type of story:

one that includes lifestyle modification but also community leadership – it becomes a community development story. 'And so what they're saying is: the things that keep spirit strong are being on country, with family, looking after your sacred sites, doing things culturally the right way (the third circle in the strategic objectives), and having good communication with communities. But you can't always predict that other world, that spiritual world, and people get jealous of each other.'

Sarah demonstrates the sign language for pointing the bone – a crooked finger. 'So if you can keep your physical body strong, if you can get infections treated early, if you can try to eat the best you can on the income you've got, and go to the clinic for check-ups, maybe your physical body is able to act as a bit of a shield . . . and your physical body can help you to fight off that spiritual attack while you work out what's going wrong.'

In this way, the discussion is still about returning people to country, looking after old people properly on country and making sure that grandkids learn their cultural heritage before the old fellas pass away. It also sends a message to look after the country and the hunting grounds properly, while looking after your family, thinking about environmental health conditions, encouraging kids to go to school, and encouraging people to go to the clinic. 'And you're fitting all those things together to have a strong individual, family and community health. Really it's someone's PhD.'

However, Sarah says that, despite the prevalence of these beliefs, she's never met anyone on dialysis who isn't keen for a kidney transplant. 'Cultures aren't static. And people have managed to survive for thousands of years in really harsh conditions – imagine being out in this weather in the desert, naked, where a sacred waterhole is literally a crack in the rock with a bit of moisture in it,' she says.

Some have incorporated Christianity into their lives, fitting a different culture and religion into their worldview. 'And you could say that that's probably one of the reasons why people have managed to survive, because if they didn't find a way to bend, they would've broken.'

'If we want to go home, they send us home'

The Purple House is literally painted purple. It has offices, a kitchen, chairs for patients and regulars to sit, and a large yard area in which a chicken waddles around. Towards the back is a room with two dialysis chairs. In a smaller place across the yard, Teresa, the 'bush medicine queen', works her medicine magic, creating bush balms that are popular with the regulars.

'It's the only dialysis centre where people come in on their non-dialysis days to hang out with us,' Sarah tells me as she takes me on a tour. There are a number of other people who work here: there's Colin, a dialysis nurse who gets everyone ready for their trips home, out bush; and Jen, a care coordinator who does primary healthcare. They're a welcoming, friendly bunch, who tell me I'm certainly going to see a different side to ageing and illness in Australia.

'Can you smell that?' Sarah asks, breathing deeply as we step inside the kitchen Teresa works from. It's *irmangka irmangka*, or scented emu bush, which will go into a bush balm with beeswax and olive oil. 'You can use it for everything,' says Sarah. It's made to provide relief for arthritis, muscle pain, joint inflammation and dry skin. You can also use it as a chest rub for cold and flu – it smells like a much nicer version of VapoRub.

Sarah tells Teresa why I'm here – to talk about ageing and illness in Indigenous communities. In her quiet voice Teresa quips, 'We leave them, we dump them,' before erupting into laughter. But then she gets more serious. 'Sometimes we take them out, old people, and look after them on country.'

Teresa's husband was on dialysis before he passed away. It was through him that she discovered the Purple House. 'I was sad for a while,' but, she tells me, he lived for a long time on dialysis – five years. 'I was just counting yesterday. I was shocked that he lived five years. A lot of people only live two years or three years.'

Teresa and I talk while she brews a beeswax concoction. Making *irmangka irmangka*, she explains that it's also for the skin. 'And our grandmothers used to drink this; put it in, boil it up and drink it.' She tries to teach me how to say it quickly, the proper way. I flub it and she laughs warmly, repeating it.

There are several products in the bush medicine range, all part of a social enterprise that grew out of the dialysis patients' desire to have it on hand. 'They had stories to tell about bush medicines that their grandmothers used to eat, and they and their mothers have used as remedies out bush, which they really wanted access to as an important part of their wellbeing.'

Patients would ask family to pick the herbs and send them into town on the bush bus. 'These would come to the Purple House in a plastic bag, and they grind them up and make them into a bush medicine.' Packaged into plastic takeaway containers, they would deliver them to the hospitals, hostels and town camps near Alice as a present to the other dialysis patients in town.

'And then we realised there was a real danger – because people were off country – that the cultural knowledge about these plants would be lost. And there wouldn't be opportunities for these older women – because this is women's work – to pass on the cultural knowledge to their kids and their grandkids.'

Thus a social enterprise was born. The bush balm shop provides income for dialysis patients. It not only gives them something to do on their non-dialysis days, it is another way of telling the story about the Purple House, that they are not passive recipients of care, sitting and waiting for their blood to be cleaned. 'These are people who are running our company, who are looking at ways to improve their own health and the health of their family, and are valuing the cultural knowledge that they own.'

The Catholic charity Caritas came on board about five years ago to help develop the social enterprise. Money raised goes back into more dialysis out bush. 'Also, we've linked in with some Indigenous traineeships, so we have young Aboriginal mainly women coming [to the] Purple House, studying business and management. Working on their marketing. [Learning] how to run a business. And either [they] continue on to work at the Purple House or go on to do other things. So it's a beautiful thing.'

The bush balms are sold on the organisation's website, through Oxfam's online store, in art gallery and museum gift shops, and at the Purple House. It pleases Teresa to see the products out in the world. 'Especially [for] people on dialysis, they love it.'

Teresa, who has help running the business at the Purple House, still worries that younger generations will lose this knowledge. 'We've learned a lot from our grandmothers. They were so special, in the old days. But it's different, it's different . . . no one's interested.'

Teresa emphasises the importance of hunting in her culture, and passing on stories. 'We've got our own fairy tales our grandmothers used to tell us at night-time. All those things gone. They're disappearing.' Bush medicine is an attempt to continue tradition and maintain knowledge. 'We are the last ones, I reckon, to keep it alive.'

✦

Over two mornings, I meet with some regulars at the Purple House. For some of them English is a fourth or fifth language. There's Kaylene, a long-time renal patient who is readying herself for a brief return home to visit family. She's missed a few dialysis treatments and has some catching up to do to get well enough to go home next week.

'Are you going to Mount Liebig?' she asks me.

Unfortunately not, I tell her.

Kaylene tells me that she comes to the Purple House for lunch, and occasionally she will do dialysis there. She's been in Alice Springs for three years, but she likes the bush and talks briefly about hunting. It's a huge story for her to be going home. They're waiting for her at aged care, Raewyn tells me.

There's Ivy, who's fifty-four. She speaks to me while her favourite gospel music plays in the background. The music is soothing, she says. From Wanarn Community across the border in Western Australia, about an hour-and-a half-flight south-west of Alice Springs, she's waiting for dialysis in order to get home. She's been in Alice Springs for around two years, since she got sick in 2015.

'I'm feeling right, but this and this . . .' She points to her legs – they're weak. 'But everything is okay.'

She likes the Purple House, and its people are friendly. 'I'm happy to be here,' she says with a grin. But she says her family gets lonely for her. 'My family is waiting for me to go back.'

Ivy likes two- to three-week visits, then to return to Alice Springs.

'Why are you writing this story?' she suddenly asks me, her expression mildly amused.

I tell her and she goes on to talk about her brother, who used to get dialysis here, on his way to Darwin.

Ivy repeats that she's content here – people get together, they're friendly, and they talk. She's made a lot of friends. 'And they're making me happy.' She beams. She even has praise for the hostel she lives in. 'We talk and laugh, make jokes and all that,' she says.

Josephine, sixty-three, is another Purple House regular and a renal patient. The first time she went to Adelaide and Darwin, she was shocked. 'Because I'm a desert woman, see; I've never been in cities.' She doesn't like them. 'Too far. They make you homesick. People want to stay with family.'

She talks about the importance of family; of family looking after each other – only her teenage daughter looks after her. 'I'm happy,' she says. 'My daughter's close to me and I'm close to her.'

She comes here every week, and has been doing dialysis for many years. She says the staff are helpful. 'And if we want to go home, they send us home.' Like the others, she lives in a hostel in Alice Springs. She even gives me directions to it. But she gets homesick despite the 'big mob' at the Purple House. Her parents have passed away, and her brother and sister, an aunty; another aunty is very sick, a renal patient who will be passing away soon. Her cousin, also a renal patient, has passed. 'They weren't looking after her properly. She wasn't looking after herself because she used to drink a lot, and not eating the right food, you know? Buying takeaway.'

I ask Josephine about her kidney issues – what led to them? She tells me she used to be a drinker. 'Then I got sick. And diabetes.' She felt a kind of pain in her body, like she was being punched. She demonstrates, touching her body. 'I felt that.'

At hospital she discovered she had kidney problems. She can't remember how old she was at the time. But she's taking care of herself now. 'Like taking pills. Eating proper food. Doing exercise. Walking around, you know?'

Josephine is a positive presence. She finishes by telling me about the things she likes: visiting family, visiting other places, painting, though it's not a huge passion, she says.

Irene is a director of the Purple House. She offers community support. She speaks several dialects. She's an advocate for her community. Raewyn tells me Irene is always the one who stands up and makes sure everyone understands what's being talked about in a meeting. She's smart, and likes people to listen carefully – 'because it's a big story, this one'.

Before we chat, Raewyn plays us a video of Carers Week at Mount Liebig, when the women were treated to a day of pampering (they dyed their hair), and hunting. Irene watches approvingly but she's not expressive. She has a commanding presence. We speak while in the background everyone goes about their day: staffers making cheese sandwiches for patrons; slicing up fruit, which gets covered by a net to keep away the flies; chatter and friendly banter. The Purple House is very much about social interaction. Both mornings I am there, I observe the camaraderie between staff and regulars. Irene talks about this, how she likes seeing doctors at the Purple House; to see the workers there; to meet families when they come in.

Originally from Papunya, Irene joined the new community of Kintore in the 1980s, establishing a school in 1981. Now she's at the Purple House.

She vividly recalls when she got sick, she thinks in her forties (she's now fifty-eight). 'I feel my body's getting weak. I can't walk. Didn't know what was happening, you know.' She didn't realise that fluid was building up in her legs. 'The doctor said, "You have too much fluid, you maybe need renal, you know, dialysing on the renal."'

She tells me with a smile that she didn't believe the doctor. It was only when she grew very ill that she took him at his word. 'My friend told me – he was crying – that I should have had this done before.'

So she went to Alice Springs to receive dialysis. It was difficult – it took her away from her community and her home. 'It's important for me because they started missing me. Not only one person. Even the little kids – grandchildren, nieces, nephews.'

She missed them, too. 'Not only a few. I've got family all over.'

Irene reflects on how there used to be more respect for older people. 'Not now, today. Today people just want to take money from old people.'

There's silence for a moment before suddenly Irene declares, 'My story's finished.' She has work to do, after all.

Friday

It's a Friday in December, but I'm not with my folks. I'm in Brisbane with my husband, Chris, visiting his family over the Christmas break. I call Mum and Dad, of course; check in, hear about their day, which my mother can timetable for me with precision – down to who ate what, with a rating for service and ambience thrown in for good measure. I will be back in time for New Year's, to see off the year with my family as fireworks light up the night sky.

For now I'm with Chris's family, negotiating the Brisbane summer heat and catch-ups with his relatives and our friends.

Chris's grandmother, Hazel, is impressively independent for someone in her nineties, and my in-laws, Ross and Judy, are solicitous with her. She lives on her own, still plays piano at concert recitals, keeps up with her favourite television shows and authors. Chris's parents ensure her fridge is always fully stocked – Hazel calls it 'Aladdin's cave', a plentiful treasure trove of her favourite foods and delights.

My in-laws are affable, kind and considerate people. They allow me to turn their dining table into a makeshift office whenever I come to visit and need to write. And I love to hear their stories.

This time, knee-deep in ageing and illness, I'm reflective. For months my world has been filled with other people's lives of loss; their memories; photos of former selves who seem distant and almost idealised. I recognise how privileged some of us are to have the capacity and circumstances to curate a good life, one of meaning and purpose. One that is generally safe and expansive. One in which many of us take our health for granted in our younger years.

'I've never seen pictures of you when you were young,' I say to Judy and Ross over dinner. There's a scattering of framed photos around the house, but none of the sepia-toned or black-and-white ones I always find so fascinating. I'm suddenly curious to have a glimpse of them as they were when they first met, of Ross as a cadet engineer on a ship. He speaks fondly of his days at sea – pre-containerisation. 'Got out just in time,' he says. He has strong memories of what it was like to live on board: the rules, official and unofficial; the camaraderie between men, and how they were like family (nobody could come between them). I hear about how when the couple were newlyweds Judy joined Ross for a trip to England. Judy loved it, had no issue being on board, and was afforded respect from the men.

Later Judy finds me at the dining table working on the book. 'Come here, I'll show you those photos,' she says, with a smile. She retrieves a box and a carefully preserved album wrapped in tissue paper – the past enshrined. It's odd seeing these pictures; they have the same effect on me as those of

FRIDAYS *with my* FOLKS

my parents when they were young and their future brimmed with potential. Why do they move me so? Is it because the images are romantic? Is it their beauty or the hint of idealism? The idea that then life was idyllic?

On their wedding day Ross and Judy beam at the camera, youthful and happy. Judy is all class, her hair beautifully coiffed; Ross, a tall man, towers above Judy. He has a full head of hair and his recognisable cheeky grin. He joins us as we excavate the past, chuckling at some of the photos, he and Judy talking about various people in them – who they were to them then, where they are now.

It's lovely to see how easily they dive into their histories. The beauty of youth. The intoxicating sense of possibility. In the same way photos of my parents affect me, I'm warmed by the history that these photos contain. The way they commemorate and speak to you all at once, a tangible reminder of the different parts of you. An honouring, and a way not to forget all that has been as you look ahead.

10.

GETTING TO KNOW MY PARENTS

*You don't learn in good times. **It's difficulty that clears your sight.***

It seems appropriate that my explorations of ageing come to a soft landing in Alice Springs. By this point something in me has been transmuted from shock to acceptance. I ponder this as I sit at the desk in my hotel room, hunched over my computer screen, waiting for that conversation with Minister Ken Wyatt. How to talk to a politician after hearing so many real experiences, surrounded by notebooks filled with these disparate and extraordinary stories to piece together.

I think of the many ageing women who recounted years of physical troubles and the stress of managing children, parents and their own wellbeing. I am reminded of the carers I met who are grappling with their own stories, trying to make things right with themselves in order to take on their new responsibility to parents. My thoughts move to Stephanie, one of the most striking interviewees, a woman in her forties who's put her life on hold while she deals with two ageing, sick parents. Her mother has a vital, able mind, but a body reliant on oxygen 24/7. Stuck. Knowing, seeing and loving as always, but imprisoned in a body that has lost its agility. She is barely living, but Stephanie can't bear the thought of her physically dying. 'I will be devastated,' she told me. 'She's my

273

soul mate.' Her father has suffered a terrible degradation of mind, his memories lost, preserved only in photos. A day out to the theatre can bring up moments of joy and communion for him, but these moments disappear within hours.

This is not to say that either of her parents are living a life less valuable. Who is anyone to determine that? But the pathos runs deep. We sat opposite each other in a café, Stephanie gradually pouring out her grief, the way her parents' losses have become her own, the way each limitation pares away her freedom and ability to live a full life. But the love, so powerful and full, remains.

My phone rang when I was with her, and because it was my brother Hossam, and Dad was only freshly out of hospital, I took the call. Hossam let me know that Dad and he were back at the hospital, though it might be 'nothing'. Yet that surge of emotion, that plunging emotional grief still took me by surprise and wet my eyes in an instant. Stephanie nodded, knowing, when I had to excuse myself. She had already been moved to tears during our conversation, but she started afresh as she took in my sudden change in composure. No longer compassionate interviewer; now a grief-stricken daughter.

You get used to it, I remember thinking. But it was Stephanie's kindness that I left with; it was her enquiring, empathetic message to me later that uplifted me with a feeling I can't quite put a name to. And months later, it's the agony in her expression that stays with me.

It is this commonality that is so affecting; the way, as humans, we so often smash into each other, but also stand beside one another. You might get used to it, but you're changing and learning as you go. That much I understand. Sitting alone in my hotel room, enveloped in sadness, I really do understand. We seek a life of meaning, connection and purpose. Loneliness kills, and disappointment at our mortality shreds us. Life is a series of negotiations. Me, ever the deep diver into what motivates people, our flaws and hopes, I'm coming to a sense of equilibrium, of being okay with life not always being okay. All of these negotiations and explorations take on new resonance as I excavate the fears and beliefs that surround the body's descent, even when the mind remains fresh – or vice versa.

My mind locks on to the many Fridays that have passed in the last couple of years, Fridays that have profoundly changed my life and how I view it. I have learned not only how to listen, to provide and be present without forcing others to be something they simply are not, but I have also received an education in elders' experiences. My mother, and her grief, are taking shape in new ways in my mind, and I think hers as well. My father's dogged determination to be a success became multi-layered in light of his relationship to his father, an at-times difficult one that can bring tears to his eyes in a moment. He is a son in the way that I am a daughter. My brothers and I, all finding our own ways to navigate a new reality.

My parents are dispossessed in Australia, yet so at home. Their similarly dispossessed daughter, I am between worlds, between cultures, looking for meaning that isn't always there, but somehow learning, growing, seeing the different shades of colour in every experience.

The dispossession in Alice Springs is not the same, of course. It is a place populated by many people who are far from home, family and community. It is a place where grief is deep and fresh. Where so many are grappling with the failures of body and the way it affects the mind.

When the minister calls, he gives me a generous amount of time. His voice is sincere, clear. He seems to care. He says the right things. Even if a lot of what he says is to be expected, he speaks like a human being invested in his portfolios; he, too, has a stake in all of this. That in itself is enough for me. But then, as we approach the end of the interview, he surprises me. He asks me about my book. I explain *Fridays with My Folks*: now I am speaking to him less as a journalist and more as an ordinary Australian citizen who has ageing parents.

I'm touched by his empathetic response. 'You're speaking like a daughter who loves her parents, and who is now giving back to them time; but in doing that has gained an understanding of them as individuals who contributed to her life, but, more importantly, contributed to the society in which they lived. And they are two unique people who still contribute to your knowledge, and your growth. And through that process, the closeness you have with them is because you now understand the two adults who gave you your uniqueness. And that's a very powerful emotion, and a very powerful recognition of acknowledging that, "Hey, my mum and dad are two incredible people."'

As I hang up, an odd memory takes shape in my mind. Watching the Food Network with my parents during one of Dad's hospital stays. It was normal life in an abnormal setting. It was ordinary joy wrapped in a bit of sorrow. But there was a fullness to it all, bolstered by moments of communion, even in simple things. Like a plump fruit that is both sweet and sour.

A segment came on about an American brand of jelly beans famous for its whacky flavours. We laughed at some of them – barf, rotten egg. And the moment also proved bittersweet. I realised that I'd never look at those jelly beans and not remember this. An association had been forged. The way bagels are synonymous with the hospital, because that's the only place I eat them, usually with Mum. The way Sydney's reconstruction never looks like a series of cranes and detours because I hear Dad's observations as I pass them by, so now his perspectives are inextricably linked to them.

And Fridays with my folks and all each one of them conjures. The flooding of vibrant purple that comes with the blooming of jacaranda trees in Sydney. Mum's stories and observations from the back seat, the occasional Arab proverb thrown in ('The camel doesn't see its bump', 'Before he eats me for dinner, I'll eat him for lunch', and so on).

I am far from where I began, when I felt like I was stumbling through a fog, subsisting on fumes, going through the motions. I'm more grounded now. More grateful for the little things, and the large. More attuned to improving my own health, to broadening my mind on how I can seek and achieve a life filled with purpose and meaning, a healthy life.

But what has shifted most is my relationship with Mum and Dad. After all this time, my parents have become increasingly, simply, more themselves. People whose emotions aren't solely measured by their connections to their children; whose experiences are not bound by their roles as parents. They don't exist for me, for their other children. Their own histories are as rich as my own; their spirits as complex and wandering.

My mind travels again to the millions of people dealing with similar situations, or worse. My heart has stretched out as I've lingered on my daily treks into town in Alice Springs, the punishing heat beating down on me, the land seeming at odds with its population. The way some people are out of place, like their spirits are elsewhere, far from their physical bodies.

I am heartened and amazed and moved by human resilience. By the compassion we exhibit to others (a choice, given we can also withold it). The way humans try to mend fractured relationships, to re-energise spaces so that life remains beautiful and hopeful. So that people feel they matter, even when they are dealing with the ephemeral nature of life.

Among our most complex negotiations in life, surely, are those of our relationships with our parents and close family, people we may one day become carers to, regardless of our history.

And of course, our relationships to ourselves must be negotiated. This deep-dive can happen at any time, perhaps, but certainly much of it comes tumbling out when we start to see evidence of our mortality.

It seems clear that if we're ever going to truly get to know our parents, in particular, it's most likely to happen during adulthood, long after we've tested each other's limits and found a meeting place. We feel tied to family members through fate. But when certain events bring us closer together, often a more enriching journey begins.

After all this time, I am seeing my parents as their distinct selves. I'm not romanticising them, or spinning false narratives about their lives. We exist in the same space together, developing new ways of being and dealing, and seeing each other. I'm meeting them where they're at, as a daughter, not a carer. I'm getting to know them.

And I think to myself, what a gift.

ACKNOWLEDGEMENTS

This book would not have been possible if it weren't for my Fridays with my folks. They have changed my life, and I am immensely grateful that my parents have allowed me to share their stories, and our Fridays, in this book.

Thank you to my husband, Chris, for being the patient partner of a writer. Thank you to my family and friends, who have shown great support and offered invaluable insights during the process of researching and writing this book.

There are so many people who have been extremely helpful in my research – from suggesting interviewees, to sharing their own stories, no matter how difficult. Thank you for your contribution, whether directly or simply through your support. I hope this book offers something to you in return.

Finally, a heartfelt thank you to my agent, Tara Wynne at Curtis Brown, and the wonderful team there, especially Caitlan Cooper-Trent. And at Penguin Random House, immense gratitude to my publisher, Meredith Curnow, for shepherding me through this exploration from its inception with so much empathy and good advice, and to my editor, Catherine Hill, who is always a guiding voice, insightful at every stage.